D1020734

EDUCATION AT AMHERST

EDUCATION AT AMHERST
The New Program

EDITED BY

GAIL KENNEDY, Chairman

Faculty Committee on Long Range Policy

Ralph A. Beebe	Vincent Morgan
Bailey LeF. Brown	George Rogers Taylor
George B. Funnell	Peter H. Odegard (Alternate)

AND

Review Committee on the New Program

George B. Funnell
George W. Kidder
George Rogers Taylor

HARPER & BROTHERS, PUBLISHERS, NEW YORK

EDUCATION AT AMHERST

FIRST EDITION

H-E

Library of Congress Catalog Card Number: 55-8552

ACKNOWLEDGMENTS

The printed report of the Committee on Long Range Policy (January, 1945) contained the following statement:

"Those who have contributed to the making of this report are too numerous to name, but the committee is deeply grateful to them all for their kindness and their patience. We wish in particular to acknowledge our debt to:

"those members of the faculty who have served since last February on the Curriculum Committee, who have attended many meetings and helped in many ways;

"the various groups and individual members of the faculty who have given us their opinions and their advice;

"the administrative and fiscal officers of the college, who in answering our questions have provided data that must have taken many hours of preparation;

"the alumni and other persons from outside the college who have talked over some of our problems with us."

The committee responsible for this book wish to acknowledge a similar debt to many members of the faculty and the administrative officers of the college.

We wish also to acknowledge permission to use quotations from the following:

John Dewey, *Experience and Education* (New York: The Macmillan Company, 1938), p. v. Used with the permission of the publisher.

Herbert G. Espy, *The Public Secondary School* (Boston: Houghton Mifflin Company, 1939), p. 64. Used with the permission of the publisher.

Luther H. Gulick, *Education for American Life: a New Program for the State of New York* (New York: Regents' Inquiry into the Character and Cost of Public Education in the State of New York, 1938), p. 12. Used with the permission of the author.

A. N. Whitehead, *The Aims of Education* (New York: The Mac-

millan Company, 1929), pp. 41-42, 58. Used with the permission of the publisher.

John Dewey, *A Common Faith* (New Haven: Yale University Press, 1934), p. 87. Used with the permission of the publisher.

A. N. Whitehead, *The Aims of Education* (New York: The Macmillan Company, 1929), p. 58. Used with the permission of the publisher.

Alan Valentine, "Problems of an Admissions Office," *Educational Review*, 16 (1935), 63. Used with the permission of the author.

William James, *Memories and Studies* (New York: Longmans, Green & Company, 1911), pp. 287-288. Used with the permission of the publisher.

Gregory Zilboorg, *Mind, Medicine, and Man* (New York: Harcourt, Brace & Company, 1943), p. 21. Used with the permission of the publisher.

"Youth in College," *Fortune*, 13, no. 6 (1936), 101. Used with the permission of the publisher.

"1940 Statement of Principles on Academic Freedom and Tenure," American Association of University Professors *Bulletin*, 29, no. 1 (February, 1943), 79. Used with the permission of the publisher.

George Rogers Taylor, "Meeting the Social Studies Where They Are," *The Journal of Higher Education*, 23 (March, 1952), 68-78. Excerpts from this article are used with the permission of the publisher.

"Victory at Amherst," editorial in *The New York Times*, March 15, 1948. Used with the permission of the publisher.

CONTENTS

FOREWORD

BY CHARLES W. COLE

President, Amherst College

The Amherst College faculty has always shown a willingness to experiment and to introduce forward-looking and even daring innovations. In 1826, when the college was barely five years old, two faculty reports to the trustees outlined a plan of education which, if it had fully succeeded, might have "modernized" American higher education a half-century earlier than was actually to be the case. In the first report on general principles the faculty said:

> One fact, we take it, is becoming more and more obvious every day. The American public is not satisfied with the present course of education in our higher seminaries. And the great objection is, that it is not sufficiently modern and comprehensive, to meet the exigencies of the age and country in which we live. . . .
>
> Why, it is demanded, such reluctance to admit modern improvements and modern literature? Why so little attention to the natural, civil, and political history of our own country and to the genius of our government? Why so little regard to the French and Spanish languages, especially considering the commercial relations which are now so rapidly forming, and which bid fair to be indefinitely extended between the United States and all the great southern Republics? Why should my son, who is to be a merchant at home, or an agent in some foreign port; or why, if he is to inherit my fortune, and wishes to qualify himself for the duties and standing of a private gentleman, or a scientific farmer—why, in either case, should he be compelled to spend nearly four years out of six, in the study of the dead Languages for which he has no taste, from which he expects to derive no material advantage, and for which he will in fact have but very little use after his senior examination?

In the second and more detailed report, the faculty, under the leadership of the twenty-three-year-old Professor Jacob Abbott (later famous as author of the twenty-eight volumes of the "Rollo" books) proposed a new course of study paralleling the traditional curriculum. It was to stress English literature, modern languages (French and Spanish), "Mechanical Philosophy," chemistry and "other kindred branches of Physical Science," elementary engineering, "Natural History," modern history, and "Civil and Political law embracing the careful study of American Constitutions." From the old curriculum were to be retained ancient history, geography, grammar, rhetoric, oratory, mathematics, "Natural, Intellectual and Moral philosophy," anatomy, political economy, and theology. The new subjects were brought in largely at the expense of Latin and Greek.

The "parallel course" was actually introduced in the academic year 1827-1828 and was elected by eighteen of the sixty-seven incoming freshman. But so great was the prestige of the older studies that in the following year few freshmen chose the new curriculum. In 1829, the "parallel course" was abandoned and Jacob Abbott resigned from the faculty. But the experiment left some traces behind it. French, for example, was made one of the regular studies in the curriculum.

In the century and a quarter which followed this educational venture, the Amherst faculty repeatedly showed its eagerness to try out new ideas. This experimental attitude was never better illustrated than in the adoption of the "new curriculum," which was actually put into effect in 1947.

As early as October, 1941, President Stanley King saw the opportunity for educational reevaluation offered by the war period and appointed a Faculty Committee on Long Range Policy. Its work was interrupted by Pearl Harbor, but early in 1944 it was reconstituted under the chairmanship of Professor Gail Kennedy, of the Philosophy Department. In the ensuing two years, it performed the monumental task of recasting the whole curriculum of the college and the even more spectacular feat of persuading the faculty individually and collectively that the new course of study should be adopted.

Nor was it just the curriculum that the Committee on Long Range Policy dealt with, for its final report discussed admissions, scholarships, social life, religion, and student government in an effort to sketch a postwar college in which the student's whole experience might be one of rounded development and vital growth.

During the same period the work of the faculty committee was reinforced by a similar study undertaken by an alumni committee of six members which worked with four subcommittees (Admissions and Scholarship, Curriculum, Religion, Student Activities) to produce a report entitled *Amherst Tomorrow*. The alumni committee was originally suggested by E. S. Wilson, '29, then secretary of the Alumni Council. It was appointed by the Executive Committee of the Alumni Council, of which Claude M. Fuess, '05, was then chairman. In its study of the past, present, and future of Amherst College it had the enthusiastic support of President Stanley King. Its report, though less specific, paralleled and reinforced the recommendations of the faculty committee in most areas.

Amherst College was fortunate that its plans and preparations for postwar changes were complete by 1946-1947, for it was possible to inaugurate the reforms in many non-curricular matters in 1946 and in the curriculum for the academic year 1947-1948. The time was ripe. The College, flooded with veterans, had not had a chance to lapse back into its old routines after the unsettlement of the war period. Thus in June, 1951, the class that was graduated had had its full four years under the new curriculum.

By 1951 the world situation was again so tense and problems of the draft and of military training were so pressing that large-scale changes would once more have been difficult, and those tensions and problems have persisted down to the present. But because of the timing of the reforms and experiments, we have now had experience with them for seven years or more. Thus 1954 is a good year to study the changes made at Amherst since the war with the idea of seeing how they have worked out in the light of the original plans laid a decade ago. We have had time enough to learn a great deal about the effectiveness of the new curriculum, but not time enough drastically to modify its intent. It was with such considerations in mind that Professor Gail Kennedy with the assistance of a small committee was asked to look hard at our brain child in order to describe it as a seven-year-old. The story told in these pages of an educational experiment at a small college should be of some interest outside Amherst circles. It should be a document not wholly without significance as a record of educational theory and practice in the mid-century.

REPORT OF THE FACULTY COMMITTEE ON LONG RANGE POLICY, 1945

INTRODUCTION

To the Members of the Faculty:

Your Committee on Long Range Policy herewith submits its report. Having completed the assignment given it, it considers itself discharged, leaving its members free to act as individuals expressing their personal views in the coming discussion of the questions this report brings before you.

It may perhaps be useful, as a preface to the body of this report, briefly to recall the genesis of the committee and the history of its activities. It was appointed by President King, with the approval of the Committee of Six, in October, 1941. The original members were Professor Chandler, chairman, and Professors Beebe, Funnell, Kennedy, and Vincent Morgan. Pearl Harbor put an abrupt end to its leisurely deliberations. It did not resume activity until February, 1944, when President King, after consultation with the Committee of Six, reconstituted the committee with its present membership, Professor Kennedy, chairman, and Professors Beebe, Brown, Funnell, Vincent Morgan, and Taylor. During Professor Taylor's absence in Washington Professor Odegard was appointed as alternate for him. The chairman was given a leave of absence for one term that he might have time to visit other colleges and to do a considerable part of the preparation of materials for discussion in the committee. Since February the committee has met, on an average, about twice a week. A number of these meetings were held with various groups of the faculty and administration. The chairman also held three meetings, one in Cambridge and two in Washington, with eleven members of the faculty who are on leave of absence, and conferred with various officials and teachers in a number of other institutions.

In order to benefit as fully as possible from the views of the faculty we early sent out a request to all its members, including those on leave of absence, for letters giving us their suggestions on every topic which would be relevant to our work. To this request a majority of the faculty replied. Their letters were most helpful in giving us an indication of the range of opinions held by members of the faculty and contained many concrete suggestions which were discussed in our meetings.

On the central question of the curriculum, the members of the committee found themselves, somewhat unexpectedly, in more substantial agreement than they had supposed. They were therefore able to send out to the faculty as early as June 12 a memorandum making a number of concrete proposals, particularly for the freshman and sophomore years. The subsequent discussion and criticism of those proposals enabled the committee still more accurately to gauge the "climate of opinion" in the faculty and served to make it more fully aware of the many difficulties confronting those who attempt to frame a curriculum.

The mandate of the committee was not, however, to attempt merely the adjudication of differences on this and other matters within the faculty. Such an attempt would on the face of it be impossible. What was expected of the committee was that, taking as full cognizance of faculty opinion as possible, it would attempt to formulate a comprehensive and far-reaching set of proposals which would, in its own opinion, be for the good of the college as an educational institution functioning in the postwar world. This charge was expressed by President King in two paragraphs of his letter appointing the original committee:

> We all realize that the present emergency is likely to produce profound changes in our social fabric. These changes are likely to affect our program of higher education. It seems to me of vital importance that Amherst College should be considering now how best to adapt itself to meet the changed conditions. It may well be that we shall wish to make radical changes in our present practices and procedures. A study of these questions is the function of your Committee.
>
> Amherst College was founded in a time of profound national unrest. It has survived succeeding crises in our national life. It has adapted itself to meet conditions of each generation. I do not need to emphasize the seriousness of the problems which will face us in years which lie immediately ahead. I am confident, however, that with foresight and prudence and flexibility the College can adapt itself to serve with even greater usefulness the society of tomorrow.

Wars frequently uproot and destroy the basic institutions of the vanquished while at the least they tremendously accelerate changes already under way in the social organization of the victors. The immense changes which have come about within the short period since World War I will undoubtedly seem almost trivial in comparison with those likely to occur during the next few decades. Your committee felt, therefore, that its approach to the problems it was confronted with should be radical, that it would not be realistic complacently to assume a "return to normalcy" immediately, or ever, after this war. If it were true that the effect of the war would be greatly to speed up certain social trends which were more slowly emerging before it, then the committee should try, however inadequately, to discover what sort of education the small liberal college can offer that is most relevant to these postwar conditions. We have endeavored, therefore, to take account of certain basic trends in our society which have become more and more obvious in recent years, and more particularly to study the rapid developments now occurring in education, both in the public schools and among private and public institutions of higher education. We have made no more than a summary reference to a few of these developments in this report, but what study we have been able to make of them has greatly influenced our opinions.[1]

Education today, as everyone knows, is in a state of intense ferment. One's first impression is that of a phantasia of competing theories and practices. Your committee's attitude toward these has been from the start a horror of all panaceas and gadgets. We have not become enthusiasts for a "plan" or "cause." The principle we have tried to follow in our inquiries has been well expressed by John Dewey:

> It is the business of an intelligent theory of education to ascertain the causes for the conflicts which exist and then, instead of taking one side or the other, to indicate a plan of operations proceeding from a deeper level and more inclusive than is represented by the practices and ideas of the contending parties.[2]

The work of the committee has obviously been limited by the time at its disposal and the competence of its members. Our function has been largely, as a representative group of the faculty, to render *qualitative* judgments. Many if not most of our specific recommendations

[1] Although we have consulted or read, as a committee or individually, a large number of documents of various sorts, some unpublished, relating to the subject of our study, the whole body of material dealing with these problems is so large that it did not seem feasible to attempt to present a bibliography.

[2] *Experience and Education* (New York, 1938), p. v.

represent our *opinions*. We have not the special knowledge or experience to judge in detail their worth. In some cases these recommendations should be given further study by the Curriculum Committee or by specially appointed committees before they are submitted to the faculty. Our role has been to agree, if we could, upon a set of fundamental proposals, thus serving as a means of bringing squarely before the faculty as a whole the question: What should be the Amherst of the future?

Most important innovations occurring in the colleges have been the result of long and gradual historical growth, or on the initiative of a determined and persuasive president, or by the foundation of new institutions. Here at Amherst we are attempting something that has rarely if ever been done: to secure through the democratic processes of study, report, and discussion the cooperative agreement of the whole faculty upon a comprehensive long-term policy for the college. It is certain that this is the most opportune occasion we are likely ever to have for that attempt. The normal life of the college has been almost wholly interrupted. The crust of custom has been broken. Traditions are in abeyance. The members of the faculty, both those here and those on leave, have discovered that they can quickly adapt themselves to doing successfully many new and unusual things. There is ample time for the fullest consideration of all proposals, since it is unlikely that military service for eighteen-year-olds will be discontinued soon enough for us to have a "normal" freshman class before the academic year 1946-1947. The college is passing through a critical period during which it is possible to plan and carry out on a democratic basis an intelligent reconstruction of its whole pattern of organization.[3]

It is said that the Chinese write the word "crisis" with two characters meaning "danger" and "opportunity." Although even the existence of many privately endowed colleges is today threatened by powerful social forces, there is no danger that so well established an institution as Amherst cannot survive.[4] The real danger is that it will

[3] This committee has consciously refrained from making recommendations concerning the problem of the returning veteran. This problem does not seem to us to be a part of the long-range policy of the college, and an *ad hoc* committee has been appointed to deal with it.

[4] See Frederick P. Keppel's article, "Will the American College Survive?" *The American Scholar*, Spring, 1942.

survive merely as "another good college." The college has suffered from too much of a certain kind of success. We need to recall that "though a private college Amherst is a public institution." It was founded "to civilize and evangelize the world by the classical education of indigent young men of piety and talents." How to implement that ideal in terms of the new society that has been emerging from thirty years of unparalleled technological changes accompanied by two catastrophic wars is the issue this report should serve to bring before the faculty.

PART I

OBJECTIVES OF THE LIBERAL COLLEGE IN A CHANGING SOCIETY

THE NINETY-YEAR WAR ON THE COLLEGE

The American college, though it was established in imitation of European models, especially the residential colleges of the English universities, soon became a peculiarly American institution. In the great majority of cases the colleges were founded by or affiliated with church organizations. They were intended primarily to be preparatory schools for the learned professions, in particular the ministry. This gave them a specific moral purpose which the first president of Amherst, Zephaniah Swift Moore, stated in his inaugural address:

> While we use our efforts to conduct those under our care in the paths of literature and science, we are always to keep in mind that it is of primary importance that we be correct in our moral and religious instruction. We are never to forget that an essential and primary object of this institution is the promotion of Christian knowledge and piety.[2]

By the earlier years of the nineteenth century there were three conflicting opinions in American thought on education: first the earlier religious and exclusive conception which had led to the development of the Latin schools and colleges; then Jefferson's ideal of a democratic elite—the provision of universal elementary education for all citizens, and of free public higher education on a competitive basis for everyone who had the ambition and capacity to profit by it; and finally what may be called the Jacksonian demand for a system of education, universal and public, but primarily vocational and utili-

[1] This part of the report considers some things that have happened to *American colleges*. The statements made in it are in general not intended to reflect particular conditions at Amherst except as Amherst is viewed historically.

[2] Quoted from Claude M. Fuess, *Amherst* (Boston, 1935), p. 49.

tarian. The competition of these bodies of opinion was to have momentous effects as the century progressed. As they operated upon and within the colleges they produced a gradual though reluctant transformation.

In terms of their origin and purpose the colleges were essentially conservative institutions. Being for the most part privately endowed and controlled, and under the fostering care of the churches, they could and did resist the currents of secular opinion. It was slowly and under the pressure of irresistible social trends that they were changed into what they now are. From the first they found themselves in a kind of unwitting opposition to those forces which were working for the creation of a more popular and democratic education. Standing as it did for the antique and bookish learning of the humanistic schools, the American college was a narrowly conceived and aristocratic institution which could offer little that was relevant for the education of men of affairs.

There were two ways of dealing with the situation. One was the creation of a new set of secondary schools, the academies, which in contrast to the Latin schools would give a more popular and useful type of instruction though, in fact, they often provided also substantially the equivalent to a part of the college curriculum. The other took the form of an alteration in the nature of the college itself. The demand for a new type of curriculum led to various forms of compromise, parallel courses, and, later, scientific schools such as the Sheffield and Lawrence schools at Yale and Harvard. Amherst College, which had itself developed out of an academy, took the lead and was one of the first to establish a parallel course. The famous *Report of the Faculty of Amherst College*, presented to the Board of Trustees in 1826, points out the dissatisfaction of a

> . . . large class of enlightened men [who, however they] may differ in regard to the practicability, or expediency of modernizing our Colleges, in one thing . . . are entirely agreed. These Institutions do not, at present, afford all the facilities which they want, for the liberal education of their sons; and we are convinced, that if the Colleges cannot so modify their systems, as to meet the public demand, or if they do not choose to do it, other seminaries, equal in rank and of surpassing popularity, will spring up by their side. How detrimental this would be, to the prosperity of existing establishments, especially such of them as derive their support

chiefly from tuition, we need not stop to inquire. Let our Colleges promptly lead on in the mighty march of improvement, and all will be well; but let them hesitate and linger a little longer, and many of their most efficient friends will go on without them.

[Why then, they ask, is there] such reluctance to admit modern improvements, and modern literature? Why so little attention to the natural, civil, and political history of our own country and to the genius of our government? Why so little regard to the French and Spanish languages, especially considering the commercial relations which are now so rapidly forming, and which bid fair to be indefinitely extended between the United States and all the great southern Republics? Why should my son, who is to be a merchant at home, or an agent in some foreign port; or why, if he is to inherit my fortune, and wishes to qualify himself for the duties and standing of a private gentleman, or a scientific farmer—why, in either case, should he be compelled to spend nearly four years out of six, in the study of the dead Languages, for which he has no taste, from which he expects to derive no material advantage, and for which he will in fact have but very little use after his senior examination?[3]

The new parallel course of study was duly instituted, but difficulties developed and, after two years of trial, it was abandoned.[4]

Meanwhile, the same forces which had generated the Jeffersonian and Jacksonian points of view were under another form infiltrating the colleges. The course of required studies was gradually being enlarged to the point where the curriculum was becoming overcrowded. The influence of the German universities was beginning to make itself felt. With the multiplication of subjects of study and the growing interest in the development of knowledge, a new idea of education was implanted within the colleges.

It was the golden age of laissez faire, and the worth of each person was indicated by his proficiency in a chosen vocation. Education, which always tardily apes the dominant pattern of the age, became increasingly individualistic. It began to be felt that everyone should be free to pursue a course of study in accordance with his inclinations and aptitudes, and that one could rely on the individual

[3] *Two Reports of the Faculty of Amherst College to the Board of Trustees* (Amherst, 1827), pp. 6-8.

[4] Fuess, *op. cit.*, pp. 98-101.

as the *end* of education—that the criterion of success in education was expertness in a particular field.

This new individualistic and secular ideal of scholarship and research, the idea of a university, was inaugurated by Jefferson in the South and by George Ticknor in New England. The two collaborated in their efforts, one to establish a true university in Virginia, the other to graft the university type of organization on Harvard College. Ticknor was one of a group of young intellectuals who began the migration of American students to the German universities, attracted by their growing reputation for freedom of thought and original contributions to knowledge. After several years of study in Europe he was appointed in 1819 to a professorship of the French and Spanish languages at Harvard. His efforts to introduce the elective system and university methods of teaching in the department of foreign languages led to a prolonged and fluctuating struggle between the defenders of the old and the proponents of the new. Ticknor, discouraged, resigned in 1835, but his successor, Longfellow, and some others, notably Agassiz, carried on the battle, and eventually won it with the election of Eliot to the presidency in 1869. Eliot was a chemist and a professor at M.I.T. His election symbolizes the turning point in the history of higher education in America. Here the colleges faced the parting of the ways. They were forced to choose. Should they remain essentially what they had been or should they become assimilated into the German university system? The results of this historic impact of the German university upon the American college were complex and momentous.[5]

It had apparently been the hope of its founders that Amherst might itself develop into a university. That was the title prospectively given it in the charter, and the new plan of 1826 was adopted with that prospect in mind.[6] But after the failure of the new course the issue did not seriously recur until the seventies. Then John W. Burgess tried what Ticknor had attempted more than fifty years earlier at Harvard: to develop graduate work in the college. However, opposition in the faculty was so strong that after three years of effort he resigned and went to Columbia, where he founded the graduate school of political science.

[5] Within a short period of time a large number of universities, private and public, were established.

[6] *Two Reports* . . . , p. 22.

As a group, the new university presidents as well as the new university type of professor displayed a rooted antagonism to the traditional sort of college. It was a barrier that had to be broken down to make way for the new learning. Thus began what W. H. Cowley has termed "the ninety year war on the college." Wayland of Brown in 1841, and Tappan of Michigan a decade later, published proposals for its drastic reformation; Eliot of Harvard, White of Cornell, Barnard of Columbia, Gilman of Johns Hopkins, Jordan of Stanford, and Harper of Chicago all continued and pressed the attack. Professor Burgess, in an essay, *The American University*, published in 1884, well expressed this attitude:

> I confess that I am unable to divine what is to be ultimately the position of colleges which cannot become universities and which will not be gymnasia. I cannot see what reason they will have to exist. It will be largely a waste of capital to maintain them, and largely a waste of time to attend them. It is so now.[7]

Several alternatives to the traditional college were proposed. One, the way usually followed, was to "integrate" the four-year college with the university by adopting a purely elective system which would allow the student to concentrate his field of studies in much the same way as the graduate student did, and to do in his last year at least some of the same kind of work as the graduate student was doing. Another was the device of combined degrees, which allowed the student, after two or three years of undergraduate work heavily loaded with preprofessional courses, to enter a professional or technical school. The most radical and persistently advocated idea, however, was to realign the American educational system on the Prussian model, either by making the secondary school a six-year institution, the educational equivalent of the German *Gymnasium*, from which the student might directly enter graduate work in the university, or by the institution of two-year junior colleges which would achieve the same purpose of completing the secondary education of the students.[8] An impressive list of university presidents then advocated and have continued to advocate this realignment. The western universities, public and private, especially attempted to foster it in terms

[7] Reprinted in *Reminiscences of an American Scholar* (New York, 1934), pp. 349-368.

[8] Johns Hopkins established an undergraduate division only after it was found that there was no other way of securing students adequately trained in the sciences.

of the four-year secondary school and junior college, but no university went so far as to grant the A.B. degree at the end of two years' collegiate work until the recent action of the University of Chicago.[9]

The majority of those colleges which did not become universities, for whatever reason, adopted compromises which were in principle a partial acceptance of the new education. They introduced more and more of the elective system, preprofessional courses, honors work, and so forth, enabling students to anticipate graduate work or easily to transfer to universities offering advanced degrees. In addition, they increasingly distinguished between the first two and the last two years, in effect offering the combination of a junior college course with the anticipation of graduate work in the last two years. Many colleges which could not develop a full-fledged graduate school did offer, at least in their strongest departments, a fifth year leading to the M.A. degree. Thus they hoped to assimilate something of the university type of training and yet remain true to the original purpose of providing liberal education.

THE IMPACT OF THE COMMON SCHOOL

While the development of scholarship and research was infiltrating the colleges from above, primarily through the influence and example of the German universities, an opposite pressure was cumulatively being exerted upon them from below. For a new population flooded into the colleges, producing an inevitable change in the interests and attitudes of the student body.

The movement for free public education was largely confined, during the first half of the nineteenth century, to the field of elementary education, although high schools were early established in many of the larger cities. After the turn of the century, however, the movement rapidly gained momentum. In the past fifty years we have gone through a period of immense educational inflation paralleling the equally phenomenal development of our industrial economy. The

[9] The University of Chicago now admits students at the end of the sophomore year in high school for a four-year course leading to the A.B. degree. This carries to their conclusion the ideas long advocated by President Harper and partially put into effect by him by the establishment of a "junior" and "senior" college at the university and of Joliet Junior College (1902).

following table shows the almost incredible growth in the schools on all levels:[10]

Year	Elementary	Secondary	College
1890	14,181,415	357,813	156,756
1900	16,224,784	695,903	237,592
1910	18,457,228	1,111,393	355,215
1920	20,864,488	2,494,676	597,857
1930	23,588,479	4,799,867	1,100,737
1936	22,770,351	6,435,703	1,208,227

Expenditures for public schools went up even more rapidly: from 63 million dollars in 1870 to over one and one-half billion dollars by 1935. In the half-century from 1870 to 1920 the per capita expense for public education rose from $1.64 to $9.80 and continued steadily to increase. Yet it is still true that "not more than 50 percent of the population finish high school, that seldom more than 25 percent of those who finish high school enter college and that less than half who enter college ever graduate."[11] To provide education for all youth up to the age of eighteen would increase high school enrollments to approximately ten million and add another half-billion dollars to the bill for public education.[12]

There is no reason to suppose that the social forces which have produced this enormous change will not continue to operate. America is rapidly becoming a nation of high school graduates. The public schools have become more and more like the family—the only way you can get out of them is by becoming legally of age. Hence they are an area of life in which it is practically impossible to fail. Everyone must remain until the school-leaving age; many feel that they ought to continue for reasons of prestige or in hope of eventually getting a better job. To remain in school, to be duly promoted, and to graduate, if necessary with the help of "maturity credits," has now become the young citizen's vested right. Small wonder that one American educator has bitterly remarked: "Many of our schools today

[10] Herbert G. Espy, *The Public Secondary School* (Cambridge, Mass., 1939), p. 64.

[11] C. Robert Pace, *They Went to College* (Minneapolis, 1941), p. 52.

[12] Harl R. Douglass, *Secondary Education for Youth in Modern America* (Washington, 1937), p. 113.

resemble a cross between a playground and a juvenile detention home."

In contrast with the European practice, which has been to have different types of schools for different social groups, we have sought to develop a common school, one for all alike. What has happened is that the common school has been gradually moving up to include another four or five years. The result has been, on the secondary level, the emergence of the "comprehensive" high school, a school providing for youth of every degree of ability and from all kinds of homes and backgrounds. A generation ago the high schools were predominantly college preparatory institutions. Now that only a fifth of the students go on to college, the high school curriculum is being redesigned to fit the needs of those who finish their formal schooling when they leave the secondary school. The college is no longer the governing deity of the high school. Its needs have become comparatively trivial and unimportant. The smaller high schools, more conservative by nature and without sufficient resources to expand, still give, in the main, the college preparatory course, but in a diluted form, accommodating it as best they can to a group of pupils to whom it is of little profit since they have neither the type of interest nor the competence that would fit them for college studies. It is no doubt for this reason that the principal of a small New Hampshire high school recently reported with pride: "We've got rid of two years of Latin and now we're working on the other two."

Since the new high school population is neither interested in nor able to undertake the conventional college preparation in languages, mathematics, the sciences, and history, the larger high schools, partly from desperation and partly from conviction, have developed great numbers of quasi-technical, vocational, and practical courses designed to provide young people with school experiences supposed to be more closely related to goals they believe to be relevant and important. A large suburban high school today will offer, in contrast to the two score given fifty years ago, some 200 courses ranging from cooking and carpentry to typewriting and tap dancing. Its program of studies will present six to a dozen curricular patterns besides the college preparatory course, patterns intended to give some sort of preparatory training for nurses, secretaries and clerks, mechanics, and housewives.

These changes reflect our commitment to the goal of secondary education for all. The population of our schools being what it is, they are inevitable, and one must agree that the public schools have succeeded remarkably well when one considers their enormous and rapid growth—what they had to do and what they had to do with. Now that they are entering upon a period of comparative stability, as their goal of universal secondary education comes within sight and as a relative decline in the numbers of children and youth in our population makes itself felt, there appears to be a growing consensus of opinion among students of the secondary school as to how it should be organized.

Studies of the ways in which secondary school students as a group spend their leisure time before and after graduation, and of the failure of the usual curriculum to produce any kind of social and civic competence, have convinced many that the first need is an effective general education. What is meant by "general education" is well described in the report of the Regents' Inquiry into the Character and Cost of Public Education in the State of New York:

> What these boys and girls now need is a broad general education which will give to all alike at least the same minimum essential tools of intercommunication and thinking, the same minimum up-to-date scientific acquaintance with the world in which we live, both natural and social, an appreciation of the culture and standards of our civilization, the beginnings of the ability to work well with others, a common understanding and belief in the democratic process, and the desire to preserve and defend self-government. In addition to this, boys and girls need as individuals some understanding of their own bodies and minds, and the opportunity under proper guidance and stimulation to develop their individual capacities, interests, and possibilities for growth. The first need is common to all; its fulfillment is essential to society. The second is different with each, but its satisfaction is likewise necessary to the growth and enrichment, not only of the individual, but also of society.[13]

Since the school has now, perforce, taken over many of the functions formerly fulfilled by the home, the church, and the small local community, no one who realizes the situation would presumably dispute this need, though how it is to be achieved is another matter. In any case, building on this foundation, secondary school education would,

[13] *Education for American Life: a New Program for the State of New York* (New York, 1938), p. 12.

particularly in the last two years, diverge in two directions, providing for the academic groups the preparation necessary for college and technical school and for the nonacademic groups a form of general and basic vocational training which will prepare them for in-service training in a wide variety of occupations.

The comprehensive high school *should*, by more clearly distinguishing between students with different abilities and expectations in life, find the time and the means to remedy its scandalous neglect of the ablest students, now for the most part submerged in the mass and largely ignored.[14] But in any event they are not likely to get much more than the equivalent of two years of college preparatory work in the high school of the future.

THE JUNIOR COLLEGE

No sooner had our school system settled down to the eight years of common school, followed by the four years of high school and the four-year college course, than new conditions arose which tended to make this organization obsolete. One purpose of the junior high school movement of the 1910's and 1920's was to provide a terminal course for large groups of young people who would go no further in their education. Interest then shifted, as we have seen, to making the high school itself the normal terminus of education. Now many educators are looking to the junior college to give these young people a combined general and vocational training analogous to that once advocated for the junior high school. In four decades they have raised their estimates of the proper levels of education for all, or nearly all, by five years. Thus the American Youth Commission believes that

> . . . in looking to the future we should think in terms of a unified public school system, beginning with such provision for nursery schools and kindergartens as may be possible, and continuing without special break through the fourteenth grade. . . . For the purpose of making the final years of secondary education accessible to all youth who want them and whose records promise that they will put them to good use for individual and social benefit, the Commission recommends that public junior col-

[14] Every reader of this report must know of instances where parents have, despite their belief that children should go to public school, been forced, often when they could ill afford it, to send them to private schools because they were getting little or no stimulus or discipline from their high school studies.

leges and technical institutes be added to the local school systems in every state.[15]

Meanwhile the growth of junior colleges of all sorts has been phenomenal. By 1928 there were 408 such colleges with a total enrollment of over 50,000 students. In 1943 there were 624 with an enrollment of over 300,000.[16] Since 1928 the number of such colleges has increased more than 40 per cent, while their enrollment has increased over 500 per cent. Although many of these colleges are private institutions, it is becoming more and more apparent that their future growth will be largely as extensions of the public schools. There is an increasing tendency toward the reorganization of our school system on a 6-4-4 basis which would make the public junior college a four-year institution embodying the last two years of the present high school.

There is little doubt [says President Coffman] that the junior college movement is a movement toward public education. What is more, in most places the junior colleges are established as a part of the public school system and not as a part of the university system. The prediction seems fully justified that the whole junior college movement is a transition movement and that in the course of time the work done by the junior colleges will become part of the curriculum of the high school.[17]

The relation of the junior college to the four-year colleges is therefore partly complementary and partly competitive. As it is developing, it is a more comprehensive institution than the college. Its natural affiliation in that respect is with the high school. It serves to drain off many students of the nonacademic type who are not really suited for regular four-year college work, to provide further general education at an inexpensive local institution for able but impecunious youths who hope to transfer later to a regular college, and finally to provide a terminal course combining general education with vocational training preparatory to being a member of one of the numerous semi-professions, such as commercial artist, interior decorator, drugstore manager, civil service worker, etc., which are becoming a more and more pervasive feature of our economy. The junior college as it now exists does compete with many of the weaker four-year colleges. As a com-

[15] *Youth and the Future* (Washington, 1942), p. 120.
[16] *School and Society*, June 10, 1944, p. 413.
[17] Lotus D. Coffman, *Freedom Through Education* (Minneapolis, 1939), p. 27.

petitor it represents another infiltration of the older liberal arts college, this time from below. These weaker institutions must now accept largely the lower third of the college student body and are in effect really junior colleges, since more than half of their students usually drop out at the end of one or two years or transfer to a better institution. In many cases these colleges would be benefited if they recognized their real position and became exclusively junior colleges.

The junior college then tends to free the stronger colleges from the dilution caused by the invasion of nonacademic students who are merely seeking more general education,[18] and from the pressure for vocational training from students who would be more properly accommodated in institutes or technical schools. As the function of providing terminal education for a semi-profession becomes, as it probably will, more and more the primary function of the junior college, it may well prove a factor that indirectly strengthens the position of the four-year college.

THE LIBERAL ARTS COLLEGE TODAY

There are now more than 650 colleges and universities of every size and character unevenly scattered over the country, varying immensely in type of control, material resources, nature of the student body, competence of the faculty, and pattern of the curriculum. They are attended by about a million and a half students. Although the greater number of these colleges are small, only one third of the students go to institutions having an enrollment of less than 2000, another third attend institutions having an enrollment of 2000 to 10,000, while the eleven universities with a full-time student enrollment of more than 10,000 absorb the final third of the students. Only 19 per cent of our youth now attend colleges with an enrollment of less than a thousand and only 9 per cent attend colleges with an enrollment of less than 500. This increase in enrollment from the 150,000 of fifty years ago again shows how the rising tide has overflowed the secondary schools and flooded into the colleges and universities. One young person in seven of college age now attends college, whereas but one in every twenty-five was doing so at the beginning of the century. The

[18] The General College at the University of Minnesota is of course a junior college installed for this purpose by the university on the campus.

increase has been out of all proportion to the rise in population or national income.

The typical college was once a small and intimate community bringing students and teachers into a close relationship. Now it is a great impersonal organization on a mass production basis. In the larger universities, hundreds and even thousands of students are enrolled in the introductory courses. The result is indicated in the figures for institutions of all types on student load. Student-teacher ratios in ten-year intervals from 1899 to 1939 are respectively 8-8-10-13-15. In general the teachers of today have nearly twice as many students as did those of forty years ago.

What is the composition of this host of new students? At present, as we have seen, not over 50 per cent of the general population finishes high school and not over 25 per cent of those who complete the high school course enter college, while less than 50 per cent of those who enter college graduate. On the face of it this looks like a highly selective process. In the opinion of the American Youth Commission, however, at least 15 per cent of the students who enter college lack the ability to do real college work, while on the other hand, as a number of studies show (for example, the Pennsylvania Study of the American Youth Commission), less than half of the students whose mental abilities promise a high degree of scholastic success do go to college.[19]

There are thus two factors determining college attendance: intellectual competence and economic means. Of these two the second has come to predominate over the first. The weaker colleges have to accept incompetent students in order to survive, while the great public universities are faced with the major problem of discouraging the incapable from entrance. In addition there is a great number of students who, while they may have a fair degree of intellectual capacity, are by temperament and habit incorrigibly nonintellectual. The in-

[19] Thirty thousand high school students in Pennsylvania were studied, with the following significant results: "While 105 out of each 1,000 high school graduates went on to college and successfully completed the first two years, there were 174 out of each 1,000 who did not go to college, usually because they were financially unable to do so. *The 174 who did not go to college were found to have mental abilities that promised as high a degree of scholastic success as the 105 who did.*" Howard M. Bell, *Youth Tell Their Story* (Washington, 1938), p. 96.

crease in students of this sort has produced an effect on the colleges akin to that we have seen in the secondary schools. The earlier homogeneity of the students in ability and interest has been largely destroyed.[20]

This increasing emphasis upon economic means rather than intellectual ability in the composition of a student body is particularly aggravated by the increased cost of education. President King illustrates this point as follows:

> My father attended Amherst College seventy years ago. He believed, I think, that he acquired as good an education in Amherst as could be had at any American college of his day. Tuition was $100 a year. Today it is $450. The entire cost of operating the college in his day was less than the salaries paid to our Biology Department today. The entire plant of the college in his day (buildings and land) amounted to less, amounted to 25 per cent less, than the cost of our present Chemistry Laboratory. The library then had only one-tenth the books it has today. Today the library budget is as large as the whole college budget in his day. In seventy years our endowment has increased twenty times; our plant fifteen times; our library ten times; our budget thirty times; and our student body three times.[21]

In part these increasing costs are paid by the student but they are also paid in part by taxes or endowments. A large proportion of those who can afford to pay the tuition fees are having another part of their way paid for them and are thus preempting places which could be more competently filled by others. Public institutions through taxes and private colleges through their endowments are subsidizing the education of many students manifestly inferior in interest and aptitude to other students unable to attend college for economic reasons.

It is primarily in response to the demands of these new students, and the public opinion they represent, that many of the colleges, particularly those within universities, have introduced different curricula, combined degrees, and vocational courses, to such an extent that they have become almost unrecognizable for what they once were. At institutions of high standing one may count toward an

[20] In the class of 1834 at Amherst, then a typical college, there were forty men, eighteen of whom became clergymen, nine teachers, five lawyers, and four doctors, while the other four went into some sort of business.

[21] *Alumni Council News*, March, 1944, pp. 181-182.

A.B., or at least a B.S., courses in such subjects as "newspaper reporting," "drugstore practice," "kinesiology," and "sales administration." Other colleges which have not sunk to these depths at least allow courses in "biography," "writing for motion pictures," "problems in the administration of a school system," and "the art of the book" as appropriate subjects for undergraduates to study. Even in the cases where such absurdities are not tolerated, the courses of study have multiplied, ostensibly under the influence of "student demand," to the point where virtually all coherence has disappeared. The number of courses appears to increase not in proportion to the number of students but directly in proportion to the number of instructors, each of whom must have his special niche in the curriculum. Though there remain a few colleges such as Haverford, which (no doubt because it is far behind the times) has a small student body and offers only a few courses, in the largest and most progressive institutions the curriculum has been enriched to the point where the announcement of courses resembles a mail-order catalogue.

Moreover there is hardly a pretense at maintaining a core of essential studies for all students. The common requirement of a group distribution during the first two years usually includes so many possible elections, in deference to the vested interests involved, that it is a sham. The only real requirements usually come down to something or other for a "major," the ability to write the English language (defined as passing a composition course), and to be able to swim fifty yards. This is now the most common definition of the A.B. degree. The student *may*, of course, plan a coherent and comprehensive program of studies and elect it, but he may scatter his elections (subject to the requirement of some sort for a major or field of concentration) on the basis of some such principle as "nothing before ten o'clock or up more than two flights of stairs," or he may concentrate his studies to the point where his last year at least is almost wholly in courses of graduate type. Thus these double forces of disintegration, working from above and from below—the demand by the public for *ad hoc* courses, for preprofessional and vocational subjects, and the increasing departmentalization of subjects and professionalism of teachers under the influence of the universities—had by the twenties virtually destroyed the liberal character of the majority of the larger colleges and of the weaker small ones. Only a few of the better endowed small private colleges, a few university colleges which had partially succeeded in resisting the influence of the university surrounding and pressing upon them, and a few "experimental" colleges preserved much if anything of the earlier atmosphere and spirit. These surviving representatives of what had once been the sole type of higher education have now become a comparatively insignificant part of the whole educational structure.

THE AIMS OF LIBERAL EDUCATION

The result of all these developments has been a chaotic and overlapping school system. The elementary school, the junior high school, the high school, the private secondary school, the junior college, the liberal arts college, the graduate school, and the technical and professional schools all anticipate or duplicate work done in the others. The result has been universal confusion and uncertainty about the aims of all these institutions. This confusion and uncertainty exists generally and is the effect of the increasing disintegration in our society, a result of the fact that in our rapidly changing culture existing institutions must be as quickly transformed to meet new conditions. This modification of their functions entails new conceptions of their significance, which cannot be adequately defined in advance. Institutions must change in a rapidly altering social environment whether they will or not. Family, church, government, business organizations are taking on new functions and dropping old ones. Those institutions which persist in their older ways—which refuse to adapt themselves to an altered environment—perish, while those which passively accommodate themselves to conditions lose their original utility and become parasites in the social body. Only those institutions which attempt to preserve their original character in an altered form, by intelligently reforming their methods of achieving their essential aims, can hope to realize those aims successfully. An institution, like a vital organism, must intelligently adapt itself to its changing environment if it is to continue to realize its purposes. Every institution therefore needs, and is getting, drastic criticism from all quarters.

The chaos of discordant opinion among educators at the present time reflects this disintegration of contemporary society. In particular, the conventional type of liberal college is being subjected to iconoclastic criticism. Many people now regard it as a historical anachronism. They would say that, having begun as a higher preparatory school for men seeking to enter the learned professions, the ministry, and the law, it has steadily lost its usefulness as social conditions have changed. Irresistible social forces, they allege, have gradually converted the liberal colleges into something entirely different from what they originally were: in some cases they have been saved by developing into great universities, but when they have not grown in this direction they have become, as one college president puts it, reservoirs of learning, because every student brings some knowledge with him but few if any ever seem to take any away. Thus the college relapses into a place where athletics, architecture, personality, character, and gentlemanliness are gradually substituted for the intellectual life.

Some of these critics, as we have seen, would abolish the college altogether—they would like to transform our educational institutions in such a way that the student would go on, if he goes on at all, from the preparatory school directly into the university. Others, like Stephen Leacock's horseman, busily ride off in all directions at once in search of a new type of college. Within a comparatively few years there have been such radical, and radically different, departures from the conventional mode of collegiate education as Bennington and Antioch colleges, St. John's College, and the new colleges at the University of Chicago and Northwestern University. Taken collectively, these experiments have nothing in common beyond a total disillusionment with existing collegiate institutions. These radical reformers must usually therefore start anew, either by taking over and completely reorganizing an insolvent institution (as was the case with St. John's), or (as with Bennington) by establishing an entirely new institution.

Those, however, who have not lost their faith in the traditional aims of the liberal college will prefer to operate within the framework of existing institutions and will be content with advocating more moderate reforms. This committee would be satisfied with the liberal college as it *is* if we believed it were effectually achieving its end. It is of course always possible to reply to critics as did an editor of *Punch*. A reader had written to the *Times* complaining that *Punch* was not as good as it used to be. The editor replied that the critic was no doubt right in his assertion, only he had forgotten to add what was also true, that *Punch* never had been as good as it used to be. We would agree with unfriendly critics in this respect, that the liberal college is today less successful than it has ever been; but we would want any reforms within the college to be conservative reforms, conservative in the sense that they attempt to restore to the college those original functions we fear it is gradually and consistently ceasing to perform. In a word, we would like to recapture the colleges for the cause of an intellectual education. As a preeminently intellectual institution the college has an essential role to play in the total life of the community. It should exist as a place where that minority of the youth who can genuinely profit by an academic education, prolonged to the age of 21 or 22, will have the opportunity to enlarge their intellectual perspectives. The supreme aim of a college education is to promote the growth of generalization. On this point one can do no better than quote A. N. Whitehead. What he says of the English university would apply to the American college:

> For those whose formal education is prolonged beyond the school age, the University course or its equivalent is the great period of generalization. The spirit of generalization should dominate a University. . . . A well-planned University course is a wide sweep of generality. I do not mean to say that it should be abstract in the sense of divorce from concrete fact, but that concrete fact should be studied as illustrating the scope of general ideas. . . . Whatever be the detail with which you cram your student, the chance of his meeting in after-life exactly that detail is almost infinitesimal; and if he does meet it, he will probably have forgotten what you taught him about it. . . . The function of a University is to enable you to shed details in favor of principles.[22]

Professor Whitehead is here saying that a liberal education should be *functional* without being *technical* or *professional*. An education of this type aims at developing the power of using abstractions in a way that will enable the individual to deal with a great diversity of experience. Under the conditions of modern life it has become more important than ever before that individuals be able to comprehend intelligently as much of this enormously complex and rapidly changing society in which we live as it is possible for them to do. We may no longer rely with safety on comfortable precedent or blindly follow the routine of accepted custom.

[22] *The Aims of Education* (New York, 1929), pp. 41-42.

It is perilous to learn from *mere* experience, where our experience is constantly breaking the established rules. In childhood one learns chiefly from participation in an established and relatively static environment. The child acquires skills: he learns to walk, dress himself, talk, get along with his parents and his playmates. Here the two complementary phases of an education, the acquisition of essential skills and the intellectual comprehension of the environment, are one and indivisible. With increasing intellectual maturity, however, his education tends to become less a process of learning by direct participation and more a process of comprehending those remote and indirect forces that *condition* his environment by means of the symbolic interpretation of his immediate experience. "I have often wondered," says Santayana, "at those philosophers who have said that all our ideas are derived from experience. They could never have been poets and must have forgotten that they were ever children; for the great problem of education is how to get experience out of ideas."

In terms of this definition one's general education must become progressively more and more intellectual in character, i.e., a general education is in the direction of constant growth of comprehension. The period of life during which this growth is most truly possible is that of late adolescence and early maturity. Between the education of infancy and childhood, which should be primarily a matter of acquiring essential skills by direct participation, and the subsequent training that one receives by the direct method of apprenticeship in technical and professional schools, there lies a period of late adolescence and early maturity when at least the ablest and most gifted members of their generation should be given the opportunity to develop the kind and quality of interests which will enable them to understand how their specific functions, as businessmen, teachers, artists, lawyers, physicians, engineers, etc., fit into the whole complex changing pattern of the Great Society. This is what is meant by saying that a liberal education is functional but not professional or technical.

If a liberal education is to be comprehensive, it should be organized in such a way as to *unify* the most fundamental cultural interests of the society in which we live. The curriculum, we believe, should be organized around three basic foci of interest: the mathematical, physical, and biological sciences, history and the social sciences, and literature and the fine arts. The organization and exposition of subjects should be in terms of these great divisions rather than in terms of a number of diverse departments and a multitude of separate courses. Every student should be required to do at least as much work in each of these three divisions of the curriculum as will give him the sense that he has a community of knowledge and interest with all of his fellow students. Nothing is more in contradiction with the purpose of a liberal education than a curriculum composed of a large number of discrete and uncoordinated courses, all treated as if they were of equal importance. This kind of laissez-faire program is a confession of intellectual bankruptcy. That a faculty should not prescribe certain courses as an essential part of a liberal education is as if a physician should refuse to prescribe specifically for his patient on the ground that all the available remedies would undoubtedly have *some* effect. It is the elective system more than any other single thing that has led to the disconnected way of treating subjects which has done so much to destroy the vitality of our modern curriculum. If students are taught fragments, they cannot learn to think in terms of wholes. This means that the curriculum should be strictly limited in character. There should be far fewer courses than there are now in the program of the average college. To limit the number of courses is not to say that a knowledge of excluded subjects is undesirable. Everything, obviously, is worth knowing in some relation or for some purpose. But some things are in general better worth knowing because they have more relations and fulfill larger purposes than do others.

All the pressure, naturally, is for the multiplication of courses and the creation of new departments to satisfy a hypothetical demand on the part of the students. But it would be better to multiply a few standard courses rather than to add new, different, and presumably less important ones to the curriculum.

Much of the waste and futility that exists in the colleges, according to their critics, is due to the fact that for the most part the student is simply put through a routine of lectures, readings, and examinations, crammed with unassimilated facts and inoculated with inert ideas. It is no wonder, say the critics, that many students emerge from their college career with minds permanently dulled to the reception of new experience.

The difficulty may be that the student too often has a wholly inadequate opportunity to react to the material that he is given. Except in most of his instruction in the sciences, and to a more limited degree in the fine arts, the student does not get, save in occasional seminars during his last two years, any direct stimulus to deal actively with ideas. He is given book learning which is largely secondhand, learning which to be assimilated must of necessity be supplemented by actual laboratory practice. In the mathematical and natural sciences laboratory practice is recognized and established. Students are not expected to study those subjects without learning to solve actual problems. But the application of similar practice in the social sciences or in literary subjects tends to be ignored. Professor Garman many years ago realized this need, and much of his great effectiveness as a teacher was due to the unique way in which he applied such methods to the teaching of philosophy. There should be less of the routine of lectures, recitations, and assigned readings, and there should be constant parallel exercise in the discussion of the materials, with the assignment of individual problems to be worked out and presented by the student. This would involve cutting down the number of conventional courses and the substitution for them of a comparatively small number of fundamental courses pursuing their subject in the spirit of research rather than in the spirit of passive inert acquisition. The majority of students, we believe, would take more interest in their own education if they were given more to do about it. In any case, whatever they actually learn is only that which they have actively acquired for themselves.

In giving a certain type of intellectual education, in striving to promote the growth of generality, the college by indirection is trying to achieve a moral end, the promotion of a certain type of character. President Moore was putting first things first, though some of us prefer to talk of them in a newer idiom, when he defined the "essential and primary object" of Amherst College as the promotion of "knowledge and piety." John Dewey in a passage of his book, A Common *Faith*, intended to describe the religious attitude, has likewise expressed the fundamental intent of liberal education:

The ideal ends to which we attach our faith are not shadowy and wavering. They assume concrete form in our understanding of our relations to one another and the values contained in these relations. We who now live are parts of a humanity that extends into the remote past, a humanity that has interacted with nature. The things in civilization we most prize are not of ourselves. They exist by grace of the doings and sufferings of the continuous human community in which we are a link. Ours is the responsibility of conserving, transmitting, rectifying and expanding the heritage of values we have received that those who come after us may receive it more solid and secure, more widely accessible and more generously shared than we have received it. Here are all the elements for a religious faith that shall not be confined to sect, class, or race. Such a faith has always been implicitly the common faith of mankind. It remains to make it explicit and militant.[23]

So far as an education is truly liberal it inevitably fosters this attitude; not, today, the passive acceptance of an "eternal truth" or a "great tradition" but the active determination to control by intelligence a changing world. There have been many attempts to define the liberally educated man, but none better than Milton's. "I call, therefore, a complete and generous education that which fits a man to perform justly, skilfully, and magnanimously all the offices, both private and public, of peace and war." Toward such an education the college can and should contribute much more than merely the acquisition of knowledge. It must also teach its proper use, that a man's knowledge and skill are his only to serve the good, public and private, of the community. It is the intellectual life of the college as a whole, as itself a community, which must insensibly convey this. Every activity, curricular and extracurricular, within the college will contribute to or detract from it. If the atmosphere of the college is false, one only learns there how to enjoy himself and exploit others; if the atmosphere is true, one may acquire by a sort of contagion a new attitude, the liberal attitude. For "in education it makes all the difference why a man does or learns anything; if he studies it for the sake of his own development or with a view to excellence it is liberal."[24]

While, then, it is the first business of education in general to conserve and perpetuate the past, it is also its duty on the higher levels of liberal and professional education to be consciously progressive. There is a real analogy between liberalism in politics and liberalism

[23] *A Common Faith* (New Haven, 1944), p. 87.
[24] Aristotle, *Politics*, book V, ch. 2.

in education. Liberalism in politics has always asserted faith in intelligence as the only just means of handling social and political affairs. The alternatives to it are the appeal to authority, reliance upon force and deceit, or muddling through. Its historic function therefore has been the *mediation of social change*. Henry George, speaking of modern ships, remarked:

> There is nothing whatever to show that the men who today build and navigate and use such ships are one whit superior in any physical or mental quality to their ancestors, whose best vessel was a coracle of wicker and hide. The enormous improvement which these ships show is not an improvement of human nature; it is an improvement of society—it is due to a wider and fuller union of individual efforts in accomplishments of common ends.[25]

It is the function of the college as an intellectual society within the greater community to foster the growth of this socialized intelligence. Upon its growth the preservation of democracy depends. Education has a unique function in a democracy for, as Dewey has said, "Democracy must be born anew every generation and education is the midwife."

THE ROLE OF THE PRIVATELY ENDOWED COLLEGES

What then is the part of the small endowed independent college? It now enrolls but a small proportion of the whole body of students. It occupies the anomalous position of being uneasily joined to the secondary school on the one hand, to the graduate schools on the other. Its integrity has been assailed by them from above and from below.

Though privately endowed it is a public institution with the historical function of educating an intellectual elite. It should try to preserve its integrity by continuing under changed conditions to perform that function today. In the past the contribution of its graduates to society has been out of all proportion to their numbers. While *Who's Who* no doubt provides but a rough indication of this fact, it is well known that the study by Kunkel and Prentice of college and university graduates included in the 1928-1929 edition showed the smaller colleges as a group to rank far above the great universities,

[25] Here quoted from John Dewey, *Liberalism and Social Action* (New York, 1935), p. 68.

with the exception of Harvard, Yale, and Princeton, in their percentage of living alumni.[26]

It is the duty of the small colleges to strive to continue that influence, to provide, out of all proportion to the numbers of their students, intellectual leadership for our society. That they have done this in the past must be due in part at least to the fact that as small selective institutions they can provide certain conditions for the breeding of a natural aristocracy, one elected, in Jefferson's words, "for genius and virtue," to serve our democracy. To maintain this role, however, they must continue to be what they once were, evangelical institutions. That means, today, that they should become consciously and deliberately experimental in character as some of them, such as Antioch or Swarthmore, already have, endeavoring to make themselves communities which actively prepare their students to play a constructive part in the great social changes now occurring. Professor Whicher has clearly asserted the claims of this ideal:

> As long as the nineteenth century current of liberalism retained its force, it was possible for American colleges to stand aloof from political questions. No basic changes in the structure of human society were involved. Whatever side won, the fundamental values of humanity remained secure. Now, however, the possibility of such aloofness is rapidly diminishing. It seems not unlikely that in the post-war era this college and other institutions that cherish a liberal tradition cannot afford to take an indifferent attitude to the social and political changes that affect the society in which we have our being. They must either become schools of moral and political reform, or they must acquiesce in a growing contempt for things of the mind, and sink to the level of mere nurseries where young Americans congregate to pass through an unthinking larval stage as complaisantly as caterpillars. Certain political tendencies are now abroad which if they become dominant involve the extinction of every value for which the liberal college stands. They are not the peculiar property of German Nazis or Japanese imperialists; the seeds of Fascism exist in every human heart. So it is not impossible that the Fascist system, if checked in Europe,

[26] A similar study made ten years later still showed that, except for Harvard, Yale, Princeton, M.I.T., the two military academies, and such small universities as Johns Hopkins, Virginia, Vanderbilt, and Brown, the top thirty rankings of percentages of living graduates went to the smaller colleges. Amherst ranked second in both studies, below Hampden-Sidney College in 1928-1929 and Harvard in 1938-1939, though her percentage of living graduates had declined from 7.40 to 5.55.

will next manifest itself in some equivalent form in the Western Hemisphere.[27]

It is not the introduction of new courses or the attitudes and interests of some individual teachers and students that we are at this point considering, but the *quality and character of the life of the institution as a whole.* All questions concerning the college, its size, the curriculum, scholarships and admissions, fraternities and athletics, must be judged with this in view. The college was founded to promote knowledge and piety. Piety has been defined as loyalty to the sources of our being. If the college can make itself a democratic intellectual community, profoundly interested in the welfare of the society of which it is a part, its future will do honor to its past.

[27] "Education for Democracy," *Alumni Council News,* July, 1944, p. 207.

PART II

RECOMMENDATIONS OF THE COMMITTEE

THE CURRICULUM

We come now to the specific suggestions and recommendations of the committee. As was indicated in the Preface and in Part I the committee finds itself disposed to start from where we are and build on what we have. We have found it useful and suggestive, however, to learn so far as we could what other institutions, whether comparable or not, are doing. Such knowledge has enabled us to become more explicitly aware than we might be otherwise of the full scope and results of the various possibilities we have considered.[1]

While the committee has studied any proposal which seemed worth its attention, no matter how radical it might appear to be, it has done so with certain precautions in mind. It has tried to avoid being seduced by mere fashions or trends, to remember constantly that no amount of tinkering with the curriculum can be a substitute for good teachers and able students dealing with significant material, that any practicable program for Amherst College must be one which will enlist the support and cooperation of the faculty, and that any recommendations the committee might make would be subject to the provision that the college could obtain funds to put them into effect without increasing the present teaching load of the faculty or preventing ample opportunity for members of the faculty to engage in study and research. We have regarded the reconsideration of the

[1] Among the institutions visited by the chairman or other members of the committee are Antioch, Brown, Columbia, Dartmouth, Harvard, Princeton, St. John's, Swarthmore, Wesleyan, Williams, and Yale. The chairman, or some other member of the committee, has attended a number of intercollegiate conferences on educational problems. The members of the committee have also done a good deal of reading in the extensive literature dealing with the problems of colleges and universities.

curriculum as our central problem and have treated the many other problems we were instructed to study as ancillary to that. Our view has been that policies with respect to such problems as those of admissions and scholarships, the social life and activities of the students, and the organization and government of the college should always be discussed by this committee in the light of their bearing on the aims of the college as an educational institution.

With these things in mind we set forth below a series of recommendations. In making these recommendations we have been guided by the general considerations set forth in Part I of this report as well as by our experience as teachers and our knowledge of the traditions and practices of the college.

Recent Curricular Developments at Amherst

Amherst's present curriculum is a conservative example of what has come to be the usual pattern of organization among the majority of liberal arts colleges. In the abolition of required courses in the first two years, enlargement of the offerings for freshmen, and reliance on a group distribution requirement to take care of the students' general education, while strengthening the requirements for the major and making greater provision for honors work, in order better to insure some proficiency in one field at least—in all these respects Amherst was responding, as were nearly all colleges of her type, in the easiest and most obvious fashion to the increasing demands made by the more recent subjects for parity in the curriculum. As a majority of the faculty know, during even the past fifteen years several departments have been increased and some new ones added. Economics, political science, music, fine arts, psychology, and geography are examples. In his report for 1940-1941 Dean Porter summarized the changes in registration over a decade by comparing the years 1931-1932 with 1940-1941. In those years the percentage of their total number of courses taken by the students in the Division of Languages, Literature and the Arts fell from 47 per cent to 41 per cent, and in the Division of Mathematics and the Natural Sciences from 22 per cent to 21 per cent, while in the Division of Social Studies and Philosophy it rose from 30 per cent to 38 per cent. The number of course elections rose (in all cases, owing to the increase in the size of the college) from 1614 to 1848 in the first of these divisions, from

756 to 954 in the second, and from 1034 to 1715 in the third. Some individual instances indicate even more clearly what was taking place. The percentage of the student body taking Latin declined from 40 per cent to 3 per cent, German from 32 per cent to 18 per cent and mathematics from 39 per cent to 25 per cent, while fine arts increased from 8 per cent to 14 per cent, music from 3 per cent to 15 per cent, political science from 12 per cent to 30 per cent, and psychology from 7 per cent to 12 per cent. These changes indicate the increasing dispersion of the interests of the students and the consequent growth of the curriculum.

As this process has gone on in every institution it has increasingly come to be recognized that the curriculum is losing definition and coherence. There has been more and more concern therefore with the problem of general education. In Amherst this concern became particularly manifest during the academic years 1937-1938 and 1938-1939. In those years there was prolonged discussion, within the faculty, of academic policy. Individuals and groups made various proposals for consideration.

Two principles were generally recognized. As expressed by a group of the faculty in a communication to the Curriculum Committee these were as follows:

> [1] Freshman and Sophomore years are the period when students should range widely and should be brought into contact with all of the broad fields of knowledge included in our curriculum.
>
> [2] Choice is not free when the range of choice is unexplored and unknown. It is the function of the liberal college to require at least an intelligent consideration of a few of the fields of knowledge which the college, by the fact of its teaching them, has marked as significant.[2]

In accordance with these two complementary principles the curriculum for the first two years was thoroughly reorganized:

1. The offerings in the freshman year (previously limited to English, certain foreign languages, history, mathematics, physics, chemistry, and biology), were broadened by allowing freshmen to elect courses in any subjects except economics, dramatic arts, Italian, Spanish, psychology, philosophy, and religion. These remained sophomore electives. In addition, three new courses were introduced into

[2] Communication to the Curriculum Committee, from Professors Atkinson, Beebe, Funnell, Kennedy, Packard, Plough, and Sherman, 1938-1939.

the first year as further enrichments of the freshman curriculum. These were Anthropology, Classical Civilization, and Problems of American Democracy. Some consideration was also given to a proposal for an introductory course of a general nature in the physical sciences especially designed for freshmen who expected to major in another division.

2. In recognition of the second principle the course of study was divided into three broad groups, (a) Mathematics and Natural Science, (b) Social Studies and Philosophy, and (c) Language, Literature and the Arts. The former sequence requirement, that a student must during his three last years elect two courses in two subjects in which courses were taken the preceding year, was replaced by the provision that freshmen and sophomores should elect each year at least one course from each of these groups. At the same time the requirement for the major was expanded from three year-courses in the same subject during three consecutive years, or during the junior and senior years, to five courses, two of which might be in related fields. Concern for the principle of distribution was evinced by the further provision that during the last two years juniors and seniors should elect each year at least one course in a group outside their major.

The Curriculum Committee, in making these proposals, said of the group distribution requirement in its report: "The spirit of this requirement calls for courses broad in scope and by the nature of their subject matter suitable as introductions to the fields of knowledge and experience covered by each of the three major divisions." It was this consideration that led the committee to recommend the approval of the new courses in Anthropology, Classical Civilization, and Problems of American Democracy and to study the possibility of a general course for freshmen in the field of the physical sciences.

The attention of the faculty was also given to the problem of providing a better organization of the curriculum during the last two years. The first steps were the stipulation of five courses instead of three for a major and the approval of two interdepartmental majors, in American Studies and in Renaissance Studies. It was felt, however, that more than this should be done. Accordingly two committees were appointed, one to make a study of comprehensive examinations as used in other colleges, the other to reexamine the relation between special work for honors and the practice of awarding honors at graduation. As the result of the reports of these two committees the present regulations for honors work leading to the degree with distinction were put into effect beginning with the class of 1942.

It is the opinion of this committee that every one of the changes we have just reviewed was a significant improvement over the earlier practices. We should like to go on from there with a further application of the principles which were employed in making those changes, attempting to apply them even more comprehensively in order to secure a still more complete organization of the curriculum. These principles, as we understand them, are as follows:

1. The college should be more or less definitely separated into a lower college and an upper college.

2. During the first two years the student should be primarily concerned with the continuation of his general education. In part this must consist in making up the deficiencies of his secondary school training, particularly in mathematics and languages. In addition, the student's general education should be rounded out by a group of basic courses which will at once complement the work he has done in secondary school and provide an adequate foundation for the work of the last two years. These courses should be both so distributed and so related to one another that by the end of the sophomore year the students will have accomplished two things: they will have a common body of knowledge in each of the three great fields of the curriculum; and each will have been able to make a sufficient beginning in work preparatory to a major, or major with honors, to be able to conclude work for that major during the last two years.

3. The student body should be clearly divided at the end of sophomore year into a "rite" and an "honors" group.

4. During the last two years the student should concentrate on a particular field, departmental or interdepartmental. If he is a "rite" student, this concentration should be limited in such a way that, while he attains a broad general competence in that field, it may be regarded as the conclusion of his general education. If he is an "honors" student, a considerable portion of his work should be done in small seminars and tutorials. It should lead to a comprehensive examination in the field as a whole which will test his competence irrespective of the particular courses he has taken; and it should be crowned by a

"masterpiece" (in the literal sense of the term), a piece of laboratory research or a thesis, the result of original work by the student, which will show his ability to continue his studies further independently of his instructors.

Abstractly considered, the principles of this curriculum, as we have just stated them, demonstrate a real coherence. While many colleges, as we have indicated in Part I,[3] have been infiltrated from below by the secondary school and from above by the graduate school, Amherst still provides a curriculum which completes the general education of all students and at the same time prepares for graduate school the "honors" students, the great majority of whom go on to some kind of professional studies.

The committee considered, for that reason, that any changes or reforms it might propose should be changes in detail designed to improve the implementation of these principles. It soon concluded that, on the whole, the work of the last two years and, in particular, the existing requirements for a major and for the degree with distinction were sound in theory and operated well in practice. We decided, therefore, that we need make no recommendations for any important change in these respects, though later in this section we shall make some suggestions for possible new majors of the "area" and interdepartmental type. The real problem we felt was to be found in the first two years. Despite the changes made regarding distribution of courses and enrichment of the curriculum to which we have referred above, we felt that the demand for an adequate program of general education during the first two years had still not been fully met. In order adequately to meet this demand, we eventually decided, fairly radical changes would have to be made.

The First Two Years

During these first two years at least four things need to be done. First, certain basic skills in the liberal arts, particularly in English, foreign language, and mathematics, must be reinforced and developed. Here, in some instances, whether we like to or not, we must largely continue and supplement the work of the secondary school. Second, there should be, at the same time, as sharp a break as possible with the student's secondary school experience, in the sense that he does in

[3] Cf. pp. 9-18.

his courses a new kind of work and on a higher level, what may be denoted as "college work" in contradistinction to the usual type of secondary school course. Third, there should be on the side of content a body of really common knowledge of the first importance, the kind of knowledge which will give one a broad basis for later specialization in every field of the curriculum though the student will, of course, normally specialize in but one. And, finally, we felt that, as a further meeting of this need for an adult departure, there should be a beginning *at the beginning* of the "honors" type of work.

This last provision would have the merit, if it could be effectively applied, of giving every student an opportunity during the first two years to demonstrate clearly whether or not he was willing to do and capable of doing honors work. Many students, and everyone can think of examples, succumb to a routine of "lessons." They do not discover what real college work entails until they take more advanced courses or commence doing individual work for honors. The introduction of an "honors" type of work into certain courses at the outset should, in many instances, awaken their interest and avoid a good deal of this educational waste. More students should be interested in and able to do "distinction" work as a result. The best students at the beginning of the junior year would enter upon their work for the degree with distinction more advanced in their training for such work. This would be particularly true if the abler students were put, as we believe they should be, into special laboratory or seminar groups, where they could undertake projects of a more difficult sort than those given in "average" sections. In some cases they might well be able to achieve by the end of the junior year the ability to do individual work in a given field that we now expect of them at the completion of their college course. We came, therefore, to regard this last provision as the most important of all. Our discussions of ways and means of organizing the curriculum were largely guided and controlled by the belief that of all things we might do the discovery of some means of putting into effect a "laboratory" or "seminar" type of course for a good part of the work during the first two years would be the greatest improvement we could suggest.

Our problem, then, may be briefly defined as follows: first, adequate provisions for the reinforcement of certain skills, particularly in languages and mathematics; second, the rounding out of the student's general education by the requirement of certain basic courses which would introduce more order into the work of the first two years and provide a body of common knowledge which might be considered as a basis for later specialization in any particular field. In each of these basic courses, so far as possible, there should be provided an interaction and mutual reinforcement of information and skills. These courses should teach both *methods*, in an elementary way at least, and *results*. This, as we saw it, could be best achieved by a *combination* of the usual classroom procedures of recitations, lectures, and discussions with laboratory or seminar periods for small groups on the model or analogy of the usual courses in the laboratory sciences.

The "Laboratory" or "Seminar" Type of Course

We recognize the usual criticism of "survey" courses as superficial omnibus affairs. What we have in mind is not survey courses. Several of the new courses we are proposing should be, we think, organized around certain broad topics or problems chosen for their value as means of introducing the students to the *kind of work* one does in that particular field. Apprentice training in this kind of work would be done in the laboratory or seminar sections; the comprehensive background for the work would be supplied by the lectures and the readings assigned in connection with them.

The most important objectives of the work done in the laboratory or seminar meetings would be to give the student training in the elements of certain skills and at the same time lead him to acquire toward the subject matter of the course something of the attitude of the inquirer who views that field in terms of problems to be solved rather than as merely so many achieved results to be assimilated. We believe that the student will get far more out of the lectures and comprehensive readings he is assigned, will realize more fully that these represent the cumulative result of the research of many workers in that field, if he has been doing at the same time some work himself, in however elementary a way, on similar though less complex problems. These, we believe, are the reasons why laboratory work is given in the introductory courses in the natural sciences—to train the student from the beginning in certain techniques and to confront him with the elementary but significant problems upon which those techniques can be exercised.

The natural sciences are taught with a full realization that it is not enough merely to rehearse what has already been done. The primary thing in science is the use of these results as a basis for further inquiry. Properly to educate a scientist one must instill this attitude from the beginning. This principle has likewise come to be realized and applied in every field of professional and technical training. The beginning law student or medical student is immediately confronted with cases or laboratory and clinical practice. In business and government agencies likewise, the in-service training given the beginner immediately, or almost immediately, puts him to work on the details of actual affairs. He is expected to learn in and through working on the job. This is "realistic" education. The problems created by practical situations allow no bungling or inept solutions. They teach respect for consequences.

The greatest criticism of liberal education has been that it represents the passive acquisition of inert ideas. This is because too much of the usual college program, particularly during the first two years, is a routine of "taking" courses and accumulating "credits." As a rule, the student is given little to do except to listen, to read, and to "integrate" if he can, but at any rate to repeat, in the examinations. His role is that of industrious accumulation. The professor does all the rest of the work *for* the student and brings his finished product to the classroom. Quite literally he too often "gives" the course to the student. Good teachers try to avoid this sin, for they know that teaching by any method is effective only as it reaches the individual student, arouses *his* interest, and guides *him* in the study of the subject.

> In my own work at universities [says Professor Whitehead] I have been much struck by the paralysis of thought induced in pupils by the aimless accumulation of precise knowledge, inert and unutilized. It should be the chief aim of a university professor to exhibit himself in his own true character—that is, as an ignorant man thinking, actively utilizing his small share of knowledge.[4]

And elsewhere he pungently remarks, "Knowledge does not keep any better than fish."

To emphasize practice in introductory courses is to give the subject greater meaning and vitality. It is to restore apprenticeship, which

[4] A. N. Whitehead, *The Aims of Education* (New York, 1929), p. 58.

has always been the natural and effective relation of student to teacher, to *all* levels of college education. It is to give meanings to the abstract portions of a subject by relating them both to the experience of the student and to the concrete details to which those abstractions pertain —for we understand the real meaning of a generalization only in so far as we are able to perceive its specific consequences. It should be unnecessary to add that this emphasis upon practice really makes education more liberal. Professor Christopher Columbus Langdell recognized this principle when he introduced the case method of teaching law at Harvard as "a distinct revolt against regarding the school as a place to get the mere tools of the trade."[5] Any truly educative procedure confronts the student with problems that will arouse his interest and self-activity. Nothing is really more impracticable than merely giving the students results. These are truisms at least as old as Aristotle. Characterizing the teaching of the sophists, he says:

> The teaching they gave to their pupils was ready but rough. For they used to suppose that they trained people by imparting to them not the art but its products, as though anyone professing that he would impart a form of knowledge to obviate pain in the feet, were then not to teach a man the art of shoemaking, or the sources whence he can acquire anything of the kind, but were to present him with several pairs of shoes of all sorts: for he has helped him to meet his need, but has not imparted to him any art.[6]

There does not seem to have been sufficient recognition in college teaching that, if "learning through doing" is essential to the training of the scientist or engineer and the business or professional man, it is equally important in the field of the humanities and social sciences. Because we believe it is essential to the teaching of every subject, we are recommending that it be made an essential element of the general courses proposed in this report.

Since the kind of work done in different fields varies greatly, there would be no uniformity in the character of the laboratories or seminars. In some courses the emphasis would naturally fall upon the acquisition of certain skills while in others it would be mainly upon

[5] A. Lawrence Lowell, *What a University President Has Learned* (New York, 1938), pp. 53-54.

[6] Aristotle, *De Sophisticis Elenchis,* quoted from I. A. Richards, *Interpretation in Teaching* (New York, 1938), p. 3.

subject matter presented in the form of topics or problems. In beginning language courses the laboratory hours might be devoted chiefly to oral practice in the language, in fine arts or music to training in certain basic techniques, in history courses to the analysis of texts and preparation of papers and reports dealing with certain selected problems. English 1-2 as it is now given is, in our opinion, what we mean by a laboratory course. The two courses in humanities that we are proposing, since they would be taught in small sections and would deal with the problems involved in learning how to read a text, are also laboratory courses. Courses in mathematics can presumably be taught in no other way. The entire program which the committee is recommending for the first two years, so far as it concerns those courses *specifically* required, is made up of courses which, in our broad usage of the terms, are of the laboratory or seminar type.

As soon as we tried to think out a program meeting these requirements in detail, we came squarely up against the fact that all curricula are irrational. If everyone could do everything that is important, there would be no difficulty, but the whole problem of intellectual education is controlled by lack of time. All of our choices, therefore, have involved some element of sacrifice. They have been between rival goods. What we can propose is clearly inadequate but we believe it to be better than any of the alternatives we have considered.

The Four-Course Program

The committee soon decided that if general courses of the laboratory or seminar type, that would have both comprehension and depth, were to be established, it would be necessary to institute a four-course program. This is obvious for the first two years. The committee, at the time it made the tentative proposals to the faculty in order to elicit criticism and suggestions, was preoccupied with the problem of the first two years.[7] Partly for that reason and partly because we did not then perceive as clearly as we do now the full implications of these proposals, we suggested in that memorandum a compromise arrangement whereby the first two years would be organized on the four-course basis while for the junior and senior years the present five-course plan would be retained. This asymmetry bothered us because it contradicted our desire to present as simple

[7] Letter to the faculty of June 12, 1944.

and uniform a program as we could. More important than that, the four-course and five-course arrangement would lead to difficulties, we believe, in the scheduling of courses, in the election of more advanced courses by sophomores, and in the election of basic courses by juniors or seniors. Again, we should like to see the introduction of more semester courses, and the four-course and five-course plan would tend to prevent this. Finally, it would also tend to prevent the introduction of the seminar or laboratory type of organization in intermediate and advanced courses. If the proposal for courses of this type is a good one, there should be the opportunity to organize classes in that way on every level.[8]

In addition to these specific objections to the five-course program for the last two years in terms of the type of curriculum we are proposing, there is a more general one. We believe that the average student cannot take five courses that are intensive in character and do justice to them. We also believe that courses offered in the last two years should be fairly intensive. In general, the curriculum for upperclassmen would, in our opinion, be a richer and fuller one if the students took more intensive courses.

We recommend, therefore, that the requirements for graduation be redefined in terms of sixteen year-courses or thirty-two semester-courses.

Semester Courses

The introduction of more semester courses would, we believe, meet criticisms that might be made of the limitations of the four-course program. If a sufficient number of semester courses were added to the curriculum, many students might take as large a number of separate courses during the last two years as they do now. The introduction of more semester courses makes for greater flexibility. It would be more

[8] In the application of the four-course plan we have in mind a maximum of flexibility as regards the number of class meetings a week, or how many of them shall be class meetings and how many laboratory or seminar meetings. Each course would be designed to take one-fourth of the student's time. How that time is to be used is a matter for the instructor and the department concerned to determine. In general we believe that, particularly in many advanced courses, more emphasis should be placed on independent work by the student and less on classroom hours. Under a four-course program many of these courses might well be organized (as they now are) on the basis of three regular class meetings or one two-hour seminar meeting a week.

easily possible for students to accelerate in their studies and to take a larger number of courses outside the field of their major.

If the four-course program is adopted, it seems to us imperative that each department and each group of teachers participating in an interdepartmental major should reconsider *as a whole* their offerings, and that each teacher giving an independent course should study seriously the possibility of recasting it. Courses should not be simply "contracted" or "expanded" to make them fit in as semester or year courses under the new plan; rather, course offerings should be reconstructed in terms of the new plan.

We recommend, therefore, that each department be asked to reconsider its course offerings and to submit to the Curriculum Committee its proposals for the new courses to be offered under a four-course program.

Proposed General Courses

The problem of general education may be approached from the point of view of method or from that of content. Because of the enormous complexity of our present knowledge, some people believe that it is hopeless to attempt to deal with the problem on the side of content. There is no longer any coherent and manageable body of adequate knowledge which can be taught as the core of a liberal education. Individuals who suppose that there is and who attempt to construct a curriculum embodying it are only too apt to substitute a narrow and rigid orthodoxy of "learning" for the living reality of socialized knowledge.[9]

We believe, however, that this point of view is mistaken in what it denies. The question is one of degrees of adequacy. Even if Leibniz was, perhaps, the last man who could hope to know everything important about the liberal arts and sciences, it is not hard to explain why we still have requirements in our curriculum. It is more important, in acquiring a general education, to know some things than it is others, just as it is more important to be able to do some things than it is to be able to do others. Even inadequate knowledge of these important things is better than none. We see no contradiction in approaching this problem, not from the point of view of method or content, but from that of an interaction of method *and* content in

[9] Cf. Part I, pp. 24-31.

which there will be a mutual reinforcement of knowledge and skills. The emphasis upon one or the other phase will vary with the particular course, but in every course there should be, quite naturally, something of both.

As regards the first point, training in methods and in certain basic skills, we agreed: (1) that English 1-2 has proved itself an effective course which should, so far as possible, be required of every student; (2) that, if possible, every student should acquire a real working knowledge of some language other than his own (if this is a modern language, then he should have at least some speaking knowledge of it); (3) that every student should have further training in reading, both in the careful interpretation of written texts and in reading of the more extensive sort; (4) that every student should have some further training at the beginning of his college course in mathematics and in the kinds of methods imparted in a laboratory science; and (5) that every student should have some training, of an elementary sort at least, in the kinds of methods employed in the historical and social sciences.

To a considerable extent, of course, the student already receives training of these different kinds in a variety of courses; but there is not as much order and proportion in the amount of training in each as we should like to see realized, nor is there any requirement at present such that each student receives at least a minimum degree of training in all of these disciplines.

On the side of content, the committee has endeavored to decide (to its own partial satisfaction) what are the more important things which the student might reasonably be expected to know at the end of his first two years. We believe that in some ways it is more significant that the students have a common body of knowledge than it is they have just this particular knowledge as against some other. A common body of knowledge plays an essential part in the creation of an intellectual community. In graduate or professional schools one learns as much, perhaps, from living in a group of students all engaged in a common task and constantly discussing it with others as one does from the formal instruction given.

Furthermore, we have said earlier that it is a fundamental purpose of the college to develop in our students what we have called "socialized intelligence."[10] To us this means that there are certain things

[10] *Ibid.*

they all should know. Granted that we cannot teach them everything they should know, or anything like it, we still should endeavor to teach them as much as we can of what we think they need most to know.

These two requirements, the acquisition of certain fundamental skills and of a body of common knowledge, are what has determined both form and content of the program of courses we are proposing for the first two years. On the side of content we have tried to apply more completely the principle implied in the group distribution requirement by proposing a set of "general" courses, the majority of which would be required, in the fields of mathematics and the natural sciences, history and the social sciences, literature, and fine arts, music, and drama. On the side of skills and method we are proposing the requirement of English 1-2 for virtually all students, a continuation of the requirement of public speaking, foreign languages for students who cannot satisfy the language requirement at entrance, and laboratory or seminar work in the general courses to which we have just referred.

To a large degree the suggestions we are able to make as to the tentative organization and content of these general courses have been derived from our meetings and consultations with groups of the faculty and with individuals in the faculty. A statement of the considerations leading to the proposal of each of the general courses and a tentative description of the content and mode of organization of the courses follows.

A Two-Year Sequence in Science

It is the belief of this committee that the curriculum offered, in the years immediately preceding the war, in the division of the sciences and mathematics was very satisfactory for those students who were taking preprofessional work in these fields, providing them with adequate preparation for graduate work. On the other hand, it is doubtful that the results have been equally satisfactory for the students whose major interest lay in one of the other divisions. The present requirement of two courses in mathematics or science does not insure that such students will obtain any common core of education within this division, built up logically step by step. The most frequent error under the free elective system has been that the study of physics has been postponed beyond the first two years or omitted altogether. Because this subject is fundamentally important to the development of the general field of science, it should come early in the student's college experience and certainly should not be omitted.

With these considerations in mind, the committee recommends to the faculty a program for the first two years in the division of mathematics and the sciences. This program comprises a sequence of topics from the following fields in the order listed: mathematics, physics, astronomy, chemistry, biology, geology. No attempt would be made to include all the material offered in the present first-year courses in these subjects, but rather the inclusion of topics would be based upon the following criteria: (1) Does the topic relate to the other parts of the course, especially to topics from other fields of science (e.g., atomic structure, differential equation for the rate of radioactive decay)? (2) Does the topic illustrate especially well the mathematical or scientific techniques or methods (e.g., laboratory exercises in qualitative analysis)?

The committee realizes that the mere act of putting together a sequence of subjects or even a list of interrelated topics into a two-year course would fall far short of the optimum in establishing connections within the course or between the work of the course as a whole and the student's experience outside the division of mathematics and science. Obviously, whenever possible the teachers in the course should make a conscious effort to establish these connections both by special lectures (e.g., discussion of the fundamental concepts of units of matter and energy applicable to all sciences; general discussion of scientific hypotheses, theories, and laws drawn from several fields of science) and by reference throughout the course to related fields. It would seem desirable that the teacher, who may take a leading part in the presentation of topics from his own field, should assume a minor role in the instruction in related fields; for instance, the professor of physics might present the principal lectures in that subject but take section meetings in mathematics or act as laboratory instructor in chemistry. If different teachers, in occasional years, had this actual teaching experience in fields outside their own, it is felt that much would be accomplished toward insuring that the teachers themselves would make the connections expected of the students.

In spite of the fact that the desirability of establishing connections is generally recognized, we believe that this is not the only objective which should be borne in mind. It seems to us that a comprehension of the methods of science even when dealing with an isolated topic will make the student better able to accomplish his own integration of his educational experience.

The careful organization of such a program would be vital to its success. It would be desirable to set up a small committee to agree on the plan for the course even down to the selection of topics for weekly assignments throughout the two-year period. It would be understood that, during the period when the topics were largely from a specific field, let us say physics, the Department of Physics would play the major role in instruction with the help of some members of other departments especially in handling section meetings and laboratory periods. On the other hand, the selection of topics from the field of physics would be based on the advice of representatives from the departments, let us say, of mathematics or biology as well as physics. It would seem that, in so far as possible, the department primarily concerned should have a major influence in deciding upon the methods of instruction in any specific part of the course. Thus, the one-fourth of the student's time allotted to the course might be very differently distributed among lectures, small section meetings, laboratory work, and outside reading and study at different intervals during the two-year period.

Because of the unconventional nature of the proposed course in science, it is natural that doubts should have been expressed in the faculty as regards the suitability and feasibility of such a course. It is reasonable that the faculty, in considering the adoption of the proposed course, should take into account these or any other possible criticisms with great care. For that reason we have listed below some of the major criticisms which have come to our attention, and have given our answers to them.[11]

[11] Criticism of the proposed science course.

A. It would be superficial if it covered as much ground as planned.

Answer: Time can be saved by eliminating duplication and especially by omitting many topics now included in our elementary courses, which do not meet criteria (1) and (2) cited above.

B. You can't impose the same methods of instruction on such different departments as mathematics and biology.

Answer: We wouldn't try to. See above.

The committee recommends that this two-year course in science be established as a required course.[12]

A Two-Year Sequence in History

One-fourth of the work of the first two years of college would lie in the general field of history. The purpose of this sequence would be to help the student (1) to understand the development of western Europe and the United States and thereby to achieve some appreciation of the forces and values which have contributed to the making of present-day Europe and America, and (2) to think clearly and exactly about problems and controversies which have played an important role in our history.

According to this plan, the freshman year would be devoted to European and the sophomore year to American history. In the brief description of these courses which follows it will be noted that, while both years are similarly organized with provision for lectures and laboratory work, the emphasis in the first year is upon the general survey of historical development and in the second year upon the analysis of selected problems. This difference in emphasis is sug-

---

C. Students enter with varying degrees of preparation in a given subject, e.g., no chemistry, or a good preparatory course; three, or four, years of mathematics.

Answer: Sections should be made to meet this criticism, e.g., so that students having trigonometry would be in a separate section. Resectioning would be necessary when they got to physics or to chemistry. It would be more easily accomplished than under the present system because of the simplification of a program in which all students take virtually the same courses. We should be prepared at all costs to avoid having students repeat the study of material already familiar to them.

D. If required of all students in the first year, the course would be too easy for the student with special aptitude and interest in mathematics and physics.

Answer: Let him take more advanced work if qualified, e.g., a student especially gifted and well prepared in these subjects might take the sophomore course in physics or mathematics in place of the general freshman course.

E. The course would be too difficult for the student who has no special aptitude or interest in science.

Answer: If he has been admitted to college, he ought to be able at least to pass such a course. Bearing this problem in mind the faculty should be prepared to admit to the degree with distinction program any student who does outstanding work in one field even though his work may be mediocre in others.

[12] Certain exceptions to this requirement are recommended by the committee. See "Exceptions to These Requirements" below.

gested in part because of the teaching staff which is likely to be available for this work. We believe the students may well gain from having experience with two somewhat different approaches to the teaching of history but wish to emphasize that a considerable use of the laboratory technique would be made in both courses.

Description of History 1-2. History 1-2 attempts to provide an introduction to the principal, general phases of the development of our Western or world civilization. Beginning with the European heritage from Greek and Roman antiquity, emphasis is placed primarily on the following broad subjects: rise of Christianity and the Church; medieval civilization; Renaissance; expansion of Europe to the New World and to the Far East; intellectual achievements of the seventeenth century; the great revolutions in commerce, industry, politics, and society; and on the results of the foregoing as manifested in the nineteenth century and in the subsequent wars and revolutions of the twentieth century down to the present.

The work consists of lectures and weekly installments of reading. This reading is assigned in a considerable variety of different types of books and is tested in a weekly written exercise. Laboratory periods are employed for:

1. Questions and discussion based on lectures and reading.
2. Individual oral reports, or essays, prepared on specially selected topics designed to:
   a. Supplement and amplify important subjects presented in lectures or reading.
   b. Afford an opportunity for reading and explaining books which are peculiarly representative of certain periods or trends, or which are unusually influential.
   c. Give at least an introduction to what is known as documentary or "source" material, and to the nature of the "scientific" process with which this material is, or ought to be, employed in the presentation of "history."

Description of History 3-4. (Problems in American Civilization). This course should enable the student to gain a fair appreciation of the evolution of American civilization, with topics chosen as far as possible to conform to this objective. However, the main emphasis of the course should be upon the careful study and analysis of a series of important problems in American civilization.

The course should be organized along the following lines. A series of major topics would be selected and about two to four weeks devoted to each. The student would be expected to do little or no reading on these major topics but significant aspects of the topics would be covered by lectures. The seminars, one or more of which should be held in connection with each major topic, would be focused on some problem or controversy having to do with the major topic. Assigned readings on this problem would be required of all students so that they would have a common factual background for the laboratory examination of it. Ordinarily, the student would prepare for each seminar a short paper analyzing the problem. This paper should not be a statement of facts but rather the student's reasoned conclusions based upon his mastery of the facts.

For example, a major topic for a three or four weeks' period might well be Jacksonian democracy. Lectures by the teachers participating in the course should deal with such subjects as the following:

1. Survey of banking history of U.S. emphasizing the struggle over centralization and providing a brief explanation of the nature of banking.
2. Political aspects of the period.
3. Economic aspects of the period.
4. Social and educational changes.
5. American thought and literature.
6. Andrew Jackson or Webster, Clay, and Calhoun.
7. Jacksonian revolution compared with the triumph of Jeffersonian democracy and the Populist revolt.

A suitable seminar problem might be the struggle over the re-chartering of the second U.S. bank. In connection with this problem, the student would be assigned such reading as Jackson's veto message, Webster's reply in the Senate, and selected surveys and analyses of the problem both by contemporaries and by later writers. Other seminar problems which might be used in connection with this major topic are the Nullification controversy, a comparison of the objectives of Jacksonian democracy and the measures advocated by the New Deal, etc. Seminar problems should be chosen so as to bring out various aspects of our civilization, not only political and economic but philosophical, literary, and sociological. But they should be sufficiently narrow in scope to permit the student to get a firm grasp of the situation through his reading.

The committee recommends that these two-year courses in history be established as required courses.

A Two-Year Sequence in Humanities

The third main division of the curriculum is more extensive than the first two and is difficult to define or to delimit. It is the field of "the humanities"—a somewhat battered term, if not without meaning, which we retain for convenience to include literature, philosophy, and the arts.

We believe that it is important to give this field a prominent place in the required curriculum of the first two years. We do not argue the point. Though some may believe that the education of the future should be predominantly scientific and sociological, we do not share this view. The humanities, taken together, constitute an expression of the potentialities of the human mind that beggars description. They have made a contribution of inestimable importance to countless men for thousands of years. They need no defense from us.

It is hardly to be expected, of course, that they will ever again occupy the central position that was once theirs, in that more or less aristocratic education where a certain sector of this great body of material made a real "core" for a gentleman's education. A young man was nourished on Greek and Latin letters and, if affluent, crowned his formal education with "the grand tour." Often enough this had little effect, no doubt, though examples abound to indicate that it was frequently an excellent preparation for intellectual achievement and for public life. But a return to it can scarcely be advocated seriously, though we might remark in passing that a tour, whether "on the continent" or elsewhere, and even if not on the grand scale, may still be a valuable way to round off a young man's education. We are suggesting in this report too many other ways of spending money to go farther on this point.

So we propose no attempt to return to the humanities as they were once understood in a narrower sense. But we do propose to include them. In fact we should like to see the college go farther in the direction of requiring some contact with them than it has gone in the recent past. We say "requiring some contact with them" because precisely that seems to us one of the duties of a college with a conscience. It is not only a matter of a balanced diet; it is also a matter of *tasting* to discover the possibility of liking. This principle applies also, of course, to the other large fields of the curriculum. It is clear that a boy who has had no contact with chemistry cannot know whether he has it in him to be a chemist, and it is equally clear that a boy who has never listened to Beethoven cannot know whether he likes Beethoven, and that a boy who has never been shown what there may be in a book cannot know whether he really likes to read.

The opportunity to make discoveries is clearly one of the most important things in education. Making discoveries, which are often surprises, is a part of development. The child who refuses a dish which he has never tasted, saying "I don't like it," is merely immature. But the adult who believes himself unresponsive to music, for example, may be merely ill educated. If he has investigated it and found in himself no interest and no response, he has a right to his position. If he has not tried it, possibly through a flaw in his education, he may have been denied access to something that might have enriched his life, he may have been cheated of the opportunity to make a discovery of very great importance to him. It is a part of the business of a college to offer this opportunity, to provide this access.

And we think it the college's business, further, to see to it that this shall hold for every student. It is of course true that the proportion of the population that reads good books, listens to good music, or takes art as a natural thing in life is a small minority, though it is increasing and there would seem to be no reason why it should not constantly increase. But we are not concerned with the whole population. We have said that we have in mind a college for students of superior intelligence, even more consciously so than in the past. This enlarges our responsibility. In the field now being considered, just as in other fields, interest and response are as likely to be awakened in the son of a mechanic as in the son of an "intellectual." We consider it imperative, therefore, not merely to offer an opportunity but to require a contact for all students. The opportunity must be really equal.

We should not expect that writers or composers or painters would result. They would probably appear in smaller numbers than the chemists or biologists or historians who might be produced by the proposed requirements in the other fields. What we should hope for would be a larger and more aware audience for the artists, to the greater satisfaction of the audience itself.

Proposed Course Requirements. The committee has been in agreement from the first on the principles just stated. The question of how these principles should, or could, be applied in practical terms has been a difficult one. In the field of the sciences, though details were left to the experts, as they had to be, it was possible to see in general terms what a sequence of two years, for every student, might include. Similarly the introductory course in history, followed by the proposed Problems in American Civilization, seemed to present a reasonable program, for the first two years, in the field of the social studies. In the humanities it has been hard to be certain that one solution was better, or more practical in local terms, than another, and consequently to be certain what was the best solution to recommend.

In considering this problem we have talked with some groups and with a number of individuals. We have examined various programs, intended to be solutions, in other institutions.[13] At least three main types of program exist. One is the course in the straight reading of books, of which the best-known example is probably that at Columbia College. In that course the books are chosen to represent different historical and cultural backgrounds and are read in chronological order. No one method is employed, each teacher using his own devices, though common examinations are given. The course, which is required of freshmen, parallels the first year of the course in Contemporary Civilization, which is approximately the equivalent of our History 1-2, and is followed in the sophomore year by a course in music and fine arts.

A second type of course is one which combines history, in the narrower sense, with the reading of books. An interesting example is the course given to freshmen at Stevens Institute of Technology. In-

[13] For these programs, and various approaches to the question, see Patricia Beesley, *The Revival of the Humanities in American Education* (New York, 1940), and Francis Shoemaker, *Aesthetic Experience and the Humanities* (New York, 1943).

evitably a smaller proportion of the reading is in "primary sources," though the amount that is is impressive. Such a course is in a sense a course in history studied so far as possible through original documents, and some books are read which might not be included in a course where the primary emphasis was on the reading as literature.

There exists at Scripps College an unusual course which might be taken as a unique example of a possible third type. In this course, which runs through three years and is required, the framework of history is used to contain not only works of literature and philosophy but also parallel developments in the fine arts and in music.

A Proposal. The committee considered the possibility of a combination course in which a carefully selected series of readings might be, as it were, inserted in the frame of history, but we reached the conclusion that it would be impractical in Amherst at present. We propose therefore another type of course, which we believe to have a number of positive values. This is a course, essentially of the "Columbia type," in which a series of books, chosen by common agreement among the teachers of the course and from a variety of historical and cultural backgrounds, would be read in chronological order. The teachers participating would have to agree on the books to be read, on the amount of time to be given to each book, and on ways of examining. In general, however, we should expect each teacher to find his own method and to approach the book in his own way. If this produced variety in the sections, that might be to the good. It is a good experience for students to realize that there are many approaches to a masterpiece, and that a number of intelligent adults may each find, in a given book, a different basic significance and a different reason for admiration, which may well not be those that the student himself finds.

We believe that such a course, properly conducted, should and could accomplish several worth-while purposes:

1. It should serve to illustrate and to illuminate the freshman course in history, which it would parallel but with which it would not be formally connected, by bringing the student in actual contact with some representative products of the historical periods which he would be studying elsewhere in a different way. This is a form of genuine integration.

2. It should show the student that the commonly revered but too

seldom read "great books" have something interesting and significant to say, induce a feeling of familiarity with what are called "classics," and help to break down whatever feeling the student may have that they are too august and remote for him.

3. It should show the student, at the very start of his college course, that there are other books than textbooks.

4. It should produce at least a certain number of men who have formed a habit of thoughtful reading.

The matter of integration with, or illustration of, the freshman history course probably needs no extended discussion. It seems beyond doubt that a student who reads some Chaucer or Shakespeare or Locke is likely to arrive at a different and a greater understanding of the Middle Ages or the Renaissance or the age of rationalism.

We believe that it is a desirable thing for an educated man to have acquired the habit of reading. We believe that this habit has been on the decline among college students, and, regretting this, we feel that the college should make a conscious effort to maintain or revive it. It is probably true that, because of various curricular changes, the average graduating senior of today has had less actual experience in reading books, exclusive of textbooks, than his predecessor of twenty or twenty-five years ago. In Amherst of late it has apparently been possible to go through four years without ever reading a book, except a textbook or a document of some specialized sort, merely by satisfying the group requirement in Languages, Literature and the Arts by taking English 1-2 in freshman year and an elementary foreign language course in sophomore year. It seems to us that the college has a duty here.

We believe also that it is desirable to cultivate in the college student a proper "amateur" spirit in his approach to the monuments of his civilization, in literature as well as in the arts. "Classic" literature of all sorts has become too exclusively the concern of specialists and graduate students, which its creators surely did not foresee. The professional may object that such an approach, in an amateur spirit, results in incomplete understanding and, what is worse, in a misleading belief in the young that they really know and comprehend. This is natural enough, though it can and should be combated. But the view of the professional is after all a special one. Henry Adams was probably not the first to suggest that the more a man knows, the less he understands. That the freshman may not make this discovery seems no reason why he should not be started on his way toward making it.

We should not presume to instruct any teacher in such a course as to how he should do his job—as we have said, each teacher should find his own method—but we feel that the approach should be neither pedantic nor merely admiring. The student should not be weighed down with professionalized literary history, but neither should he be told: "This is great; everyone says so; you ought to admire it." In our opinion the proper attack would be simply to take each book for what it has to say, and to try to make the student see and understand as much of that as possible within the limits of time and of his own degree of advancement. As has been suggested, few if any students would see or understand anything approaching *all* that a great book has to offer—this fact is one of the things that make it a great book. Few adult specialists would do so at a first reading. With some books it is conceivable that no one ever does. This seems to us no reason for not giving such a course.

What seems important is to look on the reading of such a book as a natural and normal thing for a layman of ordinary intelligence to do. We know of no better way to bring a college student to this view than to have him read the book with the friendly guidance of an older person who enjoys reading it with him.

The fact that these books would not be textbooks also seems important. With due respect to countless excellent and labor-saving textbooks, the fact remains that they were written as such. In connection with such a course as we have in mind we believe the student should be induced to use the library for himself, to discover that there are other books than those which are kept in a special place in seventy-five or a hundred identical copies, and even to buy books of his own, some of which he may find he wants to keep. There might be established something in the nature of a "Humanities Reading Room," where a student would find a small and carefully selected library in which he could begin to go farther on a point about which the course might have aroused his interest.

No doubt some students would profit not at all by such a course. This remark could be made of practically all courses and does not appear to us to affect the case.

The Problem of Staff. It was at first our idea that the course just discussed should be required of all freshmen. To put such a recommendation into effect a large staff would be necessary, for we believe the course should be given *only* in small sections. This staff should be recruited from the membership of a number of different departments, and the course, like other courses we are proposing, should be established as an independent entity—a "college" and not a departmental concern. Even more important, the staff should be composed exclusively of men with an enthusiastic willingness to undertake such work. No one should be expected or asked to participate unless he declares himself genuinely interested in doing so. If the proposal were approved, certain future appointments to the faculty could of course be made with the needs of this course in mind, but whether such a course could be so staffed, under present conditions, we are not certain.

An Alternative Proposal. We were therefore the more interested in a suggestion for a freshman reading course of a quite different sort, made independently by Professor R. A. Brower. The course which he suggests, and which seems to us to be worthy of serious consideration on its own merits, though its aims are not those the committee has had in mind, would be intended to develop in the student, under careful guidance, the *capacity to read.* It would be essentially a course in *method,* whereas the course suggested by the committee would be primarily concerned with *content.* According to Professor Brower's ideas the student would first be shown that there are various ways of reading a book, each possibly with its own validity; he would then read one book of some heft, fairly slowly, in such a way as to experiment in the application of these various methods of reading and interpretation; finally, and for the major part of the course, he would read a series of books chosen not as illustrating any pattern of European culture or as having any visible connection with the work of History 1-2 (though they would be read in chronological order) but as laboratory exercises, so to speak, in various kinds of reading experience.

Professor Brower's suggested course also would involve a staff of a number of teachers. More than that, it would require, because of its emphasis on method, a much greater degree of unanimity and cooperation among the teachers concerned in it than would the course contemplated by the committee. The two courses would have quite different purposes. Yet both seem to us to offer real contributions.

Recommendation. We recommend that both types of course be instituted and that every freshman be required to take one or the other. The matter of making a choice is admittedly difficult, and it would be necessary to describe both courses, as to purposes and procedures, as carefully as possible. Advisers of freshmen in electing might at times direct a student toward one or the other. It is of course possible that in time one course might generalize itself, so to speak, and the other disappear.

The one real loss in offering two courses, as we see it, would be the "common experience" of having an entire freshman class go through the same set of readings in a given year. In a freshman class of normal size, however, each of the two groups would presumably be large enough to provide some of the advantages of this experience.

Relation to English 1-2. The committee expects that English 1-2 will continue, and recommends that it be required of all freshmen (possibly with occasional exceptions). Since the freshman year would, according to our proposals, be divided into four parts, it becomes necessary *in this one place* to subdivide. We propose an arrangement whereby English 1-2 and one of the two reading courses would each occupy one-eighth of the entire freshman year. English 1-2 and the two humanities courses would be, however, three entirely *separate* courses, each taught independently and each having its own staff. We propose that in the first semester the freshman have English 1-2 three times a week and his reading course twice a week, and that in the second semester this proportion be reversed: English 1-2 twice a week and the reading course three times a week. This arrangement, which in effect would make each course the equivalent of a one-semester course, seems to us preferable to having English 1-2 concentrated in one semester and the reading course in the other semester. The comparative slowness of the reading course in the first semester, furthermore, would enable the History 1-2 course to anticipate the reading to some extent, which seems to us an advantage.

These proposals constitute our recommended program for the freshman year in the general field of the humanities. Work in foreign languages, which is discussed elsewhere in this report, would in the freshman year fall outside the divisional requirement in the humanities and would in many cases, presumably, occupy the fourth quarter of the student's program.

There remains the question of the appropriate requirement, if any, to make in this field in the sophomore year. According to some ideas this would be the proper time for a required course in the arts, since theoretically the student would have had his opportunity to make contact with the general subject of literature in his freshman year. The idea of a course introducing the student to the methods and to the matter of certain arts, and required of all sophomores, is a most interesting one and has been discussed at length. We recommend that such a course as is described below be instituted and established in the sophomore year as an elective, but we have concluded that it is inadvisable at the present time to recommend that the course be required.

An Introductory Course in the Arts. Owing to the absence of five of the seven members of the Departments of Fine Arts, Music, and Dramatic Arts, the problem of drawing up plans for a combined course has been a difficult one. All members have, however, been consulted either directly or by correspondence, and the course outlined below has the substantial approval of the group.

Believing that most undergraduates have no more than a passing acquaintance with some one of the arts, we thought it advisable to provide an introduction to the three arts represented in our curriculum the understanding of which depends in whole or in part on a largely nonverbal means of communication: fine arts, music, and drama. By including all three in a single course the student would be able to discover which one proved to be of the greatest value to him, and he would also acquire a deepened sense of aesthetic awareness.

The first part of the course would be divided into three periods during which the materials and methods of organization employed by the three arts would be discussed separately. (Frequent cross reference, however, might be found advantageous.) No attempt would be made to relate the material being discussed to its historical or sociological background. The emphasis would be entirely on learning how a man achieves articulate expression in drama, fine arts, or music.

The second part of the course would be devoted to a comparative examination of the arts in three or four epochs. Here similarities and differences in modes of expression would be noted, and the nature of the content expressible in the different media would be clarified. A careful analysis of a few examples taken from each field and demonstration of their relation to the times in which they were created should provide a clearer idea of how man expresses himself in aesthetic terms.[14]

A Sophomore Requirement. Assuming that the proposed course were established, we recommend that every sophomore be required to elect in the field of the humanities one year-course or two semester-courses to be chosen from an approved and specific list which should include:

1. An introductory course in the arts, such as the course proposed above.
2. An introductory course in either the fine arts, music, or dramatic arts, similar to the courses given before the war.
3. A course in English literature, possibly one, or one of a number, specified by the English Department as fulfilling the requirement.
4. A course in the literature of a foreign language, which should be, in the opinion of the department concerned, one in which the student would be sufficiently advanced in his study of the language to be able to give serious consideration to his reading as literature rather than as material for translation.
5. An introductory course in philosophy, in which a considerable amount of text would be read, chosen from various writers of different periods.
6. A course in classical civilization, in which a large amount of emphasis would be placed on Greek and Latin literature and philosophy, and a considerable amount of text read in translation.

This requirement would obviously allow the sophomore a choice not offered in either of the other two fields. In view of the diversity of the subject matter, and of what seem to us the legitimate variations in the personal inclinations of students, such a choice, within the indicated limits, does not seem to us improper at this point. In the

[14] DISSENT.—While I approve the recommendation of a combined course in music and fine arts for sophomores, I do not agree that drama should be included in it. It does not seem to me that drama can be rightly described as "largely non-verbal," and, so far as the term "dramatic arts" means "the arts of the theater," those arts seem to me to be by their very nature *impermanent* and not to be ranked, as creation, with architecture, sculpture, painting, or music. I also dissent from recommendation 2 in the following paragraph, in that I should not accept a course in dramatic arts as satisfying the sophomore requirements in humanities. Unlike the sophomore courses in music and fine arts, that in dramatic arts does not lead to a major, and I see no reason why a student wishing to elect it should not do so in his junior or senior year. G. B. FUNNELL.

sophomore year also, work in foreign language of an elementary nature would not be approved in satisfaction of the group requirement in the humanities field.

We believe that after two years of work in this general field, even with the amount of choice suggested, majors and honors work in the various departments within the humanities could be developed satisfactorily, and that students majoring in other fields would have a worth-while experience better, possibly, than our present group requirements can be relied on to produce.

Foreign Languages

The committee assumes that the college will maintain, possibly with greater emphasis than in the past, the position which it has always held with regard to the study of foreign languages: that they are an important element in a liberal education. We believe that the college should so construct its program that every student will have a fairly good working knowledge of at least one foreign language but that the application of this general principle should be broader and more flexible than before the war. We believe also that honors students should be in every way encouraged to acquire a knowledge of more than one foreign language.

Whatever our requirement may be, it is of course the business of the foreign language departments to put it into effect. The determination of the requirement, however, is the business of the faculty. We recall briefly some past history.

For a great many years the college required that every student study Latin for at least five years or Greek for at least three years, and in addition that he show evidence of possessing a "reading knowledge" of a modern language. So far as the ancient languages are concerned, the requirement has ceased to exist. Fairly recently the modern language requirement was modified so that it was no longer possible to satisfy it in Italian or Spanish; it became in fact a requirement of a "reading knowledge" of either French or German. Still more recently the administration of the requirement was modified so that the student might satisfy it, not only by passing a special examination at Amherst, but also by either attaining a sufficiently high score in the College Entrance Examination Board test in the language at entrance or completing certain courses, with specified grades, in college.

The usual arguments for the study of a foreign language are: (1) as a discipline in itself; (2) as an adjunct to the student's mastery of English; (3) as a "tool" for advanced work in other fields; (4) as a contribution to breaking down the student's mental provincialism. These are here discussed separately.

A Foreign Language as a Discipline in Itself. This seems to us a sound argument, which may need no great amount of comment. It is somewhat analogous to the argument for mathematics, a "beautiful" thing in itself quite aside from its potential applications. Language also is a "beautiful" thing, and properly taught it can hardly fail to do something to the mental processes of an intelligent student, particularly if he is studying it voluntarily. It is not quite as *an sich* as is mathematics, and for its fullest value to be realized it should be applied—that is, the student ideally should go to the point where he can use it for the purposes for which it exists. But even the study of a small amount of a foreign language (and when this is the case it will always be, according to our proposals, at least a *second* language for the student) has educational value and is a discipline.

A Foreign Language as an Adjunct to the Student's Mastery of English. This is one of the intangibles. Some educators take this argument as an axiom. Many teachers profess to believe in it, and some express this belief with vigor. Some teachers, perhaps those whose own work does not bring them into any large or significant contact with foreign languages, seem indifferent.

A Foreign Language as a Tool. This is a very common argument, but it may be remarked that no tool has much importance unless it is used. There seems to exist evidence that in the past considerable numbers of Amherst students have acquired (possibly in school, of course) the ability to use a foreign language as a working tool and have in fact so used it for the attainment of important results. Cases could be cited to show that the "tool" command of a language can be attained and significantly used. Disregarding men who have entered graduate work in the language field itself, the evidence seems to show that if a tool is needed a man either will have it or will get it.

Occasionally the tool may be useful before graduate work is reached. In recent years there has existed at least one course which has required and, what is more, has *used* a reading knowledge of French. Some other courses that have not published such a requirement have undoubtedly set students at work which necessitated using French or German when the student's ability to use the language and his personal inclinations made that possible.

On the other hand, some teachers have been heard to complain that their students cannot use French or German in such a way as to satisfy them. There is no telling how many students may have been prevented from doing a certain kind of work, or from doing it to a certain degree of satisfaction, because of an inadequate ability to read French or German. The evidence is lacking.

It seems possible to say, however: (1) that we have been theoretically providing all students with one or two tools which many have never been called on to use; (2) that we have been providing them with a tool theoretically in usable shape which in a practical test often does not prove effectively useful; (3) that the good and serious student who needs such tools either will have or will acquire them, even in some cases a considerable number of them.

We do not believe that the tool argument is an adequate reason for our requirement of either French or German. It seems to us desirable, however, that more use should be made of languages as tools in advanced undergraduate work, particularly for honors students. If the departments which do them lip service believe in French and German, or in other languages, as important tools they can both say so more emphatically and see to it that their students really use them. We feel that this point is a matter to be determined by the departments and divisions rather than by the college, and we recommend it to the departments and divisions for consideration.

A Foreign Language as Contributing to the Breakdown of Provincialism. To us this seems the most important point. It is important, to quote a well-remembered local phrase, that students should not leave college "with the notion that God and the Holy Angels speak English." The realization of this immensely significant point is one of the most educative things that can happen to a college student. Though it may be possible to be overidealistic in this matter, we believe that the future world will need as many intelligent people who are aware of this truth as it can have.

This being so, there seems no immediately visible way of encouraging such an awareness in a young American that will be better than putting him through a fairly intensive course (which means more than one year, and perhaps more than two years) of study of some other language than English. There may be no compelling argument for continuing to require that all our students learn at least a little something about either French or German. But there seems a powerful argument for requiring that all our students learn more than "a little something" of *some* foreign language, be able—to some extent at least—to use it, and if possible be put in some position or through some experience where they will use it. What is important is that the language be *foreign*.

The committee believes, therefore, that the college should (1) expand the list of foreign languages which may be used to satisfy a degree requirement to include a much larger number and (2) expect that the student's mastery and command of his foreign language become a matter to be taken more seriously than our present "reading knowledge" requirement. Just how seriously is a point on which the advice of the language departments would be needed.

A certain number of other points remain to be mentioned.

Ancient Languages in Satisfaction of the Requirement. The only apparent objection to this is that the student would not gain the experience in practical use of the language which we have in mind for the modern languages. The numbers concerned, however, would probably be small, and it is unlikely that a student in classics would have had no work whatever in a modern language. Otherwise we believe that a student with a satisfactory knowledge of Greek or Latin, as certified by the proper department, should be considered as having satisfied our requirement.

A Student's Native Language. In view of the possibility of a larger number of foreign students in American colleges after the war, this point acquires more importance, but we believe it to be valid in any case. A native Russian or Chinese or Brazilian who knows enough English to be a student in an American college will have quite sufficient language experience to insure that what we consider the purposes of a language requirement will have been satisfied in his case. We see no point in requiring such a man to study a foreign language, *in English,* at Amherst, unless of course he wants it. This principle should, however, apply only to students who had lived and gone to school in foreign countries, and not to second-generation Americans who may have some slight knowledge of their parents' language.

Russian. We believe that as soon as it may be feasible the college should appoint to the faculty a teacher of Russian. How much would, or should, be taught is another matter, and on that point would depend the decision as to whether Russian could be used to satisfy the degree requirement in language.

Portuguese. Since we believe that a student would ordinarily have to go beyond the intermediate stage in his study of a language in order to satisfy such a requirement as we have in mind, we doubt that it would be possible to satisfy the requirement in Portuguese, except in the case of a native. Since Portuguese is unlikely to be the only foreign language studied, this is probably not an important point.

Methods of Teaching. These are of course the concern of the language departments, who are well aware of the currents of thought started by the A.S.T.P. programs. We assume that these departments will make their own plans and in due time such recommendations as may be necessary to the faculty. We make two suggestions, however: (1) that the teaching should be so planned as to produce in the student as much ability to use the language as may be possible in each individual case, not so much that he may be able to speak to the waiter as that he may acquire at least a certain amount of *Sprachgefühl* and be aware in his reading that the language is alive, and (2) that the main emphasis in the advanced work should continue to be placed on the literature of the language, but that more should be done, possibly at the lower levels, along the line of "civilization" work, regardless of whether "area" studies are instituted in the college at large.

Though the teaching of language is a technical matter, we assume that the departments concerned would be ready to take advantage of the extra proportion of the students' time which would be at their disposal, if the four-course plan were adopted, for a specialized kind of laboratory work which would presumably, in particular at the lower levels, take the form of additional hours for drill and practice in the use of the language.

We make the following *recommendations:*

1. That every student be required, in order to receive a degree, to satisfy a language requirement which, within such practical limits as may be determined by the language departments, will insure a firmer

grasp of the language than our present "reading knowledge" requirement.

2. That the list of languages in which the requirement may be satisfied be expanded to include: French, German, ancient Greek, Italian, Latin, Spanish, and any other language which may be approved in an individual case.

3. That the native language of a foreign-born student, educated in a foreign country, be accepted in satisfaction of the requirement.

4. That the departments and divisions give serious consideration to the possibility and advisability of requiring a knowledge of more than one foreign language in connection with advanced work, particularly for honors students.

5. That the teaching of Russian be instituted when possible, and the possibility of satisfying the stated requirement in Russian be studied.

Summary of Recommendations for the Freshman-Sophomore Years

Some of the assumptions underlying the type of curriculum here recommended for the first two years are:

1. That one learns by doing something about it when confronted with a problem. The "laboratory" or "seminar" is primarily intended to supply for freshmen and sophomores in an elementary way a greater opportunity for that kind of education. In particular, the student should learn by doing it something of the methods, i.e., the *kind of work done,* in the historical and social as well as in the mathematical and natural sciences.

2. Dissatisfaction with the more or less "free" elective system and the belief that all students should be brought in contact with a certain body of knowledge, or with a certain type of experience, or both. (Provision should, of course, be made to excuse students from certain requirements where their preparatory education warrants it.) Superficiality of a sort is conceded, but specialists are not expected as the product and a minimum knowledge is better than none.

3. That every student should have a good working knowledge both of his own language and of another language than his own. (In the case of modern languages this should include some speaking as well as reading knowledge of that language.)

4. That it is essential for the student to have a thorough grounding in the fundamentals of mathematics and the natural sciences.

5. That it is essential for the student to know the "Western" or European background and also his own civilization; and that history and the humanities can perhaps be brought more closely together.

RECOMMENDED FRESHMAN-SOPHOMORE CURRICULUM

Semester				
I	Science 1	History 1	English 1 (3 hrs.) *and* Humanities A 1 or B 1 (2 hrs.)	Foreign language or elective
II	Science 2	History 2	English 2 (2 hrs.) *and* Humanities A 2 or B 2 (3 hrs.)	Foreign language or elective
			Summer Reading Period[a]	
III	Science 3	History 3 (Problems in American Civilization)	A course in one of: (a) Literature— English or foreign (b) Classical Civilization (c) Philosophy (d) Fine Arts, Music and Drama[b]	Elective
IV	Science 4	History 4 (Problems in American Civilization)	A course in one of: (a) Literature— English or foreign (b) Classical Civilization (c) Philosophy (d) Fine Arts, Music and Drama[b]	Elective

[a] See "Summer Reading," below.
[b] Or an introductory course in either fine arts, music, or dramatic arts, similar to the courses given before the war.

Requirements for Admission to the Work of the Junior-Senior Years

We recommend that:

1. The student must elect (as now) one year-course, or the equivalent in semester-courses, in each of the first two years in each of the three divisions.

2. In satisfying the group requirement, the student must ordinarily

elect in the freshman year: Science 1-2; History 1-2; English 1-2; and either Humanities A or Humanities B. In the sophomore year he must ordinarily elect: Science 3-4; History 3-4 (Problems in American Civilization); and one of the following: Classical Civilization; Fine Arts, Music and Drama 1-2; an introductory course in either fine arts, music, or dramatic arts; Introduction to Philosophical Literature; or a course in literature in English or in a foreign language.

3. The student must acquire at least a reading knowledge of one foreign language: French, German, ancient Greek, Italian, Latin, Spanish, or another language which may be approved in an individual case.

Exceptions to These Requirements. It is important that no set of requirements be imposed or administered in such a way that it will (1) force students to repeat work they have already had or (2) prevent them from carrying out a plan of studies which is consistent with the purposes that these requirements are intended to fulfill. The only instances the committee is aware of in which these two conditions are likely to arise are in cases where students are planning to major in certain sciences or where they wish to study two languages (most often it would be Greek or Latin and a modern language) during the freshman year.

To meet these conditions the committee recommends the two following "escape" clauses:

1. That a student planning to major in science may, at the discretion of the department in which he expects to do the work for the major, elect in his sophomore year a parallel course in a science in place of Science 3-4.

2. That a student who wishes to take two courses in foreign language, ancient or modern, during his freshman year, and who has passed the College Entrance Board examinations in English with a sufficiently high score, may take a second course in a foreign language in place of the English 1-2 and Humanities courses, if one of the two courses in foreign language is a course in the *literature* of that language.

The moral of these sample curricula seems to be: (1) all students in the first two years would be taking largely similar courses; (2) except in the sciences, in foreign languages, in English, and in history, students could not normally begin a major until the sophomore year; (3) few students could afford to elect more than one course per

SAMPLE COURSE ELECTIONS[a]

A. A *premedical student* who needs foreign language:

1st year	*2nd year*
Science 1-2	Science 3-4
German or French	Elective
Humanities and English 1-2	A course in literature, or the arts, etc.
History 1-2	American Civilization 1-2

B. A sample *science major*, e.g., chemistry:

Science 1-2	Chemistry
Foreign language	Mathematics
Humanities and English 1-2	A course in literature, or the arts, etc.
History 1-2	American Civilization 1-2

C. A *major in social sciences* who needs at least two years of foreign language:

Science 1-2	Science 3-4
Foreign language	A course in the literature of a foreign language
Humanities and English 1-2	Economics or Political Science, etc.
History 1-2	American Civilization 1-2

D. A *major in social sciences* who needs one year of foreign language:

Science 1-2	Science 3-4
Foreign language	A course in literature, or the arts, etc.
Humanities and English 1-2	Economics or Political Science, etc.
History 1-2	American Civilization 1-2

E. A *major in humanities*, e.g., English:

Science 1-2	Science 3-4
Foreign language	Foreign language
Humanities and English 1-2	English literature
History 1-2	American Civilization 1-2

F. A *major in humanities*, e.g., fine arts:

Science 1-2	Science 3-4
Foreign language	Foreign language or elective
Humanities and English 1-2	Fine Arts, Music, and Drama
History 1-2	American Civilization 1-2

[a] The student who needs a second year of foreign language will be able to satisfy the sophomore humanities requirement by taking a second course in that language. This means that the student is free to take half of his work, including the general courses, in the field of his major during the sophomore year.

year in any given department (aside from the "general" courses) during the first two years.

The Junior-Senior Years

We believe, as we have indicated above, that the existing provisions for the major and for the degree with distinction should be retained. If, as we have proposed, the four-course program were adopted, it would be necessary to modify accordingly the present statement of the requirement for the major.

Requirements for the Major. We recommended that the revised statement be as follows:

A major consists of eight semester-courses pursued under the direction of a department or special group. The major cannot begin later than the junior year and may begin in either the freshman or sophomore year; it must be completed in the senior year. No year without a course in the major may intervene between its beginning and its end. Each department decides whether a freshman course in the department shall count toward its major.

The major requirements can be met in accordance with either of two plans:

Plan A: Not less than six of eight semester-courses must be within a department; not more than two may be in related fields approved by the major department.

Plan B: Combinations of courses not provided for under Plan A, but similar in aim to the established group majors in American Studies and Renaissance Studies, may be made with the consent of the several departments concerned, and of the Dean.

In order to insure that the student continues his general education to some degree during the last two years and does not concentrate his work exclusively within one division, it has also been provided that during the junior and senior years the student must elect at least four semester-courses outside of the division in which he is majoring. We approve this provision and recommend that it be retained. Under the present regulations the student *can* take, during the last two years, as much as four-fifths of his work within a single division, but *must* take one-fifth of it in other divisions. Under the four-course program the student *could* take during the last two years as much as three-fourths of his work within a single division, but would *have* to take the remaining fourth in other divisions.

The Degree with Distinction

Candidates for the degree with distinction must at present have a general average of at least 80 per cent at the end of the sophomore year. If our recommendations for the first two years were adopted, we think it would be desirable to modify this regulation. Under those proposals all students would have to take certain subjects (e.g., mathematics) whether those subjects were hard for them or not. The committee believes that a great majority of the students who belong in a college are capable of doing reasonably good work in every division of the curriculum, though many of them will be more capable in one kind of studies than another. There are, however, a few students who have incurable "blind spots," whether native or acquired. These special cases should be dealt with appropriately by the Dean. A few such persons he may well excuse from taking, others from repeating, a certain required course. These requirements are not set up on Mr. Dooley's theory, "It makes no difference what you teach a boy, so long as he doesn't like it," but on G. K. Chesterton's, "What is worth doing is worth doing poorly." In consequence, there may be a few students of marked ability in one field, but so inept in another that they are unable to achieve the 80 per cent average that would make them eligible to become candidates for the degree with distinction. These few cases should be dealt with individually.

We recommend that when in the opinion of the department concerned it is warranted, and with the consent of the Dean, a student whose average is below 80 per cent at the end of sophomore year may be admitted to candidacy for the degree with distinction. Students so admitted would, of course, still be required to have a minimum final college average of 80 to be eligible to be considered for the degree *cum laude*, of 86 for the degree *magna cum laude*, and of 90 for the degree *summa cum laude*.

Individual Work for Honors

Candidates for the degree with distinction are at present allowed to take two-fifths of their work in junior year and two-fifths in senior year in "conference courses" or tutorials where they may do individual work in preparation for the comprehensive examination and carry out a project in the laboratory or write a thesis. The committee believes that it is important in working with honors students to encourage independent study of this sort.

We therefore recommend that a candidate for the degree with distinction be permitted, at the discretion of the department in which he is majoring, to substitute in his junior year a conference course or tutorial for one of the four regular courses required, and in his senior year a conference course or tutorial for one or two of the four regular courses required.

The adoption of this recommendation would change the existing practice in only one respect. It would make it possible for certain exceptionally mature and capable students to spend as much as half of their senior year doing individual work, under the supervision of the department in which they are majoring, outside of formal courses. There are always some students for whom nothing is too good. What they may need most is a fair amount of salutary neglect.

Alternative Plans for Honors Work

The committee made some study of other plans, especially the type of honors work at Swarthmore, adaptations of which have recently been put into effect by a number of institutions including Smith College and the University of Rochester.[15] There is one feature of the Swarthmore plan we suggest might now be adopted. Those departments which wish to do so might experiment with the practice of having outside examiners for the comprehensive examinations given honors candidates.

Honors Work for Everyone

It has been suggested that the honors type of work might be extended to all students during the last two years. This proposal the committee has considered and rejected. The committee believes that if the laboratory or seminar plan is adopted those students who are really capable of the honors type of work will quickly be discovered and stimulated to become candidates for the degree with distinction. The result should be that more students will undertake honors work. There have been, we believe, a good many students in the college

[15] For an excellent discussion of the various kinds of honors plans, see Frank Aydelotte, *Breaking the Academic Lockstep; the Development of Honors Work in American Colleges and Universities* (New York, 1944).

capable of honors work who never became sufficiently interested to try. If, as we shall point out in the section on admissions, ways can be found to recruit a larger number of able students, that too will foster the tendency for the proportion of honors students to increase. We hope that in this way the college will gradually become more and more of an honors college, but we do not believe that the honors type of work should be offered to students who by the end of the first two years have shown themselves really incapable of it. "Honors work for everybody" would, we feel, lead to a gradual dilution of our present standards and would involve the expenditure of a great deal of time and effort for which there would be comparatively little reward in the way of student accomplishment.

Comprehensive Examinations

For not dissimilar reasons, we have rejected the suggestion that comprehensive examinations be given to all students toward the end of their college course. We now have comprehensive examinations, both oral and written, for honors students, and these we heartily approve. However, comprehensive examinations for everybody are quite another thing. They too, we fear, would lead to a gradual dilution of standards. The experience of some institutions where this is the practice would seem to show that mediocre students cannot do well with them unless they are given special "correlation" courses or special tutorials to get them prepared for the examination. If the mediocre student still has to have his correlating done for him when a senior, the real purpose of such examinations is defeated. We believe that comprehensive examinations for everyone toward the end of the college course, like honors for everyone, would also mean a great deal of additional work with little commensurate return.

The committee views with more sympathy the suggestion that comprehensive examinations be given to everyone toward the end of the sophomore year as a prerequisite for admission to the upper college. These, we believe, would be valuable, so long as there is only a group distribution requirement to regulate the student's elections, as an additional means of enforcing a more orderly and substantial achievement during the first two years. We believe, though, that such examinations would have to be, for the majority of the students at that level of maturity, largely a review and coordination of what they have retained from their courses. We think it preferable to secure the coordination within the courses themselves. The examinations in the general courses we are recommending would in effect be a series of "comprehensives" since the courses are themselves comprehensive. Any comprehensive examination that might be introduced would, perforce, largely duplicate or repeat those examinations. Requiring a substantial number of courses of the type we have recommended will, we believe, attain the same end in a more efficient way.

Interdepartmental Majors

The faculty has already given blanket approval to the formation of additional majors of this sort by its provision that "Combinations of courses . . . similar in aim to the established group majors in American Studies and Renaissance Studies, may be made with the consent of the departments concerned and of the Dean." We believe that the existing group majors should be strengthened and that a few additional ones, carefully chosen and planned, should be established. Some of these would be of the "area and language" type. Examples, including those we now have, of group majors which might be feasible, in view of our size and resources, are:

1. Classical Studies.
2. Renaissance Studies.
3. English Studies.
4. European Studies.
5. American Studies.
6. South American Studies.
7. International Relations.

The organization of a series of such group majors in the upper college would complement the type of curriculum we have proposed for the first two years. They should help to give renewed freshness and vitality to the liberal arts program for students and teachers alike. For many students, who might be planning to enter government service or employment in the foreign branches of large business concerns, they would be the ideal foundation for later graduate or in-service training.

The committee has not studied this question in sufficient detail to make specific recommendations. We are, however, convinced that it is important to develop more of such group majors.

We recommend, therefore, that the faculty instruct the Curriculum Committee to make a special study of the possibility of establishing a few more group majors.

Some Minor Curricular Proposals

There is no end to what a committee can think of doing to a curriculum once it is given the mandate to reconsider everything. We shall bring forward in this section only a few of the many "minor" proposals that have been brought up in the course of our discussions.

The Reading Period. The reading period has, we believe, demonstrated its value in certain courses for students and teachers alike. It helps to break down the ever present tendency to fall into a "lockstep" by promoting the opportunity for individual work within regular courses. The reading period could be made more valuable, however, by making it more flexible. Its chief defect is to have a fixed period for all courses using it adjacent to the time of examinations. In fact, instructors may be able to make the best use of the reading period in their particular courses at very different times.

We recommend that the instructor in any course not open to freshmen be allowed, with the consent of the department concerned and of the Dean, to schedule one two-week reading period or two one-week reading periods each semester at any time during the semester.

Summer Reading. It would, we believe, be desirable to make the experiment of supplementing the proposed courses in humanities by requiring every student to fulfill an assignment of prescribed reading during the summer vacation. This would be a *common* list (or else two lists for the two humanities courses), and all students would take a common examination on that list in the fall. Passing of the examination could be enforced by making it a requirement for graduation. The reading list, or lists, would be designed to supplement the program of *general* education which it is the function of a liberal college to provide.

We recommend that the experiment be made of requiring every student to fulfill an assignment of prescribed reading, supplementing the proposed courses in humanities, during the summer between freshman and sophomore years.

Summer Scholarships. It would also be desirable, we believe, to establish a number of scholarships open to juniors for work on an honors project during the summer between junior and senior years. Scholarships of this sort would enable a small group of our ablest students to carry out a part of the work for honors during that time, in laboratories or research institutes, in government bureaus, in large libraries and museums, at universities, etc. In some instances, perhaps, they might reside and work in foreign countries. The opportunities for really significant accomplishment by students doing honors work could be greatly enhanced by the creation of these scholarships.

We recommend that a group of scholarships, open to juniors for work on a special honors project during the summer following the completion of the junior year, be established.

Some Practical Considerations

The committee, as was appropriate for a policy committee, was told on its appointment to think only of the good of the college and not to worry too much about practical details. This we have done; but there are certain matters that we have been forced to bear in mind and should like, at least briefly, to comment on—since they would all be entailed by the adoption of our major recommendations. The proposals we have made would involve a good deal of additional expense for instruction, both in terms of the teaching staff, particularly to carry out the laboratory or seminar plan, and for library and classroom facilities. Let us consider the most important of these first.

The Teacher. It is a delightfully utopian task to construct a curriculum, but such schemes are plans for *Erewhon* without the teachers to carry them out. It is no solution of the problem, however, to say, "Aren't good teachers enough?" Of course good teachers and good students can achieve their objectives somehow under almost any conditions. The point in trying to organize a satisfactory curriculum is to make this as easy for them as possible. If we have given in our deliberations and in this report more time and space to the consideration of curricular problems than any other, it is because we hope that the adoption of our recommendations on this subject might provide even greater opportunities than there are now for realizing the end for which Amherst exists.

The assumption which underlies many sections of our report is, then, that teaching is the most important function of the faculty of the college although we have made little direct reference to teaching and almost none to the conditions under which teaching is conducted. Therefore, we should like here briefly to consider what may be called the "economics" of instruction, the relation of teaching to research, the recruiting of teachers for the laboratory plan, and the equipment of instruction.

By economics of instruction we mean the salary problem of the present and future, as expressed by a professor at Quaelibet University in a recent number of the *Bulletin* of the American Association of University Professors,[16] the problem of teacher load, particularly in view of the proposed changes in the teaching of our basic courses and in connection with committee and advisory obligations almost necessarily incurred in a small faculty, and the future of sabbatic leave.

We should like to assume that everyone whose duty it is to read this report would without reservation agree that it is of the utmost importance for the college to make the conditions of teaching at Amherst as attractive as possible to the ablest men in the profession. Nothing that we have suggested or recommended in the report should *under any circumstances* be put into effect if it would result in lowering present salary standards in order to employ more teachers to implement the proposed program, add to the customary prewar teaching load, or curtail opportunities for study and research.

Because sabbatic leave appears to be one of the simpler forms of budgetary economy, there is need to emphasize the point that such saving may constitute a false economy. Scholarship, especially in the form of publication, has commonly provided the justification for periodic leave. Not too much consideration has been given to its equally great value for the professor as a teacher. We wish to emphasize that sabbatic leave is indispensable in the encouragement, maintenance, and stimulus of good teaching on the college or university level. An excellent teacher cannot preserve the necessary freshness or vigor of mind or the resourcefulness and interest inherent in first-class work unless he frequently draws on new sources of thought and inspiration. To those provided by books or laboratories should be added changes of scene and personnel. Travel, particularly foreign travel, and varieties of experience are essential to a high quality of instruction. Sabbatic leaves, with adequate financial assurance, are as imperative to

[16] "The Salary Situation at Quaelibet University," 30 (1944), 366-392.

this end as any other form of "keeping up" or "keeping alive" in one's profession. This is notably applicable in the broad expanse of the "liberal arts," significantly so as the world outlook becomes less and less provincial and the need for more than a national psychology becomes more imperative.

If it is necessary that a teacher have leisure for study and research, so too is it necessary to have teachers who do continue to study and perform research. The danger is that teachers who are not adequately equipped to do some type of productive work in their special field tend to become routine teachers, to repeat on the college level the type and kind of teaching characteristic of the secondary school. No matter how able and inspiring this sort of instruction may be, it is rarely more than appreciative and assimilative in character. It is perhaps appropriate to some of the work done during the first two years of college but it is inadequate for the better students among upperclassmen.

The point is that the real thinking in any field goes on at that line where the frontiers of knowledge are being extended. Unless the better students sense that their professors are professionals in their subjects and not just professional teachers of those subjects, they will be disappointed. During at least their last two years in college they will become progressively dissatisfied with knowledge about the past, even knowledge about the "best that has been thought and said" as embodied in the classics, and will want to begin modestly to become acquainted with knowledge that is still in the making. We recognize this need in our provision for the honors thesis. Many of these theses are in a humble way contributions to knowledge. They usually have the merit of enabling the student to discover something of how truth is to be obtained.

Everything that has been said about the "Ph.D. Octopus" since James' famous essay is largely true. The increasing specialization of knowledge makes it constantly truer, but we doubt whether the proper compromise in this irreconcilable conflict between the demands of teaching and those of research is to be found in a division of labor within the teaching faculty itself. Such a division of labor will in fact exist. There will always be those who are primarily interested in their teaching as teaching and those who are more interested in scholarship and research. The rarest and best individuals are those who have the energy and ability to combine both. The ideal faculty, at least for the abler students, would be composed of the last group. All of the better colleges have, we think, aimed at getting as many of these as possible. Doubtless there are not enough of them to go around. One answer to this shortage is such an increase in the incentives and opportunities as will encourage more men of first-rate ability to enter the field of college teaching.

It is virtually impossible for anyone to be a good teacher in a liberal college who is not actively engaged in enlarging his knowledge of his subject, and who does not likewise possess the cultivation and breadth of interest which will enable him to be sympathetically conversant with the intellectual pursuits of many of his colleagues. Otherwise he may have a bright beginning but he comes to a dismal end. What original knowledge he may have picked up in the graduate school grows steadily duller, staler, and more out of date with each annual repetition. His teaching will invariably become listless and perfunctory, and his students will be as sheep that look up and are not fed.

Good teaching, therefore, demands leisure and opportunity for research. The teacher must be given an income adequate to place him above the need of doing the hack-work kind of editing, lecturing, and teaching in summer schools, if he is to have sufficient time and energy to do creative intellectual work. He must have regular sabbatical leaves, must be given a reasonable schedule of courses, and must be adequately supplied with books and equipment and with such clerical and research assistance as he is likely to need. And finally, he must be secured from any kind of intimidation or restraint in the expression of his opinions, though always subject to the criticism of his colleagues. These requirements are even more of a necessity for the younger than they are for the older person engaged in academic work. It is the younger man who most needs the leisure and opportunity for research while he is yet plastic enough to build up habits of creative inquiry.

What we have said about the necessity for research on the part of every teacher does not imply the kind of quick production too often insisted upon by shortsighted administrators and heads of departments. In any faculty there will be found some fertile minds to whom expression in a form reducible to writing seems to be an impossibility. Their mode of communication is in the form of lectures or discussions, and the effect of their intellectual culture is imprinted upon the minds and character of their colleagues and students. We need only mention the example of Professor Garman, one of the greatest teachers and one of the most active minds Amherst has ever known. On the whole, though, a roughly reliable index of the quality of any given faculty is to be found in the quantity of significant writing that emerges from it.

Recruiting of Teachers for the Laboratory or Seminar Type of Course. If our proposals for these courses were adopted, it would be necessary to make a number of additions to the faculty, particularly of younger men, in order to have an adequate staff for the conduct of the numerous small laboratory or seminar sections. The following suggestion for the recruiting of some of these teachers should, we think, be considered: that the college follow a policy of awarding fellowships for graduate study to certain of its ablest students explicitly to encourage them to enter the field of college teaching, with the understanding that some at least of these students will be called back to the college, after they have had a certain amount of graduate training, as assistants or instructors for one or two years in the laboratory or seminar courses. They could then return to their university for the completion of their graduate work. This scheme would accomplish the threefold purpose of encouraging some of our best students to enter the field of college teaching, of giving them training as teachers, and of providing over a period of time a fairly constant supply of able young teachers.

The Equipment of Instruction. The non-laboratory subjects of college instruction have long been the Cinderella of the academic family in terms of housing and equipment. Adaptations of old buildings to meet classroom exigencies account for most of the space and equipment devoted to the use of by far the larger proportion of both faculty and students. Teachers and classes in English, the languages, economics, history, political science, and philosophy meet and work where they can find sanctuary. There has been little real planning for the ideal needs of instruction in these subjects.

Properly furnished small rooms for classes of from ten to twelve students, for what is called seminar work, are too few. Lecture rooms with adequate arrangements for graphic displays, maps and charts, sliding blackboards, lantern accommodation, and so on, are almost nonexistent. Not even Grosvenor House has met the need for office or study accommodation. The dream of even one modern building with reasonably up-to-date equipment for the hundreds of men studying the above-mentioned subjects is still the modest solace of those who daily pass such modern structures as the Kirby Theater, the Alumni Gymnasium, or the Moore Laboratory of Chemistry.

Reference Librarian. Another basic need is that a skilled reference librarian be added to the staff—a person having the kind of training and ability which would afford him faculty status. The need for a librarian of this sort would become the greater were the number of honors students to increase and were the laboratory plan adopted. It would be his function to give freshmen systematic instruction in the use of the library, to assist all students and the members of the faculty in locating and using research materials. The latter function requires an individual of great versatility and breadth of knowledge. The proper reference librarian would become a key person in implementing the laboratory and honors plans so far as use of the library is involved. We recommend that a reference librarian be added to the staff.

The Curriculum Committee. If our proposals in this section were to be adopted, the Curriculum Committee would presumably bear a large part of the responsibility for working out the details involved in putting them into effect. We believe that, in any event, the Curriculum Committee should assume a much more important role in determining the educational policies of the college than has heretofore been the case. Its mandate should not be merely "to watch the curriculum," to act as a board of censorship passing on proposed new courses, but, of its own initiative, to undertake studies and make reports suggesting to the faculty such innovations or reforms as it believes would improve our practices. We have in various parts of this report suggested a number of studies which we believe it would be desirable to have made by the Curriculum Committee. The Curriculum Committee should also, we think, meet with the Instruction Committee of the Board of Trustees, on the occasion of its annual visit to the college, for the discussion of problems with which both committees are concerned.

We should like to see the Curriculum Committee continually study the balance and distribution of courses among the various departments in the college and make proposals from time to time for additions to or reductions in the number of courses being offered—particularly the latter. It would seem that at Amherst and no doubt in many other institutions the curriculum is like a maze without an exit. New courses are continually getting into it but none ever seem to get out. There is a substantial body of opinion in the faculty that the number of courses in the curriculum is increasing and ought to be reduced. This committee, after discussing the problem, has decided to bequeath it with its blessing to the Curriculum Committee.

Studies of the sort we suggest usually involve painstaking and time-consuming inquiries. One important reason why the committee tends to take less initiative than we would like to see it take is that its members usually cannot spare the time from their other duties to do more than take care of the matters that are thrust upon them. If the committee is to assume a more comprehensive function, to assume a position of leadership in the development of educational policy, it will be necessary from time to time to relieve one of its members, the chairman or secretary, from a part of his teaching duties, for a semester or a year, to make special investigations and reports. We suggest that this be done as occasion demands.

Perhaps there is enough in a name to make it worth our while to recommend that the committee's title be changed to Committee on Educational Policy. This change of name would make it clear that the committee ought to be concerned not merely with matters affecting the curriculum in the narrower sense but with anything that affects the intellectual life of the college.

We recommend that the title of the Curriculum Committee be changed to Committee on Educational Policy and that the faculty instruct the committee to make an annual report.

Status of General Courses and Group Majors. General courses and interdepartmental majors cannot easily be established unless they are given *independent departmental status.* At the start most teachers in them would have plural membership, in their original department and in the new department of "X Studies." Thus Professor Y might be a member of the English Department (2/3), and also a member of the Department of American Studies (1/3). In some cases teachers might transfer wholly to such new interdepartmental departments and some new appointments might subsequently be made entirely in them.

We recommend that general courses and group majors be given independent departmental status.

Timing of Our Proposals. If any of the more important proposals that we have made, particularly the introduction of required general courses of the laboratory or seminar type, were adopted, it would be well, we think, to try to put them, or some of them, into effect experimentally with the small civilian classes we now have—before the college feels the full impact of demobilization or begins to receive a normal freshman class. Next year we shall, presumably, have a large faculty in proportion to our student body. The members of the faculty will have more time and opportunity to plan these courses and fewer distractions because of other duties than they are likely to have again for a long time to come. An experimental program of this sort would not entail any serious consequences in the way of recruiting new staff, large investments in equipment, and so on. Finally, it would be easy to modify the new program or even to discard it altogether if upon trial it proved unsatisfactory.

ADMISSIONS AND SCHOLARSHIPS

There is no subject with which this committee is empowered to deal about which the faculty has shown more concern. Teachers are primarily interested in the quality of their students. They are always aware that the success of the college as an educational institution is measured by the distinction of its graduates. No matter what the level of ability among their students is, they are always hopeful that the next class may be a little better than the last. If that hope could be realized, it would mean that this college would tend increasingly to revert to its original function, that of educating a highly selected group of students the great majority of whom were intending to enter upon a professional career.

It is still the case that about half of the students, including those who attend schools of business administration, do some sort of graduate work. The committee's views on the various topics discussed in this section are based upon the premise that, if Amherst is to maintain in the future the reputation that she has founded on the distinction of her graduates, she should do everything possible to discover and secure an *increasing* number of such students of high ability. Unless the college can enhance the repute it already possesses as an educational institution able to offer the highest quality of preparation for the various professional and graduate schools, it will, we believe, gradually decline in influence and prestige. As institutions both public and private have developed in all parts of the country, a small eastern college acquires a relatively disadvantageous position. It inevitably becomes less well known, and students are more difficult to attract from afar when there are excellent institutions in their own vicinity. Under these circumstances applications for admission tend to come increasingly from the immediate locality and from the communities of alumni in various urban centers. Some people competent to judge already think of Amherst as having no other future than that of a *community* college, in this double sense.

Amherst is still recognized as one of the leading small colleges in the country. Is it possible, however, for her to become and remain a national institution in the way that the liberal arts colleges of the great private universities are national? This, we believe, in view of our endowment and equipment, the quality of our faculty, and the history of the college itself is a legitimate goal for her to aim at; but it will be a difficult ideal to implement. It would mean that Amherst must be so well known as a place where students can obtain the best possible start toward an administrative or professional career that she can successfully compete with institutions like Yale and Harvard for the most energetic and ambitious young men throughout the country. Fully to achieve an end of this kind may well be impossible, but, unless we make every effort, the alternative of a gradual decline in our comparative importance is equally inevitable. We believe that Amherst's best chance for a bright future lies in trying to become predominantly an *honors college*, offering a general education preparatory to the professions of such excellence that it can command nationwide recognition. All of the comments on the various problems of admissions and scholarships which follow are based on this presumption.

Admissions in the Past Decade

Until the thirties it could hardly be said that there was an admissions problem. The formal requirements for admission were set in such a way and so little was done to attract students from new sources that the college was able to accept a very large proportion of the candidates who could satisfactorily meet the formal conditions. Despite this fact the enrollment of the college gradually rose from 528 in 1921 to 707 in 1929, when it began to decline, primarily no doubt because of the depression. In 1932-1933, after study by a faculty committee, an undergraduate committee, and a committee of Amherst alumni engaged in secondary education, the faculty adopted new admission requirements. This relaxation in the requirements, together with the appointment of a full-time admissions officer, enabled the college to adopt a more flexible method of selection. In the decade from 1930 to 1940 there was a large increase in the number of applications. Despite a concomitant growth in the size of the college the percentage of applicants rejected also rose. At the same time there was a fairly constant but irregular increase in the percentage of students admitted from private secondary schools as against those admitted from high schools. In 1931, 51 per cent of the students were admitted from private schools whereas in 1940, 67 per cent were from private schools. Similarly, the number of sons and relatives of Amherst alumni admitted to the college tended irregularly but steadily to increase. The geographical distribution of our students remained about the same.

The following tables illustrate these trends:

APPLICATIONS AND ADMISSIONS FOR THE PERIOD 1937-41

Year	Total Applications	Number Admitted	Per Cent Admitted
1937-38	534	232	43
1938-39	650	240	37
1939-40	529	241	45
1940-41	515	241	46
1941-42[a]	440	273	62

[a] War conditions.

GEOGRAPHICAL DISTRIBUTION OF STUDENTS FOR THE PERIOD 1937-41

Section	1937-38	1938-39	1939-40	1940-41	1941-42	Whole Period
New England	35 %	34.4%	35 %	33%	35 %	34 %
Middle Atlantic states	42 %	41.3%	41.5%	46%	43 %	43 %
Southern states	1 %	.8%	.5%	1%	1 %	1 %
North Central states	16 %	17.2%	16 %	13%	15 %	15 %
West of Mississippi	5.5%	6 %	6 %	5%	5 %	6 %
Foreign	.5%	.3%	1 %	1%	.8%	.8%

Admissions from High Schools and Preparatory Schools

The Report of the Alumni Committee on Admissions, Scholarships and Secondary Schools of 1934 describes the situation at that time as follows:

The number of Amherst undergraduates from public high schools, from endowed private schools, and who have received their preparation at both a high school and a private school, are in the following proportions: In the senior class, 49% come directly from high school, 27% have attended both public and private schools in the four years immediately before entering Amherst, and 25% have received their preparation solely from private schools; in the junior class, 55% received a high school preparation, 23% a complete private school education, and 22% went to both a private school and a public high school; in the sophomore class, 40% received their total preparation in high school, 30% received their total preparation in private school, and 29% received their preparation in both a high school and a private school; in the freshman class, 44% went to college direct from high school, 29% took their full preparation in a private school, and 26% went to both a high school and a private school before entering Amherst. Consequently a majority of our present undergraduates have come directly from high school to college, a somewhat smaller percentage have had a full preparatory school preparation, and a slightly smaller group have had both types of college preparation.[17]

The figures for 1933-1941 are as follows:

Year	Number Admitted	High School	Preparatory School	Both
1933-34	239	42%	31%	27%
1934-35	239	47%	33%	20%
1935-36	243	50%	28%	22%
1936-37	225	39%	31%	30%
1937-38	232	46%	27%	27%
1938-39	240	41%	32%	27%
1939-40	241	38%	32%	30%
1940-41	241	33%	32%	35%
1941-42	273	War	War	War

[17] *Alumni Council News*, 8, no. 2, supplement 2 (1934), 7.

Admissions of Relatives or Sons of Amherst Alumni

In 1934, 33 per cent of the senior class, 34 per cent of the junior class, 34 per cent of the sophomore class, and 25 per cent of the freshman class were relatives or sons of Amherst graduates. The figures for subsequent freshman classes are:

Year	Students	Relatives	Sons	Total
1934-35	239	22%	11%	33%
1935-36	243	37%	9%	46%
1936-37	225	31%	15%	46%
1937-38	232	26%	13%	39%
1938-39	240	37%	14%	51%
1939-40	241	27%	12%	39%
1940-41	241	27%	12%	39%
1941-42	273	War	War	War

Present Composition of the Student Body

What is the present (prewar) composition of our student body? Taking the four classes which entered in 1937-1938, 1938-1939, 1939-1940, and 1940-1941, all of whom were in college in 1940-1941, we have a student body approximately 33 per cent of whom were from the New England states, 43 per cent from the Middle Atlantic states, 16 per cent from the North Central states, 6 per cent from the Western states, something less than 1 per cent from the Southern states, and something less than 1 per cent from foreign countries. Of these students 39.5 per cent entered from high schools and 60.5 per cent from private schools. In the private school group 30.75 per cent were from private schools alone and 29.75 per cent had attended both public and private schools. If we may judge by the class which entered in the fall of 1939, the students came from a larger number of preparatory schools than of high schools. The members of that class were admitted from 67 preparatory schools whereas only 62 high schools were represented. Of the high school students a considerable number were from large urban or suburban institutions. Thus a comparatively small proportion of the class came from small-town high schools.

Of the students in college at that time 42 per cent were relatives or sons of Amherst alumni. Of these 29.25 per cent were relatives and

12.75 per cent were sons. If we may judge from the class of 1941, more than half (about 55 per cent) of them were sons of men engaged in business,[18] 8 per cent of doctors and dentists, about the same percent of lawyers, 3 per cent of ministers and social workers, a little over 5 per cent of engineers, architects, and chemists, more than 8 per cent of teachers or school administrators, artists, and musicians, but only 2 per cent at most were sons of farmers or laborers. No one who goes through the detailed list of fathers' occupations for the classes of 1942, 1943, and 1944[19] can doubt that Amherst so far as the composition of its student body goes is overwhelmingly a middle-class institution. This, of course, is laboring the obvious. Everyone at all acquainted with the college knows it, but not everyone may have realized the degree to which it is now true that the usual Amherst student is the son of a middle-class or upper-middle-class father engaged in a business or profession, has been to a private preparatory school or has graduated from high school in a well-to-do urban or suburban community, and is almost as often as not the son or relative of an Amherst alumnus.

Your committee feels that this is too narrowly homogeneous a student body, that our geographical and social basis should be widened. There is no controversy about the desirability of extending our geographical representation and in this respect Amherst has, as a matter of fact, done rather well. The geographical distribution of our students is about the same as that of Yale, slightly better than that of Williams, and decidedly better than that of Wesleyan, while Bowdoin by comparison is a provincial college. The committee believes that so far as the policy of becoming predominantly an honors college is successfully put into effect our present geographical distribution can be maintained and even gradually increased.

The problems with which the committee is primarily concerned are those involved in the second question: How can we enlarge our social basis? Two points, logically distinct but in fact closely related, are involved here. When the comment is made that the quality of the students admitted might be improved, those in a position to know are likely to reply that, in view of the intense competition among the

[18] In 1934 only about 35% of the students then in college were sons of businessmen.

[19] Published in the Curriculum Committee's report on the admissions problem, 1941.

colleges for good students, there are simply not enough of them to go around. In Amherst's case an adequate selection for quality would require at least 800 of the sort of applications for admission that we are *now* getting instead of the 650 received in our best year, 1938-1939. Everyone is, we believe, interested in quality from whatever source and it would be greatly to the advantage of the college if the number of these usual applications could be increased until they reached an optimum point. If the competition for boys from private schools and certain large urban or suburban high schools is getting more strenuous we might well ease that strain by supplementing our present efforts, by turning to new fields and new methods. When one recalls that there are some 25,000 public high schools in the United States, 3500 of them in the northeastern section of the country, and that one recent Amherst class drew its members from only 62 of these 25,000 schools, it becomes clear how highly restricted are the sources of our student body.

Means of Increasing Applications for Admission

The committee has considered several ways in which the total number of applications from good students might be increased. The most important of these are: (1) the provision of funds adequate for the establishment of a more complete system of regional scholarships; (2) the appointment of an assistant admissions officer to develop relations with secondary schools and in areas from which we are not at present drawing any significant number of students; (3) a greater use of the alumni to assist us in obtaining able students; (4) the adoption of admissions requirements which would make it easier, particularly for high school students, to meet the *formal* conditions of admission.

Scholarships. The most important way in which we may hope to improve the quality of our student body and broaden its social basis is through the most effective use of our scholarship funds and an increase in these funds.

Amherst has always maintained, as befits the purposes for which it was founded and endowed, a generous fund for scholarships. Approximately 25 per cent of our students receive scholarship aid. Regular scholarships range from $300 to $450. The stipend of the Lord Jeffery Amherst Scholarships is $500. A majority of scholarship holders receive less than the equivalent of full tuition, the average amount of all scholarships granted being $340. About 60 per cent of the scholarships go to students entering from public schools and 40 per cent to those entering from private schools.

It has never been the policy of the college to restrict the use of scholarship funds for students of high intellectual distinction. The funds are described in the catalogue as "for the assistance of worthy and needy students." Until 1932-1933 it was possible for any student who was passing in all his courses with an average of 70 per cent to receive scholarship aid. In that year, on the initiative of Dean Porter, the minimum requirements for scholarship holders were raised to an average of 70 per cent for sophomores, 72 per cent for juniors, and 74 per cent for seniors. In 1935-1936 the requirements were again raised, to 72 per cent, 74 per cent, and 76 per cent. Awards were rarely made, however, to students who could barely meet the minimum requirements. It is to be noted that the required minimum averages are below the actual college average of Amherst's students, which for five recent classes was 75.87 per cent. In response to an inquiry from the committee Dean Porter summarized the situation as follows:

> In general awards were not made to students who barely met the minimum requirements because of the fact that we had approximately 25 per cent more candidates for scholarship awards than we had money available for scholarship assistance, and our policy was to make our awards to the students with the better scholastic records. However, exceptions have been made where in my judgment the student was deserving of financial assistance and was at least meeting the minimum requirements for a scholarship award as stated in the catalog.
>
> In the year 1940-1941, 8 per cent of the scholarship awards were made to students with an average of 90 or better; 52 per cent to students with an average between 80 and 90; and 40 per cent to students with an average between 70 and 80. Twenty-five per cent of the awards were made to students whose average was below the college average, and 28 per cent of the awards were made to students whose average was below the average of their class. Sixteen lettermen who had averages below the college average received scholarship awards. This group comprised 37 per cent of the men of the sophomore, junior and senior classes with averages below the college average who received scholarship awards. In this particular year there were 148 lettermen in the College. In other words, the group

of lettermen who received scholarship awards who were below the college average comprised 11 per cent of the whole group of lettermen for the year.

The Dean also advocated the policy of increasing the number of large scholarship awards. This he was apparently unable to do because of economic conditions. As a result the number of ordinary scholarship awards during the decade 1932-1942 remained almost constant.

The committee is in agreement with these two policies: an increase in the minimum scholastic requirements, and a consolidation of scholarship funds that will enable us to offer a number of large regional scholarships strategically placed in such a way as to draw more students from remoter areas and at the same time positively to increase the quality of our student body by obtaining more top-ranking students.

It is the view of the committee that the only defensible theory of student aid is one that places the whole emphasis upon the worth and ability of the student.[20] "Student aid" in reality includes the whole amount of the cost to society in tax exemptions and to the institution in endowment income of the student's education, minus whatever he contributes in tuition and other fees. At Amherst, on a conservative estimate, the approximate gross cost to the college of educating a student, as of 1940, is more than $1100 per year. Of this amount the student who pays full tuition contributes less than half. Every student in Amherst College in effect receives a scholarship of at least one-half the cost of his education exclusive of living expenses. It seems to us difficult to justify granting additional aid to students who cannot fulfill the expectation that they will take the greatest possible advantage of the opportunities the college offers them.[21] The established minimum requirement for holders of scholarships should be raised at least to conform with the college average in recent years. We recommend that it be changed to 75 per cent for sophomores and that, *so far as possible,* no scholarships be made available to juniors

[20] Cf. William S. Learned and Ben D. Wood, *The Student and His Knowledge,* Bulletin No. 29 of the Carnegie Foundation for the Advancement of Teaching (New York, 1938), pp. 62-64.

[21] These estimates are based on figures furnished us by the Treasurer's Office. If one adds to this the average expenses for board and room, clothing, books, travel, etc., the total *actual* cost of an education at Amherst becomes at least $1700 a year.

and seniors who are not candidates for the degree with distinction.[22]

The problem is not simple. Some of the scholarship funds are so restricted that there may not be a well-qualified candidate for them in any given year. Moreover, the college must choose among the best who are available enough students to insure that it has a freshman class of the requisite size. This means that so long as we do not have enough really good students applying, a part of our scholarship funds must be diverted to helping students of worthy character but mediocre abilities who are able to pay a part of their way.

There are only two ways in which we can hope materially to improve the quality of our student body through the use of scholarship funds. The first is by increasing the number of applicants who are good students and who can afford to attend Amherst on a scholarship covering a part or the whole of their tuition. The other is to obtain sufficient scholarship funds to establish a number of large regional scholarships enabling a substantial group of first-rate students to attend Amherst irrespective of their means. The present Lord Jeffery Amherst Scholarships are, of course, a step in this direction.[23] But they do not begin to meet the real need. Dean MacMeekin has recently suggested that the name of these scholarships be changed to Amherst National Scholarships and the stipend be increased to $800. If this were done, Amherst would still be doing less, even in proportion to her size and endowment, than some other eastern institutions. The most conspicuous examples are the National Scholarships

[22] Dissent.—We do not concur in this recommendation. We fear that, if adopted, it might deprive of further scholarship aid too many students both "worthy and needy" in the ordinary sense of the words. To possess qualities of present worth to the college or of future worth to society, qualities which might well be strengthened by continuing his course with suitable financial assistance, it does not seem necessary that an upperclassman be a candidate for honors.

We assume that, other things being equal, scholarship preference will continue to be given to the intellectually more able. If the scholastic ability of our freshman scholarship holders should rise, there would be no problem of minimum requirements for continuation of scholarships. If it should not, then merely to raise the requisite minimum averages would not supply us with better students. Bailey Brown and Vincent Morgan.

[23] There are at present eight of these. Lord Jeff Scholars are appointed from the following areas or schools: (1) Central New York State; (2) Chicago; (3) Cleveland; (4) Philadelphia; (5) St. Louis; (6) Deerfield Academy; (7) Phillips Academy, Andover; (8) Phillips Exeter Academy; (9) the whole country outside of these areas or schools. The candidate must apply from the area in which he is attending school.

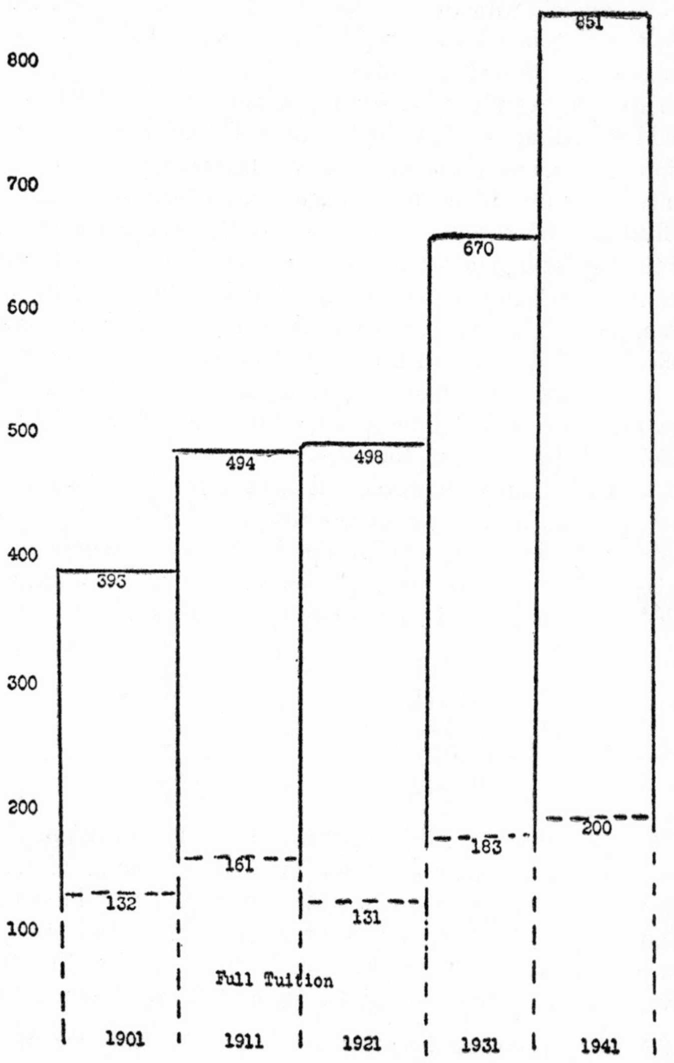

CHART A. Growth of Student Body and Number Who Could Have Received Full Scholarships, Amherst College, 1901-41

offered by Harvard. Yale and Princeton likewise have set up extensive systems of regional scholarships, and more recently seven eastern women's colleges have combined to establish twenty-one national scholarships similar to those given at Harvard. We are not in a position to compete with these larger institutions but we must try to do at least as much as Dean MacMeekin has suggested if we are going to hold even our relative position.

In its study of the scholarship problem the committee has been aided by financial data furnished by the college.[24] There is no need to go into these financial details here. We shall merely point out certain significant relationships which emerge from an analysis of these figures.

Chart A shows the growth in the size of the college since 1900-1901 and the scholarship aid which has been available to Amherst students. It will be noted that, if scholarship funds had been used to pay full tuition only (i.e., if no part scholarships had been given), 132 boys would have had their full tuition paid by the college in 1900-1901. The committee notes that, despite increased tuition rates, scholarships increased so that by 1940-1941 two hundred boys could have received full tuition from these funds.

In a relative sense, however, the college has lost ground in the granting of scholarships, for the *percentage* of the student body which could have received full scholarships has declined appreciably since the beginning of the century. The percentages of the students who could have been granted scholarships are as follows:

1900-01	34
1910-11	35
1920-21	26
1930-31	27
1940-41	24

The committee views this trend with some apprehension. If it be granted that our scholarship funds are a prime means of securing superior students, then it follows that we are not now in as good a position to attract as high a percentage of superior students by this means as we were in 1900-1901. More than one-third of the student body could have been brought to Amherst in 1900-1901 with full

[24] See the Memorandum from President King which forms the Appendix, pp. 175-176.

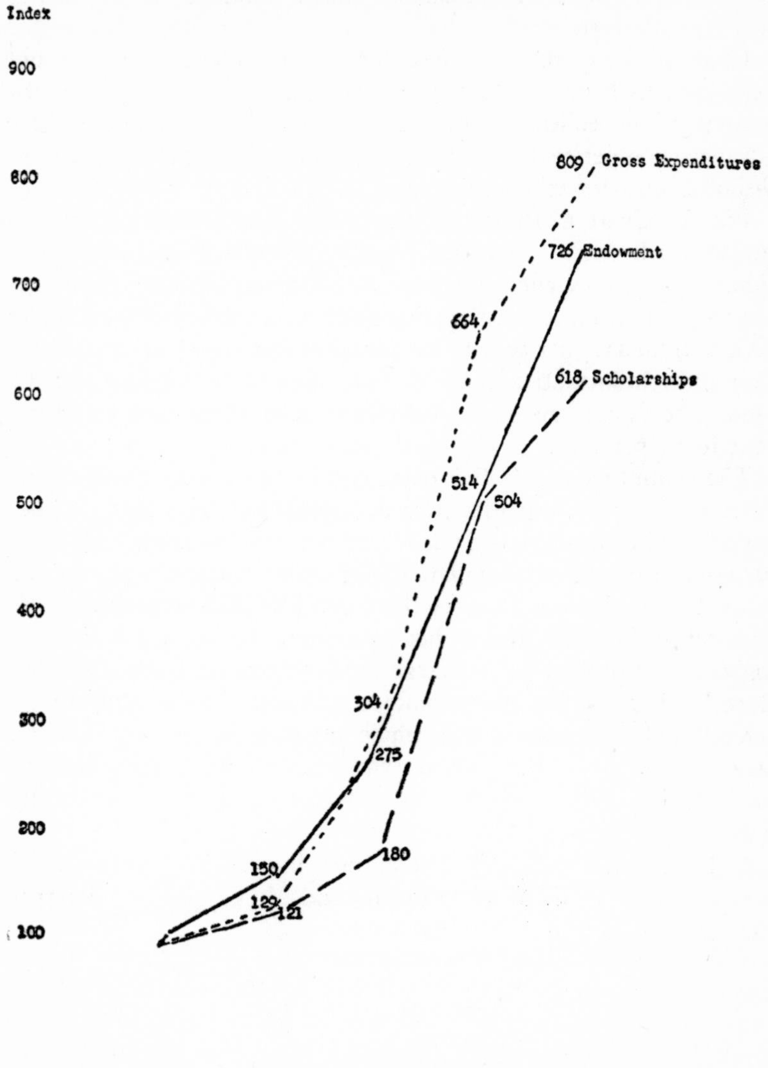

CHART B. Index Based on 1901 Showing the Relative Growth in Gross Expenditures, Endowment, and Scholarships at Amherst College, 1901-41

tuition paid, whereas less than one-fourth could be secured in this way in 1940-1941.

Chart B shows that, in percentage terms, scholarships have not kept pace with either the gross expenditures of the college or the growth of the college endowment. While gross expenditures have advanced 709 per cent since 1900-1901 and endowment 626 per cent, disbursements for scholarships have increased 518 per cent.

Finally, Chart C shows the percentage distribution of gross expenditures by three categories, namely, instruction and administration,[25] scholarships, and "all other." It will be seen from the chart that the share spent on scholarships has declined, in the forty years under review, from 11.3 per cent to 8.6 per cent, and the share for instruction and administration from 66.7 per cent to 58 per cent. At the same time disbursements for "all other" have increased from 22 per cent to 33 per cent.

The committee regrets that data are not available to permit a careful analysis of the expenses here designated as "all other." It does wish to point out that the relative increase in this item took place between 1910 and 1930 and that but little change appears in the proportionate distribution since the latter date. The committee notes with satisfaction that this earlier trend toward spending an increasingly smaller proportion of college funds on instruction and scholarships has been halted, and recommends to the administration that a careful study be made of this whole situation to the end that the facts may be more clearly known and a reverse trend established in the direction of the 1900-1901 ratio if that should prove reasonably possible.

Until recently Amherst's expenditures for scholarships compared very favorably to those of Williams and Wesleyan. For the year 1940-1941 these were:

	Scholarships	Loans to Students	Student Aid Employment
Wesleyan	$69,790	$5,999	0
Williams	70,538	2,281	$9,868
Amherst	86,616	3,957	3,300

[25] Instruction and administration have been combined in a single item because accounting allocation between the two items has not been on a consistent basis throughout the period.

90

80

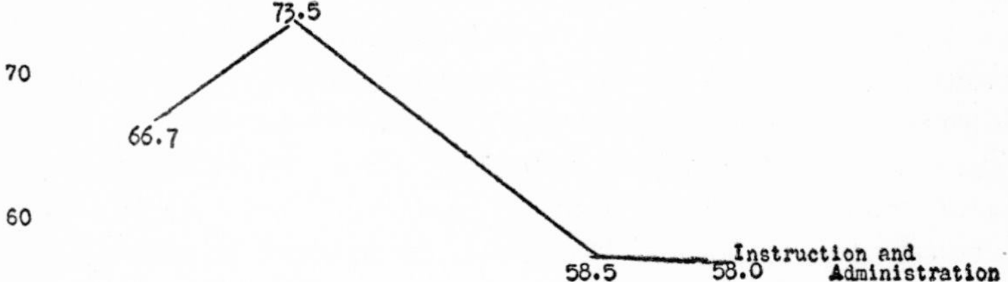

50

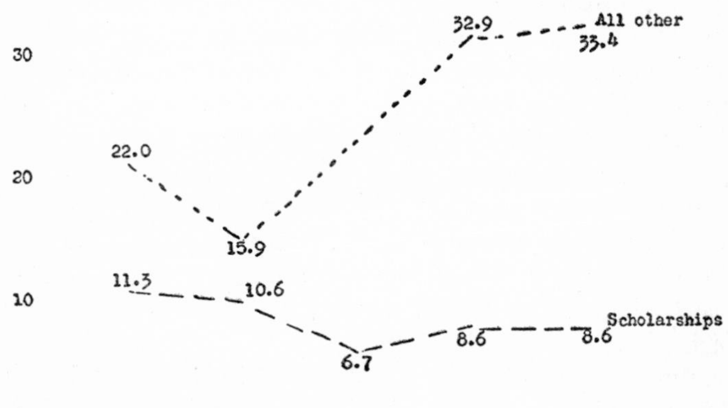

1901 1911 1921 1931 1941

CHART C. Percentage Distribution of Gross Expenditures—Amherst College, 1901-41

These might be considered reassuring figures. However, Williams College has recently been given a large endowment, the Stephen H. Tyng and Stephen H. Tyng, Jr., Foundation scholarships, expressly for students of high attainments. According to the printed description, Williams will now be able to offer a large number of scholarships providing "a full college education to outstanding students of limited means." They are on a sliding scale, the amount being adjusted to the need of the student. There is the further interesting provision that these scholarships "may be extended for post-graduate study at any recognized university."

Perhaps the greatest single present need of the college is a special endowment of this sort. This committee believes that such an endowment would be a most fitting kind of war memorial. In lieu of this, every reasonable effort should be made to effect economies that would enable us to divert more of the general funds of the college than are now so allocated to scholarships in order to establish a set of competitive regional scholarships on the sliding-scale basis with a maximum stipend of at least $1000.

An Assistant Officer of Admissions. While it is true that Amherst would find it impossible to consider promotional work on any large scale in the public high school field, it is equally true, in the opinion of the committee, that we should do everything we can to bring the college to the attention of more high schools and in particular of a certain number of carefully selected high schools in the smaller cities and larger towns. Any real effort in this direction would entail the appointment of a second admissions officer. Wesleyan, which already has a considerably larger high school representation than our own, made the experiment, for a number of years prior to the war, of sending out a young graduate of the college with experience as a secondary school teacher especially to develop relations with a selected group of high schools. Although such efforts apparently bring slow returns, it is our belief that they are worth making. We would recommend that the appointment of an assistant admissions officer to work in the high school field be considered.

Cooperation of the Alumni. Another way in which we believe both high schools and private schools might be more effectively reached is through a further extension and development of the use of alumni committees and in the smaller towns of individual alumni.

There are at present a number of secondary school committees functioning in large cities where well-developed organizations of the alumni exist. They have been, in most instances, chiefly concerned with the recommendation of candidates for the Lord Jeffery Amherst Scholarships, although some of them have also been of great assistance in helping us obtain good students from both the private and the public schools of their locality. Could not a carefully selected list of individual alumni do a like service for us in the smaller towns?

We realize that this sort of policy can lead to difficulties—not all alumni understand clearly what type of student the college wants and some may become disgruntled if a student recommended by them is rejected. This is a risk we believe worth taking if by more fully enlisting the aid of the alumni we can secure a larger and wider basis of choice among applicants for admission. It could be minimized if a beginning were made with a comparatively small number of selected individuals each of whom was individually approached and carefully instructed as to what the college wants. In particular, certain of the younger alumni who are well acquainted both with their secondary school and with present conditions at Amherst could perform this service well. Some of the eastern colleges and universities with which we are wont to compare ourselves are planning to develop greatly the use of their alumni as a means of recruiting students, particularly in more distant and smaller towns and cities. In the judgment of this committee we would do well to follow their example.

One of the most valuable means of recruiting students is, as everyone knows, through the influence of those Amherst alumni who become teachers in secondary schools. An important reason why we now admit relatively few good students from the high schools is that, over a long period, the number of our students becoming teachers and administrators in the public schools has steadily diminished until it has almost reached the vanishing point. Until social conditions change, as they may, little can be done to stimulate the interest of Amherst undergraduates in public school teaching and administration as a career. We have established a course in the History and Philosophy of Education which may indirectly help to interest a few boys in such a vocation. Individual teachers can do even more by advising certain undergraduates whom they consider well fitted for it to enter that field. We might well supplement these efforts by setting up, if the funds can be provided, an Amherst Fellowship for Graduate Study in Education. There are more real opportunities in public education for men of ambition and ability than most people realize. The existence of such a fellowship would induce a larger number of students to investigate them and would thereby help to restore a fraction of our former influence in the public secondary schools.[26]

Proposed New Admission Requirements. The committee has briefly described in Part I of this report the rapidly changing character of the public secondary schools. It is becoming increasingly common for college preparation to be confined to the last two or three years of high school. To this must be added the fact that many states now require courses in such subjects as American history, social studies, problems of democracy, etc. The result is that it is more and more difficult for the students in many high schools, and in some private schools as well, to meet a detailed and specific set of formal requirements for entrance to the college.

In 1934 the alumni committee report, in recognition of this fact, said:

> On the matter of closer cooperation with secondary schools, your committee cannot stress too heavily the importance of Amherst's building up and maintaining the closest possible relations with the good public high schools and endowed private schools of New England, New York, New Jersey and Pennsylvania. Your committee feels that in looking to the Amherst of the future, particular emphasis should be laid upon the endowed schools from which Amherst, in the past, has drawn comparatively few boys.[27]

It is this policy that was carried out during the past decade, as is evident from the statistics we have cited above. This committee believes the policy should be reversed, in which case we must lay less emphasis upon a certain uniform type of preparation and more upon the intrinsic abilities of the students applying for admission.

Formal requirements should not block the way of an able boy who is willing to try. What is needed is *general basic requirements* which will provide an adequate test of aptitude and training but will not, of

[26] It has been suggested in the committee that more contact with the secondary schools on the part of the faculty might also help to gain the desired end. Anything of this sort, however, would probably have to be done on an individual rather than a formal basis, as opportunity might occur.

[27] *Alumni Council News*, 8, no. 2, supplement 2 (1934), 13.

themselves, prevent the entrance of a good student from any school or from any state. If we are serious about wanting to get more good high school students, then we must adopt a more flexible set of admission requirements.

This fact has been recognized during recent years in the changed character of the College Board examinations, which are now designed to test both the aptitude and the achievement of the student in a way that will require a minimum of "standardization" of secondary school courses. It is particularly evident in such examinations as the one on social studies, which makes allowance for a wide variety of preparation among students.

There can be no doubt that it is to the advantage of the student to enter college with a thorough preliminary training in certain basic skills, particularly languages and mathematics; but there can also be no doubt that as between the mediocre student who is well prepared and an abler student who must make up some of his deficiencies in college, the latter is more likely to succeed. A number of studies have been made showing that the relationship between the subjects taken in high schools and success in college is too small to justify the practice of prescribing high school subjects for college entrance. Because it is true that able students tend to persist with difficult subjects, one must beware of a *post hoc, ergo propter hoc* in criticizing the results of these investigations.[28]

The experience of admissions officers has led them generally to agree that the best method of measuring the student's ability and his probable success in college work is to be found in a complex judgment which will combine his school grades and class rank (making an allowance for the size and character of the school), his scores in achievement and aptitude tests (such as those given by the college board), and the opinions of his principal, or headmaster, and teachers.

In view of these facts the committee recommends the following entrance requirements:

[28] The Dean in his annual reports for the years immediately following the abolition of the Latin requirements made a five-year study (1933-1938) of the comparative achievement in college of students entering with varying amounts of Latin. The groups of students entering with three or four years of Latin had significantly higher averages in college than those entering with little or none. It is interesting, however, to note that, if one analyzes these figures, this relative advantage in scholarship tends to diminish each successive year.

Admission Requirements

Amherst College does not have a formal unit requirement for admission. Candidates must show that they are prepared to carry on college work. It is expected that applicants will have graduated, or be candidates for graduation, from acceptable secondary schools and that their scholastic records will be of good quality. However, any student who in the opinion of his headmaster or principal is qualified to enter college after three years only of secondary school work may file an application for admission. Special consideration will be given to such applications providing, of course, the student is, in the opinion of the proper school authorities, an exceptionally capable student and one who would benefit from this special consideration.

The following program of studies is recommended for students planning to enter Amherst College:

English	4 years
Mathematics	3 years
Foreign language	2 or, if possible, 3 years of one
History	1 year
Laboratory science	1 year

It should be noted that the college stresses sound preparation in certain subjects which are important implements for the many branches of college work. English, mathematics, and foreign language (ancient and modern) are the subjects in which entering students should show proficiency.

Students with particular interests may wish to modify the suggested program by taking more work in certain subjects and less in others. Such modification is wholly acceptable, provided there is evidence of adequate preparation in each of the basic fields mentioned. Extensive deviation should be discussed in advance with the Director of Admissions.

Scholastic Aptitude and Achievement Tests

All candidates for admission are required to take the College Entrance Examination Board Scholastic Aptitude Test.

Although the Scholastic Achievement Test consists of tests in nine fields, only three of these are required by Amherst College. Applicants are expected to take (1) English composition; (2) a foreign language reading test (if foreign language is offered for entrance); (3) the test in social studies or in a science.

These tests are not only a requirement for admission but are frequently used as placement tests for work in college.

The proposed new requirements explain themselves, we hope, with perhaps one exception. The provision relating to the admission of particularly well-qualified students after three years of school work, adopted as a war measure, should, we believe, be continued. Everyone knows that some boys are more mature and better prepared for college work after three years of secondary school than many of those who graduate. The Carnegie investigation, *The Student and His Knowledge*, to which we have previously referred, amply demonstrates this fact.

A number of studies have been made on the academic achievement and social adjustment of selected groups of students entering college at an earlier age or after three years of secondary school. Both groups, those who finish high school at an early age and those who enter college with only three years of preparatory school, succeeded at least as well, intellectually and socially, in college as the somewhat older average student. Some of these studies show that the younger and able students are, on the whole, even more successful. We believe that this degree of acceleration would be beneficial to the exceptional student.[29]

The Problem of Selection

The alumni committee report of 1934 in discussing this topic warned:

> To continue in the future the kind of thing that it has achieved in the past, Amherst must guard carefully against any tendency to become an "exclusive" college in the narrow sense, and with the increase of applicants from whom it may "select" those whom it will take, it is readily apparent that the danger of such a tendency will become great.[30]

[29] For a recent summary of the studies see Charles W. Boardman, "Findings from Selected Studies on Early Admission to College," *The School Review*, vol. 51 (1943), pp. 460-470.

[30] *Alumni Council News*, 8, no. 2, supplement 2 (1934), 16.

We agree with this statement. If the proposed new admission requirements were adopted, since a much larger number of students might satisfy our formal requirements, a much heavier responsibility would be placed upon the admissions office. The new admission requirements are proposed with the intention that they will enable us to select a student body which is at once *broader* at its base (geographical and social) and *higher* in quality.

The primary criterion of admission and the award of scholarships should be the intellectual abilities and interests of the prospective student. We doubt that "character" or "leadership" are particularly significant criteria of choice. President Valentine of the University of Rochester in a paper written when he was admissions officer at Yale remarked:

> The function of a board of admissions is to present each year to its university the best available collection of schoolboys with intellectual potentialities. I use the world intellectual advisedly, not being convinced of the wisdom or success of complicating the selection problem by placing great weight upon other qualities. One is impressed by those who talk of admitting boys because of outstanding character, but one wonders how it is done, unless one determines an individual's fine character by its similarity to his own. Nothing is more subjective than estimates of character. At schoolboy age it is uncertain and changing, and estimates of what denotes good character would doubtless vary greatly among the occupants of this room. It is obvious that in addition to demanding academic achievement or promise, an admissions officer must select boys who will conduct themselves with reasonable decency, but, in my own experience, the thicker the candidate's file with earnest praises of his character, the weaker his scholastic claims usually turn out to be.[31]

Such factors as regional distribution, type of school, cultural background, and social position are likewise incidental. They may modify the choice as between candidates of approximately equal ability in the interests of obtaining as good a cross section of our society as we can within the student body, but they should not determine that choice. During the postwar period we are likely to have many more foreign students on the campus, brought here under the auspices of the State Department and such organizations as the Institute of

[31] Alan Valentine, "Problems of an Admissions Office," *Educational Review*, 16 (1935), 63.

International Education. They should be matched by a proper representation of minority groups within our own culture. We agree that it should be the policy of the college, when these choices are made as between students of equal ability, that a preference may properly be given to those applicants who are relatives or sons of Amherst alumni; for equal and opposite reasons we think it also desirable that there be a proper representation within the student body of different economic, racial, and religious groups.

In particular we would like to see a serious effort made to obtain more good Negro students than we have had in recent years. The first Negro student to be graduated from Amherst College was Edward Jones in the class of 1826. From 1878 on we have had a small but fairly constant number of Negro students who have usually become leaders among their people. Our present Negro alumni reflect great credit on the college. In recent years, however, there have been comparatively few Negro students. Between 1920 and 1944 approximately 33 Negroes entered Amherst, an average of 1.32 per class. The committee has reason to believe that a number of our alumni are in a position to recommend to us Negro students of ability. We have also been assured that although Negro colleges have improved there is a real advantage to the Negroes themselves in having some of their abler students attend New England colleges. We hope that through the cooperation of the Admissions Office with our alumni we can once more have Negro students in every Amherst class.

It may be argued by some that, while the present geographical and social distribution leaves something to be desired, the present quality of our student body is about as high as we can hope to obtain. The committee is more hopeful than this. If we examine the relative achievement of preparatory and high school students in recent Amherst classes some interesting facts emerge. In two recent classes, as the following table shows, applicants admitted from public schools made significantly higher scores in the college board aptitude tests. That students who attended both public and private schools are inferior to the other two groups is no doubt due to the fact that many of these students needed more "preparation" for college than the public schools commonly offer.

AVERAGE COLLEGE BOARD APTITUDE SCORES

V—Verbal Aptitude M—Mathematical Aptitude

Class	Public Schools	Public and Private	Private Schools
1944	529 V—542 M	510 V—525 M	525 V—532 M
1945	511 V—521 M	480 V—509 M	504 V—513 M

If the aptitude of high school students on admission to Amherst as measured by the college boards is higher, so is their achievement greater. For a number of years the Dean in his annual reports has recorded the comparative achievement during freshman year of preparatory school students and high school students, dividing them into groups according to the quarter of their school class from which they entered. Consolidating his tables for the classes entering in the years 1938-1939, 1939-1940, 1940-1941, we get the following results:

SUMMARY OF DATA FROM THE DEAN'S REPORT ON FRESHMAN CLASSES ENTERING AMHERST IN 1939-40-41

	Number		College Grade	
Standing in Preparatory School	Private Schools	Public Schools	Private Schools	Public Schools
1st quarter	184	207	77.89	79.32
2nd quarter	168	42	72.41	73.20
3rd quarter	77	7	69.95	69.71
4th quarter	37	1	69.43	71.00
	Total 466	Total 257	Average 73.91	Average 77.22
	Total number 723		General average 75.03	

The interesting point in these figures is that it is the *third- and fourth-quarter preparatory school students* who pull down the average of their group.[32]

[32] It is reassuring, however, to note that the proportion of sons and relatives of Amherst alumni among the third- and fourth-quarter students is smaller for two of these three classes than it is for the three classes as a whole.

That the inferiority in achievement of preparatory school students persists during their college career is borne out by the following tables giving the distribution among high school and private school students of (1) awards of the degree with distinction and (2) elections to Phi Beta Kappa for the classes of 1931, 1936, 1941, and 1942.

DEGREE WITH DISTINCTION

Class	Total	High School		Private School		High School and Private School	
1931	59	34	57%	15	25%	10	17%
1936	89	46	52%	23	26%	20	22%
1941	82	50	61%	16	20%	16	20%
1942	40	18	45%	15	38%	7	17%

PHI BETA KAPPA

Class	Total	High School		Private School		High School and Private School	
1931	22	13	59%	7	32%	2	9%
1936	23	12	52%	6	26%	5	22%
1941	24	14	58%	2	8%	8	32%
1942	21	11	52%	5	24%	5	24%

The comparative percentages of high school students, private school students, and high school and private school students for the last three of these classes, *at entrance,* were:

	High Schools	Private Schools	Public and Private
1936	55%	23%	22%
1941	46%	27%	27%
1942	41%	32%	27%

Comparing these figures with those above it would appear that, on the whole, as the percentage of high school students in these successive classes declined their superiority to the other two groups increased.

Some of the students near the top of the third-quarter group are boys who are slow in maturing but good college material. The remainder of the third- and fourth-quarter group exhibits varying combinations of inadequate motivation with inferior ability. It does not belong in Amherst. The committee feels that if we could increase our applications, particularly from high school students, to the point where the great majority of these third- and fourth-quarter preparatory school students could be replaced by students from the upper half of their school, public or private, the intellectual life of the college would be greatly improved.

Faculty Participation in the Determination of Admission and Scholarship Policies

In an unpublished paper, "The Problem of Admissions at Amherst College" (1941), President King says: "The admissions office is and should be subject to criticism. Some of the criticism is just. Most of it, in my opinion, is based on inadequate information or erroneous assumptions." If some of the criticisms expressed or implied in this discussion are incorrect or unjust, it is, in part at least, because the faculty has not been adequately informed of the problems and procedures of the Admissions Office. The trustees have delegated to the faculty the "power and the duty to fix the requirements of admission." President King has assumed full responsibility for the administration of such requirements as the faculty should establish. The admissions policies under these requirements are determined and are carried out by a committee consisting of the President, the Dean, and the Director of Admissions. The responsibility for the administration of the scholarship funds is in the hands of the Dean. This committee believes that, so far as the determination of policies is concerned, it would be a wise procedure to supplement the present organization by the constitution of a new committee on admissions and scholarships consisting of the President, the Dean, the Director of Admissions, and two members of the faculty appointed with the advice and consent of the Committee of Six. It would be the function of this committee to meet periodically for the discussion and revision of admissions and scholarship policies but not to deal with individual applications. It should likewise be a part of the function of this committee to interpret these policies to the faculty by publishing an annual report. This report would state any changes in policy, with the reasons therefor, and would contain an analysis of the numbers of students applying and admitted and of scholarships granted, as well as a series of continuing studies showing the comparative achievement of the various groups of students in college. A committee of this sort and reports of this nature would be of great assistance in the interpretation of admissions and scholarship policy to the faculty. We therefore recommend that such a Committee on Admissions and Scholarship Policy be established.

ORIENTATION AND GUIDANCE

What has come to be known as the "personnel movement" and "the personnel point of view" has two main sources: the development of aptitude and placement tests and of applied psychology in industrial management because of the increasingly complex specialization in our society; and the concomitant growth of mental hygiene and psychiatry as branches of social work and of medicine.

In the college of earlier days the curriculum was small, personal relationships with fellow students and the faculty were fairly close, the continuity between secondary school and college was great, the interests and abilities of the students were similar, and the occupations they aimed at were comparatively few. What guidance they might require was obtained by the way. There was no real need for a formalized system of counseling. The highly developed systems of guidance in colleges and universities today have been the result of mass enrollment. Fifty per cent of all freshmen now enter colleges or universities with student bodies of 4000 or more. The new student is confronted by a catalogue he cannot read, registration forms as complex as income tax blanks, and a course schedule that reads like a railroad guide. There are dozens of bureaus and agencies he may need to get in touch with. Classes in the majority of the introductory courses he takes will be so large that to his teachers he can hardly expect to be more than a name in a class book. He is fortunate if he knows anyone beyond a speaking acquaintance with the few students who happen to sit next to him in some class. He is bewildered and lost. Hence, as the larger colleges and universities took on the same characteristics as a large industry or army of overwhelming size, complete impersonality, and bewilderingly complex organization, it became apparent that some new way had to be devised of reaching the individual student. The personnel movement in education is an attempt to guide the student through this educational maze and to break the "lockstep" which is the effect of mass enrollments.

There are a bewildering number of offices and functions that come under this topic. They include such things as testing and placement, advising students on their course programs, the planning and regulation of the social life of the students, the remedial teaching of reading, writing, and speech, mental hygiene and psychiatric aid, religious counseling, and occupational guidance. In general they fall under three rubrics: academic guidance, vocational guidance, and psychiatric aid. These three functions are quite distinct and should never be confused, although in practice they obviously may all be involved in a particular case.

In this section we propose to discuss only the freshman orientation program and academic guidance. There is a need for some sort of psychiatric aid in dealing with certain individuals in every college but we have no clear idea what a college in Amherst's situation should do about it. If we admit students who need remedial work in reading, writing, or speech, they should, no doubt, be given the training they need singly or in small groups by members of the faculty in the departments of psychology, English, or public speaking qualified to give that sort of instruction. Occupational guidance is, we believe, satisfactorily provided for as it is carried on by the Alumni Secretary. Religious counseling we refer to in a later section of this report.

To what extent does the need for guidance exist in the small college? President King has said:

> Character, manners, relations with his fellows, the power and technique of group action are as essential as the hours spent in the class room. And these aspects are individual; they do not lend themselves readily to the technique of mass production. They are a by-product of intimate associations with and personal stimulus from the maturer minds and cultivated personalities of the faculty. So it is; so it has always been. The Greeks trained their soldiers in armies; they taught their young men and women in small groups in the academy.[33]

This we would like to think means that in the small college no elaborately developed form of counseling or personnel service is necessary; but the truth is that, to some degree at least, a small college

[33] Quoted from *Student Personnel Services in Colleges and Universities*, edited by John Dale Russell (Chicago, 1941), p. 4.

frequently neglects the individual at the time when he most needs someone to take a personal interest in him and help him find his bearings. That function largely goes by default to such social groups as the fraternities. Guidance in the small college during the student's last two years, except for vocational guidance, is not normally a problem. By this time he knows his way around, has established himself in a major, and can of his own accord seek out the advice he needs. In the first two years, however, while he is attempting to wean himself from dependence on his family and establish himself as an adult individual, he frequently needs some mature person to whom he can turn as a friend for advice and support. Every college must, as a matter of course, supply certain of the services mentioned above but this is the central problem of guidance which, irrespective of its size, exists for every institution.

Orientation of Freshmen.

It has long been recognized at Amherst that an orientation program aids the incoming freshmen to make the adjustment to college life, to acquire some perspective on the opportunities presented to them as undergraduates. We believe that this program should be expanded and developed experimentally along somewhat the following lines:

The College Catalogue. The orientation of freshmen should begin with the catalogue and the booklet for prospective members of the freshman class. Both of them should contain the sort of information that will help the student to decide not merely which courses he should take but whether he should go to a liberal arts college at all. There should be a brief but clear and persuasive statement of the "Plan of Undergraduate Study" (the Princeton catalogue offers a good illustration), which would begin with a statement of the aims and ideals of liberal education and its relation to preparation for a vocation, then go on to show how the curricular provisions of the first two years and the requirements for majors and honors are intended to realize those objectives. There should, perhaps, also be a description of certain typical courses of study constituting a major or major with honors in representative fields, e.g., a premedical course, a major in a social science, a major in a literature, etc., to acquaint the prospective student with an illustration of the sort of total program he might expect to take during his four years in college.

In a prefatory note to these sample programs the student should be advised to follow his intellectual interests in the choice of a major rather than to think of a particular course of study such as pre-law, pre-medical, or pre-business, for success in business and in graduate school is correlated with the distinction of the student's work in college but not with work in any particular field of concentration.[34]

Orientation Program. The present orientation program for freshmen could, we believe, be improved. The experiment should be tried of bringing them to the college at least several days before the return of the upperclassmen. The opportunity for beginning their acquaintance with one another without the presence of the other students would help to establish their solidarity as a class. A selected group of upperclassmen should be present to meet the freshmen and to help them become acquainted with the college and with one another.

The organization and control of this period would be worked out cooperatively by the Dean, the Freshman Dean, the Student Council, and the Student-Faculty Conference Committee. The sort of program we have in mind for this period is as follows.

They should not be talked at over much; that kind of thing gives rapidly diminishing returns. But there could be, in addition to certain social events, a series of talks or panel discussions on such subjects as:

1. The values of a liberal education, by the President or a member of the faculty.
2. The rules of the college, by the Dean.
3. A talk by the Director of Religious Activities.
4. A talk by the College Physician on some common-sense rules of health and hygiene.
5. A student panel organized by the Student Council in which three or four seniors would discuss their college experience with some reference to their vocational aims.
6. A talk, perhaps by the president of Scarab, on outside activities, the *Student*, the Masquers, managerial competitions, etc.

This orientation period might be followed up by the freshman forum we have now.

[34] Two of the best-known studies of this question are those by President Lowell of Harvard and President Gifford of the American Telephone and Telegraph Company. For a summary of both see A. Lawrence Lowell, *What a University President Has Learned* (New York, 1938), pp. 73-78.

During the first term some provision should be made for giving the students some instruction in the use of the library. If we eventually acquire the services of a reference librarian, he might give the freshmen, in small sections, brief training courses of this sort. Perhaps it might also be possible to frame a certain number of assignments in English 1-2 that would entail practice in the use of the various resources that the library affords. We have mentioned in discussing a humanities course for freshmen the possibility of inducing students, through the work of such a course, to discover and to use the library, and the possibility of developing what might be called a "Humanities Reading Room" which might facilitate the discovery.

In the second term, during the period preceding consultation with advisers and elections for the sophomore year, there should be a series of talks on courses and departments, roughly divided into three groups, natural sciences, social studies, and humanities, all dealing specifically with the requirements, type of work involved, and typical programs, and as clearly as possible outlining the purposes of a major or major with honors in that particular field. This series should be concluded with a presentation by the Alumni Secretary of the plan of vocational guidance used at Amherst.

We recommend that an orientation program of this kind be adopted.

Academic Guidance

This committee was given a copy of excerpts from a large number of letters written on the subject of the curriculum by Amherst graduates to the Alumni Committee. The need for more guidance, particularly during the first two years, was mentioned in these letters oftener than any other topic. Although most of the alumni talked about being helped in their choice of courses, etc., it is easy to see from the nature of their comments that what they really wanted most was intellectual stimulation and moral support in their efforts to mature. This coming to maturity of our students is a change that usually occurs, sometimes quite suddenly, toward the middle of their college career. How it happens or when it will is a mystery. This is what a proper adviser is most interested in and eager to see achieved. The best test of the success of an advisory system is the extent to which a student can be assisted in this process of maturation.

The adviser will try to keep the boy out of mischief or to prevent him from attempting what for him is unwise or impossible; but this is preliminary to the effort to arouse his latent abilities. Unfortunately, the impulse to master difficulties is independent of the individual's intelligence. With most boys at the age they enter college it is still to a great extent unfocused and unattached. The boy may remain for a long time at loose ends, he may fritter his energies away in a multitude of "activities," or he may gradually acquire a sense of direction, develop real interests, and concentrate his energies on taking advantage of the opportunities for his own development that the college offers. Some of this sense of self-direction the student can and should acquire of his own accord. Certain teachers and certain courses will particularly arouse his interest and aid him to do so, but most students need the additional help that a personal friendship with at least one member of the faculty can give them.

Some members of the faculty have felt that we could raise the standards of scholarship within the student body by eliminating more of those students who are at the bottom of their class. The committee sympathizes with the demand for more rigorous standards of scholarship but it would like to point out that if there is laxness, that is, in part, the faculty's own fault. A member of the faculty may frequently be tempted, in marking his students, to be far stricter when distinguishing between two students to whom he is giving grades of 90 and 93 than when distinguishing between students with grades of 55 and 60. There is no general tendency to give an honor grade to anyone who does not deserve it but there is always an inclination to let a student on the border line between passing and failure "get by." This tendency is perhaps reinforced by the competition of individuals and departments for student popularity. The introduction of a curriculum in which there are more interdepartmental and required courses such as that suggested in the section on curriculum of this report should help to remedy this situation so far as the first two years are concerned, since the grading of students in these courses would be done on a broader basis by a group of instructors.

A more important problem, however, is that of arousing the ambition of students who are working below the level of their real abilities. The drastic elimination of the poorest students can hardly affect even indirectly the potential B or A student with a safe 75. How can we bring such a student up to where he belongs? We believe that the introduction of a curriculum of the kind we have suggested, and, in particular, of the laboratory or seminar type of work, work which cannot be evaded and which the student does under the close supervision of the instructor, would greatly help to eliminate a good deal of this present waste. It should be supplemented, however, by a system of guidance in which a student is challenged to realize his potentialities.

How such a system is to be organized your committee is not certain. The whole question should be studied and experiments made as a result of that study over a period of years. Certainly the existing system of faculty advisers in its actual operation is entirely inadequate for this purpose. Some of the advisers are unwilling to give their students more than perfunctory attention. Others are not really fitted by their temperaments or interests to establish the relationship with their students which is needed. There is no obligation on the part of the student who is running away from responsibility to see his adviser except once a year to get his course card signed.

If the counseling of students is to be taken seriously, and we believe that it should be, a small group of capable advisers who are really interested in doing such work must be carefully selected. They would have to work as a corps under the close supervision of the Dean to carry the students through the first two years. We are not sure that in practice such a system is really feasible. It would take too much of the time and energy of the men who participated in it unless they were relieved of a part of their teaching duties. What seems to us to be a better alternative is the appointment of an associate dean, under Dean Porter, for the freshman-sophomore years, chosen specifically for those qualities of personality that would make him effective in counseling students. He would be appointed from the faculty or appointed to the faculty for this purpose. He could, we believe, teach one course, devoting the remainder of his time to establishing relationships with the members of the freshman and sophomore classes. He would be a person whom they could come to know well enough so that they would be able to receive from him the advice that would really meet their particular problems.

To set up an office of this sort would have the merit of fixing responsibility upon an individual instead of dispersing it among a group.

Much would, of course, depend upon the character and ability of that individual. If the right person were chosen, he could secure the help and cooperation of the members of the faculty on a voluntary basis as it was needed. His work would be arduous but rewarding, for he should be able to do much in cooperation with the faculty to create and maintain a higher level of morale and achievement in the freshman-sophomore student body. In a small college the appointment of the right freshman-sophomore dean is, we believe, the best answer to the question: How can we provide a personnel service that is truly personal?

We recommend that an associate dean be appointed to be in charge of the counseling of freshmen and sophomores.

SOCIAL LIFE AND ACTIVITIES

At the beginning of this section we shall make a few general remarks on the relation of activities to the curriculum and to the atmosphere of the college. We shall then proceed to a discussion of three important questions which may conveniently be grouped under this general head: student government, the fraternities and their relation to the social life of the college, and physical education and athletics.

Everyone will agree that extracurricular activities have an essential part to play in the total educational effect of the college experience. The question is: What kind of activities and how much of them? Do they contribute to the education of the student by providing a means of healthful recreation and the formation of good social habits, by affording occasions for the development of enduring friendships, and by the cultivation of desirable interests and tastes; or do they waste his time, dissipate his energies, and distract him from taking the best advantage of the opportunities the college affords for his development? To point the issue: Do the activities serve and express the native "resistance" of a boy to education, do they help him to prolong his adolescence and defer the arduous business of growing up; or are they a means of enabling him to reach social and intellectual maturity?

It is only too easy to find instances where college life competes with the curriculum. In such cases the outcome is never in doubt. Henry Seidel Canby in his delightful book about his own undergraduate days, *Alma Mater: the Gothic Age of the American College*, describes such a state of affairs. One would gather from reading it that the faculty might have tinkered with the curriculum till the cows came home without having the slightest effect upon those genial young barbarians living an intensely competitive, wholly absorbing life of their own, which gave no leisure to pay more than a harassed and perfunctory attention to their courses in order that they might keep the right to live as they chose.

We would agree with Mr. Canby that the little world he describes has been slowly falling into decay. Its decline began with the First World War and became obvious with the depression. Its demise may be hoped for in the postwar world. That gay and irresponsible life expressed the confidence of his generation that a world awaited them on graduation in which what they had done in college, so far as their studies were concerned, was not so very important. One could make his way in the business world, or even in a law school, by getting down to work when he got there. Such a belief was always an illusion, but it was plausible then and it has lost that plausibility now. There can be little doubt that the world the college graduate must face has steadily become a tougher and more competitive one. The number of graduates of colleges and professional schools has increased out of all proportion to the growth of population and of national income. The average college graduate now earns less than $3000 a year.[35] It has been estimated that not more than 6 to 7 per cent of the jobs available in industry require a full college education. Competition for these jobs is becoming correspondingly severe while at the same time there is a growing threat of overcrowding in the professions. We face a situation which has long since become acute in certain European countries.

The college should therefore guide the activities of the students in

[35] MEDIAN TOTAL INCOMES OF GRADUATE FAMILIES, 1939, COMPARED WITH INCOMES ESTIMATED FOR ALL U.S. FAMILIES, 1935-36

	Graduate	Total U.S.
Families including individuals living alone	$2,850	$1,070
Families excluding individuals living alone	$3,200	$1,160
Individuals living alone	$1,720	$ 830

F. Lawrence Babcock, *The U.S. College Graduate* (New York, 1941), p. 27.

such a way that they may be helped rather than hindered in coming to maturity. Activities must complement and not compete with the curriculum. This problem will take care of itself in so far as we are able to select better students and as each succeeding student generation realizes more clearly that real work while in college is a foundation of subsequent success.

In the interim, activities must be taken much more seriously than they have been by the faculty, the administration, and the students themselves as a part of the total educational plan of the college. They are not just something to be ignored, apart from a little perfunctory regulation, since all work and no play would make Jack a dull boy. While they should remain extracurricular, they must be controlled in such a way that participation in them will be widely distributed throughout the student body,[36] and useless and time-consuming routines involved in the usual "competitions" will be so far as possible curtailed or eliminated. The absurdly false emphasis on the prestige arising from success in certain activities should be diminished while those which encourage genuinely recreational, intellectual, and cultural interests should be fostered.

This does not imply that a benevolent dictatorship should be exercised by any administrative officer or faculty committee over the extracurricular activities of the students. On the contrary, we deplore the general tendency to "take over" and "do for" the student particularly evident in dramatics and intercollegiate athletics. It is this tendency that we would call "professionalism" in activities. The committee is aware why this has occurred. Intercollegiate athletics have long been recognized as too important to be safely entrusted to the

[36] To the impartial spectator it might appear that at Amherst too much attention is paid to activities rather than too little. It would seem, however, that all of this busyness is concentrated, as is doubtless true in many other institutions, in a minority of the student body. Dean Porter, in his speech at the Symposium on Activities (May 27, 1944) describes the situation (excluding intramural activities) as follows: "In the year 1941-1942, according to the statistics which have been kept in the office of the Director of Intercollegiate Athletics, 230 out of 597 sophomores, juniors, and seniors participated in athletics and such non-athletic activities as the Amherst Press, the *Amherst Student*, the *Olio*, *Touchstone*, musical clubs, dramatics, and debating. In terms of percentage this would be 39 per cent of the men of these three classes. In the freshman class of 273, 95 out of 273 participated in extracurricular activities. In percentage terms this would be 35 per cent. The non-athletic activities in which they participated were the *Amherst Student*, musical clubs, dramatics, and debating."

amateurish inefficiencies of student management and control. In recent years the Masquers has assumed a similar though not equal degree of importance. They are not matters which concern the students as a body of students alone but the college as an institution in its relation to other colleges and to society at large.[37]

The committee does not believe that these problems can be dealt with in any summary fashion. Though it may be argued, quite correctly, that quasi-professional dramatic performances are more valuable as a contribution to the cultural life of the college as a whole, and though it is obvious that quasi-professional intercollegiate athletics are an inevitable and irrepressible development of the competitive relations between the colleges, it may also be argued, and some members of this committee believe, that the growth of professionalism in activities of any sort diminishes their value as *activities* to the students who participate in them. We should like to see, in dramatics as well as in athletics, more of the "plural teams" idea put into practice, with a larger number of students participating.

The committee has no comprehensive proposals to offer for the realization of this general objective, to make activities an integral and constructive part of the total "educational" plan of the college. It can only be realized over a long period of time by the careful and patient molding of existing institutions and practices. The committee suggests that for the future it should be a primary function of the Student-Faculty Conference Committee, working in cooperation with the Student Council and the Dean, to search for means by which activities may be gradually transformed in this direction. We do propose, however, to make suggestions regarding three basic questions that bear directly on these problems—student government, the fraternities, and physical education and athletics.

[37] DISSENT.—It is our opinion that the experienced direction and control of the principal Masquers productions and of intercollegiate athletics, as they existed prior to the war, are very desirable. We believe that this direction adds to the value of the performances from the audience point of view and of the activity from the participants' point of view. That student-produced plays and student-organized athletics, on the other hand, have a peculiar activity merit is incontestable, and the opportunity for both is provided. It does not follow, however, that plays and sports, when professionally supervised, cease to be valuable as activities. Rather, they assume different and equally important values. BAILEY BROWN and VINCENT MORGAN.

Student Government

No activity can be more important than student government. This is obvious if it is the purpose of the college to give young men of superior endowment the knowledge and training that they need to make them leaders in a democratic community. Amherst was one of the first colleges to establish, under President Seelye, a system of responsible self-government in the student body. It is a confession of failure in the college that in the years before the war student government had declined to the point where it had little responsibility and even less authority.

The causes of its failure were, no doubt, subtle and complex. Chief among them was the effect of the fraternities on student government. As the result of fraternity rivalries an absurd rule governing elections was passed which forbade "combines," though it is an obvious fact that the very nature of political democracy consists in the combination of various interest groups to gain control of the government. Any regular political party is an illustration of this. Constant violation of this rule led to the engineering of a "revolution" (1938) eliminating these violations of "democracy" by amending the constitution in such a way as to substitute for the real government which had previously existed a new organization which was nothing more in effect than an interfraternity council. The result was that the student government has since been basically undemocratic. It has consisted of fifteen separate groups, including the Lord Jeff Club and (in theory) the Independents. The student body as a student body no longer had any representation. In consequence, the only important responsibility this confederacy could exercise was that of trying to adjust its own internal conflicts, chiefly disputes over the rushing rules. Since it could command no obedience, it lost the respect of the students and the confidence of the faculty and administration.

It is of the greatest importance that when the college returns to normalcy every effort be made to institute and maintain a proper form of real student government, organized on a basis similar to the one destroyed in 1938. We believe that the attitude of the administration and the faculty toward that government should be to give it as much responsibility as it can bear. As it grows in strength, it should be able properly to demand and to receive more of such responsibilities. The administration and the faculty should be ready and willing to confer them.

The difficulty with most student governments is that they are the instruments of a disguised paternalism. They have no sovereignty and are allowed to do what they want only in so far as they do what is wanted by those who have the power to abolish them. We believe that an experiment in government of this kind is too trivial to be worth making. If we propose to give the students practice in self-government, it is necessary to take the risks involved in giving them something important to do and more difficult than they may perhaps be able to do well. No student government can succeed unless the students desire to govern themselves, and they are not likely to desire that power unless they are given a taste of it. We do not mean to suggest that a responsible student government can be set up *ad hoc*, but the students can be encouraged by the administration and the faculty gradually to assume more and more of the responsibility for their own discipline in proportion as traditions and practices of the right sort are developed. The faculty members of the Student-Faculty Conference Committee and the Dean can perform an invaluable service in promoting and guiding the development of such a government.

A revived and strengthened student government will doubtless press for a restoration of the honor system. The committee's view is that whether an honor system exists or not, and, if it exists, whether it works or not, is important chiefly as a *symptom* of the morale of of the student body.

Honor systems have generally been on the decline. With the growth in size and increasing heterogeneity of student enrollments they have proved in many institutions to be unworkable. A survey of two hundred colleges and universities made in 1915 showed that all but twenty-two were using the honor system in whole or in part, or were planning to adopt it, and that none of these institutions had abandoned it. A similar survey of eighty-one institutions made in 1933 showed that forty-two of them did not use the honor system, twenty-five of them had previously used it but had now abandoned it, and none of them were planning to adopt it.[38] Still more recently, a survey of one hundred and twenty-two institutions showed that fifty

[38] L. Cole, *The Background for College Teaching* (New York, 1940), p. 186.

per cent do not use the honor system, thirty-seven per cent employ a combination of honor and proctor system, and only thirteen per cent have a full honor system.[39]

In a small institution with a student body that forms a real community an honor system can operate efficiently. It cannot, of course, be imposed but must get started as an expression of a vigorous and enlightened student opinion.

Why did the honor system come to a dismal end in 1928 at Amherst, to the mutual relief of students and faculty? The honor system has persisted in comparable institutions such as Hamilton, Haverford, Wesleyan, and Williams. We presume that it works well at all of them; we have been assured that at Wesleyan and Williams it has always done so.

The honor system will, we hope, eventually be revived. If it is, however, it should be set up in such a way that while evidence of infringements is given to a student committee the actual trial of a case is participated in by representatives of the faculty and administration. We believe this because in the delegation of responsibility to a student government it is important to make a distinction between the legislative and executive as against the judicial function. Students often bungle the judicial functions which fall to them under honor systems. They have not the experience and maturity needed for their exercise and, notoriously, their judgments are too severe. In the legislation of rules for their own government and in the management of many of their activities there is enough scope for the kind of opportunity to acquire social maturity that they need.

The Fraternities

It would be no exaggeration to say that the fraternities dominate the social life of the college. What must be referred to vaguely as the climate of opinion within the student body is primarily the effect or product of their mode of life together in the fraternity groups. To some degree, at least in a small college where the fraternities include a great majority of the students, this has always been true.

What, if anything, should be done about them is, therefore, a question of the greatest importance. It is, likewise, a most difficult ques-

[39] Basil H. Peterson, "Student Government in Collegiate Institutions," *Journal of Higher Education*, 14 (1943), 207.

tion to discuss. Since there is little or no "objective" evidence to bear out any particular opinion, one's personal feelings and experience are likely to weigh more in forming one's opinion than anyone else's argument; and so many possible attitudes on the question may be taken, ranging from approval of the *status quo* through modification and radical reform to abolition, that it is hard to achieve through discussion a real consensus of opinion on the subject.

Nevertheless, a majority of the members of the committee find themselves in agreement: we believe that they should be abolished. We propose to give first our fundamental reasons why we believe that fraternities should not be continued at Amherst, then to indicate why we think that various modifications and reforms of the fraternity system as it has existed are inadequate or impractical, and finally to make our own recommendations. The two basic charges, to quote President King, "that fraternities must face if they are to survive" are "(1) fraternities are anti-democratic; (2) fraternities are anti-intellectual."[40] We believe both these charges to be true; and we believe that in both respects the existence of fraternities conflicts with the fundamental educational aims of the college.

It is difficult to discuss these two criticisms separately, for they are in fact intimately connected. We shall attempt, however, first to state why we believe fraternities to be "anti-democratic" and then why they have become increasingly "anti-intellectual" in ways that seriously conflict with the purposes of the college.

Fraternities Are Anti-Democratic. No one can seriously deny that the fraternities are in a fundamental sense anti-democratic. Some of them, by the terms of their charters, officially exclude members of certain racial and religious groups. All of them are, in practice, exclusive in the sense that they select for membership, so far as they are able to, persons who conform to their own particular standards of value. That, of course, is the fraternity's right so far as it is a private group, but that right becomes a special privilege when it is exercised within a college community. We are not thinking here so much of the "forgotten man" (a relatively small number) as we are of the psychological and moral effects upon the "elect," the members of the fraternities themselves. The psychology of the *in* group vs. the

[40] Quoted from a speech to the New York alumni.

out group is deeply rooted in human nature, for organization in exclusive groups is a fundamental characteristic of primitive society. Social democracy has set itself against this tendency. It is basically an attempt to construct a society in which there shall be no privileges that are not earned, no aristocracy save an aristocracy of talent devoted to the service of the community. The college, therefore, as a community should be superior to the society without. It should possess some of the traits of an ideal society if its most important function is to enable students to get a certain perspective on the pattern of culture in which they are immersed, a perspective which renders them sensible to its defects as well as its merits. How else can we hope to graduate young men who will become good citizens and even leaders in a democracy? Professor Ralph Linton has said: "A society that genuinely believes in social justice can get social justice and the educator can do more than anyone else to establish this belief."[41] It is because fraternities positively impede this educational objective that they should be called anti-democratic.

Young men when brought together will mutually associate in groups. These groups will compete with one another. A loyalty to the group will be reinforced by this competition. The question is not whether there should be such social groups but whether membership in those that exist shall be accessible to all and under the control of the college. As it stands, admission to the college is not tantamount to admission to all of the rights and privileges that the life of an undergraduate affords. This is a fundamental inconsistency. Amherst College, as an educational institution performing a public service, should afford to every student the same social as well as intellectual opportunities. This it cannot do so long as the fraternities as independent social groups existing on the campus largely determine who shall participate in the various social activities and what the forms of those activities shall be.

The committee has suggested that it seems desirable to enlarge our social basis, and specifically to procure more applicants for admission from a larger number of public high schools. We were curious to see whether any perceptible connection existed between the type of school from which a boy entered college and the likelihood of his

[41] *Culture and Personality,* American Council on Education Pamphlet (Washington, 1941), p. 17.

"making" a fraternity. The figures in the accompanying table, for three recent classes at five-year intervals, appear to show that such a connection does exist. It seems to us that a general disinclination on the part of the fraternities to take in freshmen entering college from high schools may be a hindrance to the college in obtaining such students.

Class	Percentage Entered from		Number of Men in Non-Fraternity Group from		Percentage of Men in Non-Fraternity Group from	
	Private Schools	Public Schools	Private Schools	Public Schools	Private Schools	Public Schools
1934	50.99	49.01	6	37	13.95	86.05
1939	48.73	51.27	16	40	28.57	71.43
1944	63.34	36.66	11	24	31.43	68.57

Fraternities Are Anti-Intellectual. It is usual, in discussions of this topic, to contrast fraternities as they once were with fraternities as they are now. It is pointed out that at one time they provided associations for the students which served to round out their lives by offering them a means of recreation, a way of draining off their surplus energy in activities and competitions, and a basis for enduring friendships, and even supplemented the curriculum so far as they took on some of the characteristics of the earlier literary societies. In this respect they were a valuable corrective to the rather narrow environment, social and intellectual, in which those students lived. For this reason it is difficult to discuss the value of the fraternities as they are now with many older graduates of the college. Because they did not realize it then, they do not recognize now that there is any important opposition between the fraternity and the college. They did not feel any conflict of loyalties between them while they were themselves undergraduates and they remember their experience as one in which the college and the fraternity both played a vital role, each supplementing the influence of the other in their total education. If there has always been a latent antagonism between the fraternities and the college which has now become acute, that is because the conflict between the values represented by the college and those of the social groups from which the majority of these students come has grown more profound.

Youth are naturally and inevitably imitative. Coming to a college in their later adolescence, they have already received the major part of their "education." They have assumed the stamp of their parents, their friends, their home communities. Even those "in revolt" are in fact dependent upon that which they appear to oppose. Theirs is a kind of partial, negative imitation. The college can operate upon these preformed characters only within the narrow confines of their remaining elasticity. Within those limits they can be formed but not reformed. The rise of fraternities, however, coincided with a growing disparity between the aims professed by the college and the real interests of the students themselves, interests which they brought with them to the campus. The fraternity gave the student an organized means of resisting the domination of the college, a way in which he could express his own ideals and live his own life in partial independence of it. It continues to flourish as a kind of implicit protest against academic tradition and as an expression within the college of the forces of the "outer" world.

The fraternities represent an entrenchment of the world without inside the college community. They are the center of a kind of social education that reinforces the conventional values of our society in an environment where those values are being analyzed. Hence, there is a real and natural antagonism, which anyone at all acquainted with them will recognize, between the fraternities and the college.

The fraternities, which may once have helped students to mature, now more often help to breed social irresponsibility and emotional regression. They do this by putting a premium on mediocrity in the literal sense of the term. What meets with approval in the fraternity is too often that which discounts and even derides what has been said in the classroom. In a social atmosphere of mediocrity the development of intelligence and moral sense is stifled. Such an atmosphere is fostered and perpetuated by certain dominating groups of students within the fraternities. They welcome it as an anesthetic to prevent or at least alleviate the pains of coming to social and intellectual maturity.

It is also true that fraternity traditions usually influence their members in such a way as to nullify the primary purpose of the college. The social traditions of the fraternity compete strenuously and as a rule successfully with the curriculum. They serve to enlist the interest and energy of the student in extracurricular activities in a way that renders him relatively immune to any deep or lasting influence by the college. This competition, in which the college comes off, with the majority of students, a bad second best, is dramatically initiated by the rushing season.

The freshman's introduction to Amherst is one in which he is more than likely to receive the impression that the intellectual life of the college exists largely as a dim background while "college life," as exemplified by the activities of the fraternities, is the really important thing that is going on. The impression is equally serious and profound on those students who are chosen for membership and those who are not. It is not an exaggeration to say that this social disorientation persists, constantly reinforced as it is by the mode of life in both groups, with most students through the sophomore year. With some the effects are permanent.

Here, however, we must discriminate between the various fraternal groups. They vary greatly, as everyone knows, among themselves and many of them are in a state of constant change, going up and down in both the social and the academic scale. The tone of a given fraternity is determined primarily by its undergraduate members. Many a fraternity has changed radically in a short period of time, owing to the chance that some particular group of undergraduates have, as leaders in that organization, determined its character. Such changes are for the better or for the worse. A few fraternities, perhaps because of peculiarly strong traditions, have retained a relatively constant character over a long period of time.

Our support of the charge that the fraternities are "anti-democratic" was based upon their inherent characteristics as exclusive secret societies rather than upon any "objective" testimony or evidences of fact. That this exclusiveness tends also to operate in a way that is "anti-intellectual" seems evident to us from the fact that the fraternities often exclude, in addition to certain racial and religious groups, many students who, as their subsequent achievement shows, are potentially important members of the college community. This may be due, in part, to methods of rushing, which cause some students whose merits are not obvious to be overlooked. In greater measure, however, it results from the adolescent standards of many of the fraternity groups themselves. Good looks, good clothes, an air of premature sophistication, and athletic prowess would seem to be some of the criteria that are most influential in determining the students' choices. Scholarship, beyond the minimum ability to qualify for initiation by attaining passing grades, is rarely an important qualification. The following tables concerning the awards of the Treadway Trophy, the degrees with high or highest honors, and the elections to Phi Beta Kappa over a period of approximately twenty years show this.

AWARDS OF THE TREADWAY TROPHY FOR INTERFRATERNITY SCHOLARSHIP, 1924-43 INCLUSIVE

Year	Winner
1924	Delta Tau Delta
1925	Delta Upsilon
1926	Delta Tau Delta
1927	Nonfraternity group
1928	Nonfraternity group
1929	Nonfraternity group
1930	Nonfraternity group
1931	Nonfraternity group
1932	Psi Upsilon
1933	Theta Xi
1934	Commons Club
1935	Lord Jeffery Amherst Club
1936	Lord Jeffery Amherst Club
1937	Lord Jeffery Amherst Club
1938	Lord Jeffery Amherst Club
1939	Alpha Delta Phi
1940	Alpha Delta Phi
1941	Lord Jeffery Amherst Club
1942	Lord Jeffery Amherst Club
1943	Lord Jeffery Amherst Club

Recapitulation:

Lord Jeffery Amherst Club, Commons Club, or nonfraternity group	13	Delta Upsilon	1
Alpha Delta Phi	2	Psi Upsilon	1
Delta Tau Delta	2	Theta Xi	1

DEGREES SUMMA CUM LAUDE OR MAGNA CUM LAUDE CONFERRED AT COMMENCEMENTS FROM JUNE, 1924, TO OCTOBER, 1943, INCLUSIVE, ANALYZED BY FRATERNITY MEMBERSHIP

Group	Summas	Magnas	Total	Percentage
Highest fraternity	5	28	33	12.4
Next highest fraternity	1	22	23	8.6
Nonfraternity	7	58	65	24.4
These three groups	13	108	121	45.4
Eleven other fraternities	13	132	145	54.6
Totals	26	240	266	100.0

ELECTIONS TO PHI BETA KAPPA, CALENDAR YEARS 1924-43 INCLUSIVE, ANALYZED BY FRATERNITY MEMBERSHIP

Group	Elections	Percentage
Highest fraternity[a]	51	11.5
Next highest fraternity[a]	30	6.8
Nonfraternity	120	27.2
These three groups	201	45.5
Eleven other fraternities	240	54.5
Totals	441	100.0

[a] These two fraternities are the same ones as in the previous table.

During the period covered by these tables nonfraternity membership has been on the average 18 per cent of the total enrollment of the college. About 6.3 per cent of the student body were, on the average, in each fraternity. It should be noted that two of the fraternities have maintained standards of scholarship comparable with those of the nonfraternity group. These three groups representing about 30 per cent of the student body got 45 per cent of the academic honors.[42]

[42] It has seemed invidious to give a complete list or to name the fraternities. It may be interesting, however, to give the facts for the lowest fraternity, which is the same one in both lists. During this twenty-year period its members attained seven degrees *magna cum laude*, or 2.6 per cent of the total honors degrees granted, and twelve elections to Phi Beta Kappa, or 2.5 per cent of the total elections.

The conclusion seems justified: that during the past twenty years, under three different college administrations, and under various systems of granting honors, there has not been maintained a healthy and reasonable balance, in the matter of high scholarship, among the different social groups of which the college has been composed.

At this point the question occurs: What are the alternatives? Few members of the faculty, we believe, would not agree that a reform of the fraternities as they were during the period preceding the war is essential. There are, therefore, only two real alternatives. Should they be reformed or abolished? Everyone will concur that the greatest strength of the small college lies in the fact that it can influence the social maturation of its students in desirable ways by controlling the social organization and extracurricular activities of the student to a degree impossible in larger institutions. This defect of the large college has been recognized in the establishment of the house plans at Harvard and Yale. Those plans are, essentially, attempts to establish within a large college many of the social advantages of a small one.

Some Possible Reforms of the Fraternities. Those who believe that the fraternities, in view of their long history at Amherst, still provide the best mode of self-government and social training for the students, that it is dangerous for the college to acquire too much control over their social life, that the fraternity organization is the best way of enabling the administration to maintain morale and discipline, and that the fraternities are a source of loyalty to the college which cannot be replaced, will argue for changes in the fraternities which will tend in part to meet the criticisms that have been made of them.

Many possible modifications of the fraternities have been suggested. They represent varying degrees and kinds of reform. Those we are familiar with are not mutually exclusive. Conceivably all of them might be adopted. Some are far more thoroughgoing than others and any combination of them would be more drastic in its effect than any one taken singly. Some of them seem to us to be ineffective in the sense that they would be likely to effect little or no change in the present character and behavior of the fraternities. Others seem to be impractical in that we doubt if they could be instituted so long as fraternities retain their present independence. With still others there is no guarantee that they would in fact produce the results claimed for them. Let us comment as briefly as possible on each of these proposals in turn. They are, very roughly in the order of their importance as effecting substantial changes, as follows:

a. Faculty Advisers. Many houses have had faculty advisers in the past. In some cases these advisers have been of great benefit to them, but there is no uniformity or consistency in the practice. Houses which most need the help of an adviser are often least inclined to invite it. When the Student-Faculty Conference Committee made a serious effort a few years ago to revitalize the advisory system, it was predicted—correctly—that their efforts would not meet with more than token results. In any case, the faculty adviser does not and cannot affect the existing system. He can only tinker a little with it.

b. Resident Tutors. We do not believe that their institution would be practicable whether or not they were given disciplinary powers. Under existing conditions residence in a fraternity house would be intolerable to most members of the faculty and unwelcome to the students. This is another modification which would not serve to meet effectively the principal criticisms of the fraternity system.

c. Elimination of Eating in the Houses. This, we believe, everyone agrees is a desirable reform, if the fraternities are to continue, and needs no further discussion by us.

d. Enhancing the Advantages of the Lord Jeff Club. This also everyone will probably agree is a valuable reform if fraternities are to be continued. At the least, the Lord Jeff Club should be given a separate house which will provide quarters for it equal to those owned by any fraternity.[43]

e. Abolition of National Affiliation. This reform was strenuously urged by a group of undergraduates just before the war. Their arguments were principally (1) that the costs of national membership (approximately $11,000 a year—very unevenly divided between the thirteen groups) did not bring a commensurate return to the students, (2) that this cost probably helped to prevent some students from joining fraternities, and (3) that in some cases the national organizations tended actively to promote in the fraternities the kind of behavior which made them vulnerable to the charges that have

[43] The argument for this possibility has been well stated by Mr. Eugene S. Wilson, Jr., in an editorial in the *Amherst Graduates' Quarterly*, November, 1944, pp. 26-27.

been brought against them. We would urge the abolition of national affiliation in the event that fraternities were to be continued.

f. An Alumni Fraternity Council to Assume Responsibility for Morale and Discipline among the Fraternity Groups. The committee does not know whether this proposal is a practical one. Whether it would work or not would depend upon the willingness of the fraternities to delegate authority to it and upon the ability and capacity of the alumni members to exercise their authority. It seems to us that it would be undesirable for members of the faculty who belong to fraternities to serve on this board since exigencies might arise wherein they would find themselves, as faculty members, on one side of a controversy and, at the same time, as members of the board, on the other. If resident faculty members were not on the board, it seems equally difficult to see how a group of busy men living in various localities could get together often enough or come to know the details of conditions on the campus sufficiently well to serve effectively in this capacity. Such a board would not be analogous to the present organization directing the interfraternity business management. In that case the group of alumni representatives serve as a board of directors who are represented on the campus by the interfraternity business manager. They do not need to meet often nor do they need to undertake the execution of policies. An alumni interfraternity council, while we agree that it might conceivably help to improve morale and discipline, could hardly do anything about the fraternities which would meet the most fundamental criticisms of them without depriving the undergraduate members of virtually all of their right to govern themselves. Finally, to set up a third power, expressly representing the alumni members of the fraternities, between the undergraduate members and the faculty and administration of the college might have the undesirable effect of creating a situation in which the fraternities became even more independent and powerful. Their capacity to resist changes in college policy that they found unwelcome might become greater than it is now. For all of these reasons we believe that the institution of such an alumni fraternity council might well prove dangerous in principle and unworkable in practice. We should not, therefore, recommend its institution.

g. Restriction of Membership in Fraternities to the Last Three or

Two Years. Your committee does not intend to enter into the involved arguments that center about the question of deferred rushing. We believe that to defer membership for one year, or even better for two, would be a substantial reform. It would enable the freshmen, and the sophomores, if they were excluded from membership, to consolidate their friendships, thus promoting class solidarity and emphasizing a primary loyalty to their class and to the college before joining fraternity groups. It ought also to relieve them of some of the pressure to go out for activities now exerted on them by these fraternity groups. This proposal, if put into effect, would probably result, however, in an even greater "typing" of the houses than now exists. We doubt if it is practicable, since many of the houses would probably be unable to make ends meet if deprived of the dues of freshmen and sophomore members. Again, it is one that does not meet the fundamental criticisms of fraternities.

h. A "Fish-Bowl" Type of Election to Membership. A workable plan of this type for elections to membership was proposed to a special committee on rushing procedure in 1942. We do not propose to go into the details of the plan here. If adopted, it would give, in effect, equal bargaining power to each fraternity. The result would be that each of the fraternities would soon attain parity with the others in terms of the quality of their membership. Exclusiveness, or the "typing" of a house, would become virtually impossible. The defect of this plan is that we cannot imagine a majority of the fraternities, and in particular the stronger ones, consenting to such a plan so long as they have any power to resist and prevent it. Though it goes a long way, this plan does not fully meet the objections to fraternities.

i. Compulsory Pledging of Perhaps 95 Per Cent of Each Freshman Class. This reform is similar to the last. It is perhaps equally radical in that it would alter the present character of the fraternities. It might be a little more palatable to them than the "fish-bowl" method of election. We believe it doubtful, to say the least, that the fraternities could ever be brought voluntarily to accept it, though it does not compromise the freedom of election by fraternity groups in quite the same way. For this reason we believe it is impracticable. This plan like the one above, though radical, also does not entirely meet the objections to fraternities.

As we review these various proposed modifications or reforms of the existing fraternity system, we see that at best they palliate existing conditions; nor is there any guarantee that if any of them were adopted they would be permanently successful in achieving even that objective. To adopt any of these modifications, even the most radical, would be to evade an unparalleled opportunity to inaugurate a radical change, if such change is for the good of the college. The alternative, their abolition, must therefore be faced.

The Abolition of Fraternities. Abolition of the fraternities would, clearly, involve many difficult and onerous problems for the trustees and administration of the college. With such problems this committee is not concerned. We should attempt, though, briefly to answer the question: If the fraternities were to be discontinued, what would take their place? The development of an alternative form of social groupings under the control of the college and more in harmony with its fundamental, educational purposes might involve some difficulties of its own. However, we can see no good reason why, starting at a time when the fraternity organizations have been in abeyance for a number of years and when they have few if any remaining undergraduate members on the campus, it would not be possible to set up new social groupings which would afford the undergraduate most of the benefits to be derived from the fraternities and have many advantages of their own.

If the houses of the fraternities could be acquired by the college, and we presume that they could, it should be possible for the students, under an active and vigorous student government and with the assistance of the Dean and the Student-Faculty Conference Committee, to establish a workable method of self-government for the upperclassmen residing in those houses. Moreover, a method of allocation to the houses could be worked out by means of which congenial groups of students (not large enough in any case to dominate a given house) might arrange to live together during their last two years.

We consciously make no attempt to recommend a specific substitute for the prewar fraternity system. This whole question is of such importance that it would have to be studied, from every angle and at great length, by other groups as well as by the faculty before being settled.

Fraternities, as we have said, tend in their *operation* to be anti-intellectual and in *principle* are anti-democratic. We know of no sure way in which they could be cured of their natural antagonism to the educational aims of the college, and, if we did, we should still be opposed to their continuance for the second reason alone. No one has better expressed this fundamental objection to fraternities than E. B. White.

Clubs, fraternities, nations—these are the beloved barriers in the way of a workable world, these will have to surrender some of their rights and some of their ribs. A "fraternity" is the antithesis of *fraternity*. The first (that is, the order or organization) is predicated on the idea of exclusion; the second (that is, the abstract thing) is based on a feeling of total equality. Anyone who remembers back to his fraternity days at college recalls the enthusiasts in his group, the rabid members, both old and young, who were obsessed with the mystical charm of membership in their particular order. They were usually men who were incapable of genuine brotherhood, or at least unaware of its implications. Fraternity begins when the exclusion formula is found to be distasteful. The effect of any organization of a social and brotherly nature is to strengthen rather than to diminish the lines which divide people into classes; the effect of states and nations is the same, and eventually these lines will have to be softened, these powers will have to be generalized. It is written on the wall that this is so. I'm not inventing it, I'm just copying it off the wall.[44]

If Amherst as an educational institution wishes to be true to her motto, *Terras Irradient*, then she should now, when it can best be done, prohibit the revival of the fraternities on her campus.

A majority of this committee (Professor Bailey Brown dissenting) therefore recommends to the faculty that it pass a resolution advising the trustees that it is to the best interests of the college that fraternities be abolished at Amherst.[45]

[44] E. B. White, *One Man's Meat* (New York, 1938), pp. 341-342.

[45] DISSENT.—The lack of social democracy in the fraternity system is evident. But I regard this lack as inevitable in any free society whose members are not all exactly alike. The individuals will form groups according to tastes. I respect the right of such a group to choose its members. There will always be individuals in some groups who would prefer to be in another. In recent prewar years, every Amherst student has had an opportunity to join one or more social groups. It seems to me to be futile to expect more than this.

Any suitably qualified student may join a fraternity or play varsity football or graduate *summa cum laude*. The qualifications for these various privileges differ greatly, but are set in each case by a duly authorized body.

The qualifications for membership in such a social group as the fraternity ought, in my opinion, to be set primarily by the fraternity itself. The ill effects on some

Physical Education and Athletics

The subject of this part of the report might have been placed under the section on the curriculum, but it is so intimately related to student activities, forming in fact an essential part of them, that we prefer to treat it here. The committee's consideration of this problem started with the view that our program of physical education and athletics before the war was good. The vast majority of our students who were not playing on varsity teams were getting some form of helpful physical recreation either in the regular classes, where chief emphasis has always been placed on the playing of games, or in intramural sports. Physical education was required of freshmen and sophomores. With the consent of the department they were allowed to substitute in place

---

individuals either of membership or of non-membership do not seem to me to be serious enough to warrant the destruction of a system which has long been an integral part of the college and which has made an important contribution to the training of Amherst men.

I do not believe the fraternity to be intrinsically anti-intellectual. When such a tendency is manifested, I regard it merely as a defense mechanism on the part of the adolescent male, who by nature is not intellectual, against a temporary overdose of "intellect" from the faculty, whose business it is to be intellectual. At its worst, the fraternity is, of course, too efficient in this respect.

The fraternity at its best, on the other hand, offers, in my opinion, a set of values complementary to the academic training of the college well beyond what residence in a dormitory or college house could provide. Whether he gets the best or the worst depends on the member himself quite as much as on his fraternity.

During the period just before the war, the contribution of the fraternities has not been what it should be. This has been in part their own fault and in part due to causes beyond their control. But if their present inactive status appears to offer an opportunity for semi-painless abolition, it is an equally good opportunity for the fraternities to free themselves of some objectionable features, and to resume after the war a life somewhat nearer their full potentiality.

The fundamental issue to be decided on this matter seems to me to be a choice between these two alternatives: the best possible Amherst training with the fraternity at its best, as against the best possible Amherst training without fraternities. An individual's choice will depend, among other things, on the period when he was in college, on the extent of his acquaintance with Amherst men of other generations and with the college itself during other times, and on his knowledge of other colleges. If the first alternative is preferable, then the fraternity is worth preserving as a part of Amherst College. If, during a given period, it should appear that the fraternities are not contributing their fair share to the common enterprise, then the college should so advise them in a suitable manner. I believe they would respond.

To me the first alternative is preferable. BAILEY BROWN.

of the required activities participation in certain intercollegiate sports. Seventy-five to 80 per cent of the juniors and 70 to 75 per cent of the seniors, not on varsity teams in any given season, were taking part in intramural sports. This was a good record. The extensive intramural participation made it possible.

The committee, however, felt that even this program could be improved. What seemed chiefly to be lacking was that there was not sufficient opportunity for all students who had any inclination and ability to do so to participate in the more skilled and vigorously competitive intercollegiate sports. If intercollegiate sports have the values for those who participate in them that are usually claimed for them, then it should be a part of the educational program of the college to enable the widest possible participation in them for all students. The committee fails to see how if competitive sports are good for some students, those now privileged to participate in them, they should not be good for nearly everyone. Should they not, perhaps, be even more beneficial to those students who do not now have the opportunity to take part in them because they have less natural ability? If competitive sports are really good, there should be competitive sports for all.

A Carnegie Bulletin issued in 1931 stated that in the opinion of its authors there has been a decline of undergraduate interest in intercollegiate athletics as "spectator sports." "Students no longer line the daily practice field to encourage the squad; they prefer themselves to play rather than to look on."[46] We think this tendency should be encouraged because we believe that the development of moral and intellectual power in youth is to be found in the combination of a rigorous mental discipline and a rugged physical education. These are two complementary aspects of the curriculum. To say this is merely to reiterate what was obvious to the fathers of liberal education, the Greeks. Their view was that music and gymnastic, as they called them, were equally important for education. An excess of the one tended to produce effeminacy, of the other brutality. They must be mixed in the right proportions to produce a harmonious development of moral and intellectual character. The importance of this point has been brought out in still another way by William James. In his essay "The Moral Equivalent of War," he says:

[46] Howard J. Savage, John T. McGovern, and Harold W. Bentley, *Current Developments in American College Sport* (New York, 1931), pp. 15-17.

I do not believe that peace either ought to be or will be permanent on this globe, unless the states pacifically organized preserve some of the old elements of army-discipline. A permanently successful peace-economy cannot be a simple pleasure-economy. In the more or less socialistic future towards which mankind seems drifting we must still subject ourselves collectively to those severities which answer to our real position upon this only partly hospitable globe. We must make new energies and hardihoods continue the manliness to which the military mind so faithfully clings. Martial virtues must be the enduring cement; intrepidity, contempt of softness, surrender of private interest, obedience to command, must still remain the rock upon which states are built—unless, indeed, we wish for dangerous reactions against commonwealths fit only for contempt, and liable to invite attack whenever a centre of crystallization for military-minded enterprise gets formed anywhere in their neighborhood.[47]

It is because "a permanently successful peace-economy cannot be a simple pleasure-economy," because leadership in a democratic society demands moral hardiness as well as intellectual ability, that we believe it to be an essential part of the educational program of the college to provide competitive sports for all.

The training for participation in such sports requires close supervision by skilled teachers. It cannot be acquired quickly or "picked up" by taking part in intramural athletics. If the students during their freshman year were to be given this kind of basic instruction, then all of them would be better equipped to participate in intercollegiate sports during their last three years; or, if they preferred to take part in the intramural athletic program, they would because of this training benefit from the games they played far more than they do now.

While the members of this committee in its discussions arrived at these principles, they did not feel competent to formulate any detailed program for physical education and athletics. It was decided, without, however, suggesting any policy to them, to request the members of the Department of Physical Education to formulate an independent set of proposals for a program of physical education and athletics which might be considered by the committee. A letter making this request was sent to Professor Marsh, and a similar letter requesting him to make any suggestions he might have to offer to the committee was sent to Professor Jordan. Professor Jordan's reply (September 7, 1944) to the committee was in part as follows:

[47] William James, *Memories and Studies* (New York, 1911), pp. 287-288.

Not being familiar with the problems to which you refer it would be most difficult to make detailed specific proposals that would aid in your discussion. Therefore it would seem that for the present my views as given at the symposium in May would have to serve as a general background of my ideas.

The members of the Department of Physical Education who were still teaching at Amherst held a series of meetings among themselves as a result of which they submitted the following specific proposal:

Postwar Physical Education[48]

When the United States began to organize for war and to call out large numbers of young men, many of these boys were found to be physically unprepared for service except after much training. Departments of Physical Education were criticised for this. Much of this criticism did not apply to the colleges except as it was obvious that while a few of the students were well trained many others had received only a little training. During the war most men connected with this physical training and athletics have agreed that, following the war, more complete training should be given to more men. Therefore, the Department of Physical Education believes that the best program of Physical Education for Amherst College is a program which gives the most complete physical education to all the students. This includes both a fundamental and basic training and vigorous team competition for all men who are physically fit. This program should merge the two into one comprehensive plan.

This most complete training includes: Examinations; tests; special exercise for those who need it; ability to swim; general skills; fundamentals of one or more recreational games, and vigorous team games, including, if possible, outside competition. This program includes both intramural and extramural (intercollegiate) sports.

1. The Department recommends that all Freshmen for the first year (or 3 terms) shall have their program as a unit during the last hour in the morning, five hours per week, Monday through Friday. This allows for the fundamental training to be given to the younger men at the beginning of their course. This places it where it should be.

[48] Professor Marsh in his letter proposing this plan to the committee states: "This general program has been approved by the present staff here including Messrs. Eckley, Kennedy, Lumley, Rostas, Richardson, Van Petersilge and Marsh. Paul Eckley, however, would like to see contests for freshmen with Williams and Wesleyan in some sports at the end of each term. Tug favors, also, some competition for freshmen if it can be worked into the training program. The others are willing to give up freshmen intercollegiate contests for more teams and competition for the upperclassmen."

This program will consist of: Examinations; tests; special exercise for those who need it; swimming; obstacle course and practice in the fundamentals of one or more recreational games and vigorous team sports. Competition will only be within the group or college.

At the end of the first year all Freshmen will have the basis of fitness and fundamentals of swimming, one or more recreational games and one or more team sports. A sample program, generally approved, is as follows:

(1) Meet five days per week: Monday, Tuesday, Wednesday, Thursday, Friday.
(2) No changes from squad to squad except by Doctor's orders.
(3) Tests to be given at the end of each term or semester.

Complete fitness tests and examinations given all men to determine physical condition.

Fall Program (8 week period.)
(1) Obstacle course. 2 weeks. Test at end of first week.
(2) Special exercise group and men excused.
(3) Choice for remainder of term (6 weeks):
Football
Soccer
Cross Country and Obstacle.

Winter Program (16 week period.)
(1) Special exercise group and men excused. Men may graduate as soon as standards are passed.
(2) A two weeks rotation plan for all other men. (8 weeks.)
a. Basketball
b. Swimming
c. Choice of: Squash, Handball, Skiing
d. Choice of: Wrestling, Boxing, Fencing
(3) Selection of above sports or others offered by the Department (8 weeks.)

Spring Program (8 week period.)
(1) Tests for all men in either Golf or Tennis to determine ability.
(2) Men failing winter swimming test to return to pool for recheck.
(3) All men who pass either Golf or Tennis tests choose from:
a. Baseball
b. Track
c. Golf (Estimate ¾ pass tests.)
d. Tennis

(4) All men who fail both Golf and Tennis choose from:
  a. Tennis
  b. Golf

(5) Special exercise group and men excused.

2. The Department recommends that all Sophomores, Juniors, and Seniors have their physical education in the afternoon from 4:00 to 6:00 P.M. and 3:00 P.M. for men who may be free. For these classes the Department recommends keeping the basic requirements at three hours per week though many team candidates may be expected to meet daily if schedules permit. As a result of the freshman course these upperclass students should be ready for team competition. Moreover, for some time after the war many men will return to the college more mature and needing adjustment. Therefore, it is the aim of the Department to include, if possible, every man who is physically fit on some team during the course of the year and as many as possible each term. They will choose their activities and sports, subject to Department recommendation, each period from a list offered by the Department. This list will include the present intercollegiate sports for competition. The members of the Department in charge of each sport will organize the men in their activity for training and will develop as many teams for outside competition as is possible and necessary to include most of the men in the group. Some of the activities may not have outside competition (e.g., Boxing) or during certain periods (e.g., Tennis in the Fall, if offered). In this case intramural competition will be organized within the sport.

Possible activities to be offered, depending on the number of men available and in probable order of offering, are as follows:

Fall

Football	Special Exercise	Swimming (non swim)	Tennis
Soccer	Farm Work		Golf
Obstacle and Cross Country			

Winter

Swimming	Special Exercise	Boxing	Fencing
Basketball	Squash	Hockey	Obstacle and Track
Wrestling	Skiing		

Spring

Baseball	Special Exercise	Golf
Track	Farm Labor	Rugby or Football
Tennis	Swimming (non swim)	Soccer

After discussion of this proposal the committee has concluded that it is a workable plan, which, if put into operation, should go far toward realizing the objectives we have stated in the first part of this section. By providing that the freshmen are taken together as a group in the last hour of the morning for a thorough program of fundamental training during the first year, the whole staff of the Department of Physical Education would be able to devote its undivided attention to them and to accomplish much more with them during that year than it was able to do under the prewar program. Under this program, where the freshman teams compete with each other within the group, class solidarity would be promoted. Each student would have a full opportunity to learn the fundamentals of both individual sports and competitive games. Many should discover an interest in and a talent for team games they did not before know they possessed.

The opportunity to learn and to do is further enhanced by the provision, after the first year, of a number of varsity teams in each sport. Almost any student who wants to should be able to play on some intercollegiate team. The students who do not would be more proficient in their intramural sports, would get more out of them, and should, accordingly, take an even keener interest than they now do in them.

The department's proposal really merges physical education, intramural athletics, and outside competitions into one over-all program. Under it the great majority of students should have the experience of participating in intercollegiate athletics while in college and would have acquired a proficiency in at least two individual sports which would provide them with a means of healthful recreation in later years.

Finally, it is not one of the incidental merits of this plan that it should be attractive to many boys, and to their parents as well, because it offers an opportunity, which many of them under the former program could not expect to have, for participation in intercollegiate athletics.

The committee, therefore, recommends that this plan for physical education in postwar Amherst be adopted.[49]

[49] Copies of this plan have been sent to a number of other institutions, including Wesleyan and Williams, where they are now being studied.

The New England Intercollegiate Conference at Boston on December 2, 1944,

THE RELIGIOUS LIFE OF THE COLLEGE[50]

To a great many people deeply interested in Amherst no subject can be of greater interest and importance than the religious life of the college. For that reason the Alumni Council appointed a special subcommittee to consider the problem and we are devoting to it a separate part of this report.

Any discussion of this question has two phases. The broader and more important one is concerned with the morale of the college as a whole.[51] The narrower one is concerned with the specific problems of the practice and teaching of religion in the college. These two phases are frequently confused—naturally so because at one time they were less obviously distinguishable than they now are.

The terms of Amherst's charter provided "that no Instructor in said College shall ever be required by the Trustees to profess any particular religious opinion, as a test of office; and no student shall be denied the privileges of said College on account of the religious opinions he may entertain." The College was founded, however, by orthodox Congregationalists to prepare "for the gospel ministry young men in indigent circumstances, but of hopeful piety and promising talents.[52] In the fulfillment of this purpose it succeeded handsomely. According to the general catalogue for 1892-1893, in a total alumni body of 3428 there were 1164 ordained clergymen and 120 foreign missionaries.[53] The members of the faculty were themselves clergymen. The health of the college was measured by revivals. In those earlier days few students missed the experience of at least one of them during their college course. In the sixty-year period between 1822 and 1882 there

---

considered postwar physical education. The Amherst Plan was discussed as a part of this program. Postwar programs (including the Amherst Plan) were the chief topic for discussion at the annual meeting of the National Collegiate Athletic Association in Columbus, Ohio, January 12, 1945.

[50] DISSENT.—I prefer not to sign this section of the report. My decision to take this position is not based upon any serious disagreement with the specific recommendations of the committee, but rather upon my dissatisfaction with the general point of view expressed throughout a large part of this section. R. A. BEEBE.

[51] We recall President Moore's remarks on "knowledge and piety," and the quotation from John Dewey's *A Common Faith* on pp. 29-30.

[52] From an address by Noah Webster at the laying of the cornerstone of South College, August 9, 1820.

[53] W. S. Tyler, *A History of Amherst College* (New York, 1895), pp. 290-291.

were twenty revivals. Every effort was made to save those who were "unregenerate," among the student body. Under these conditions it would have been pointless, in fact impossible, to distinguish between religion in Amherst College and the Christianity of Amherst College. Today it is equally impossible fruitfully to discuss the question without making that distinction. For now only one teaching member of our faculty, the professor of religion, is a clergyman, and church and chapel are no longer the powerful institutions they once were.

If these earlier conditions cannot be restored, can a fundamental approach to the problem be made by "doing something" about church and chapel, the religious advisers, the Christian Association, or, last of all, the courses in religion? These things have steadily lost their importance so far as seriously affecting the actual beliefs of a majority of the students is concerned. No matter how excellent they are, it is only in a secondary way that they can reach and influence the students. This is not a criticism of the college or of our present specific provision for religious instruction and religious activities. The same thing has happened everywhere. Society has moved in a direction such that the church, once the rival or the partner of the state, has become more and more segregated from the main currents of social life. As our society has become secularized the colleges have moved with it. For these reasons we consider any specific recommendations which may be made about church and chapel or the teaching of religion in the college to be, comparatively, unimportant.

The problem of religion in the college is a smaller image of the problem of religion in our whole society. The nucleus of all cultures which have existed heretofore has been some form of religious traditions and practices. How can religion (we do not say the church) be restored to a central place in the community? How are the aspirations and ideals of the community to be organized and expressed in such a way that the spiritual kinship of men associated in a common life may be realized? To this question, the most difficult and perplexing which faces our vast new industrial society, we have no real answer beyond what we have already said: that the future of religion, and with it of our society itself, depends upon the growth of socialized intelligence.[54] How this can be achieved in the Great Society we do not know. Coming down, however, to the smaller, simpler, and more easily

[54] Cf. Part I, pp. 24-31.

understandable community that we call the college it is a little easier to perceive some things that are relevant in dealing with the problem.

Amherst College in earlier years graduated many young men who later attained distinction. Perhaps one reason they did so was because they came to the college during a period of ferment. Their inherited religious beliefs were being challenged. During the latter half of the nineteenth century, for example, the theory of evolution and problems of social justice were coming to the fore. It was an important part of the success of the college that while here many of these young men were able to resolve their conflicts by channeling their religious aspirations into ways that were useful to society. To use an old-fashioned term, they left the college to enter their vocation with an attitude of consecration to it. They felt that in following that vocation they were serving not merely themselves but society. Amherst does not give vocational training. It is her part to *prepare* young men for their vocations by giving them, whatever their specialized training and activity in later life may be, this common attitude toward the society in which they participate.

Each profession has its own particular ethos, its mode of consecration. The medical student, for instance, is brought into close contact with people who are ill. Working in an atmosphere of sickness and death he learns to become detached without becoming indifferent. His whole training is intended to produce

> . . . a constant cultivation of what may be called the "therapeutic intent." This therapeutic intent is not merely an intellectual perception of a wish to cure; it is a *need* to cure. It becomes an integral part of the medical man's psychology. A good doctor is distinguished from a bad one not by the relative amount of his book knowledge but by the degree to which this therapeutic intent is developed. Knowledge can always be acquired from books and from the observation of a number of cases. But unless the therapeutic intent becomes properly developed, the doctor is a failure.[55]

The proper moral intent may be identified in each vocation or profession.

In discussing the aims of a liberal education, we defined it as one that is *functional* without being *technical*.[56] What corresponds in

[55] Gregory Zilboorg, *Mind, Medicine, and Man* (New York, 1943), p. 21.
[56] Cf. Part 1, pp. 24-31.

liberal education to the specific moral intent that controls the training for each particular vocation or profession is the inculcation of a generalized attitude of respect and reverence for truth. This *liberal* attitude cannot be achieved unless the student is required to study the basic areas of human experience without any preoccupation or commitment except his interest in them as a human being. It will not be acquired as effectively as it could be unless the students pursue these studies in common, unless the student body as a community deals with the same areas of human knowledge during at least the first part of their course. The framing of a curriculum is in a fundamental sense an attempt to make of the college an intellectual community. To do this is also to fulfill the deeper religious intent of producing a common faith. In the section of this report dealing with the curriculum we have tried to meet this requirement.

The next generations of students will come to the college perturbed by the conflicts that now threaten to destroy our society. The energies released by those emotions are our stock in trade. The solution of the problem of religion in the college does not consist in direct attempts to inculcate morality and religion. These are rarely if ever successful. It does consist in attempting to resolve these emotional tensions by directing the energies involved in them toward socially useful objectives. This can be done so far as we are able to make our teaching of every subject more than mere training, so far as we make it truly humane.

The question has, therefore, been raised whether moral and spiritual character should be considered in a candidate for the faculty of Amherst College. We believe it should, but that there must be no confusion between moral and spiritual values and any particular doctrinal belief or sectarian affiliation. There are on this faculty and elsewhere a number of men who meet in every way those qualifications but who are not Christians and might be even skeptics or atheists. We do not believe that moral and spiritual leadership is in our contemporary society closely related to religious affiliation. Hence, we should like to have the college choose individuals for its faculty in terms of their personal merit, intellectual, moral, and spiritual, quite independently of their particular religious beliefs. It should be added that intellectual qualifications are basic. They are a necessary though not sufficient condition. We ought to have scholars and teachers on our faculty who are also in other respects good men but we should not ever tolerate or excuse the appointment of an individual to the faculty because, although a mediocre scholar or teacher, he is a fine person. This is true, of course, because the excellence of the college as an institution depends primarily on the professional competence of her faculty.

Nor do we believe that members of the Amherst faculty need feel a direct responsibility for the moral and spiritual life of their students as well as for their classroom work. A member of the faculty as a member of the faculty *should* feel a definite responsibility for his student as an apprentice in the subject which that faculty member is teaching. Such a responsibility does involve certain moral and spiritual values which are specifically related to the kind of work being done by student and professor alike in that subject. The teaching of every subject, as we have said, obviously involves the inculcation of such values as a respect for and love of truth. In addition, each subject has its specific values. Any reflective analysis of the curriculum proceeds in terms of the complementary values to be derived from the study of the natural sciences, the social sciences, and the humanities. In guiding the progress of the student within his own field each member of the faculty is inevitably helping him to build up certain moral and spiritual attitudes, the total effect of which should be to produce that type of mind and personality which we vaguely denote as the liberal spirit. Any member of the faculty may, and many will, assume an additional responsibility for other aspects of the moral and spiritual growth of his students than those directly related to the study of his particular subject. This is a privilege which a teacher assumes as a member of the college community. It has been our experience that in a small college almost every faculty member feels a sincere devotion to the welfare of the institution and takes a keen personal interest in his students.

In small classes and in advanced work the close relationship between teacher and student which frequently develops inevitably spreads over and beyond the confines of "subject" and affects the whole personality of the student. This influence can be good or bad. It becomes bad if the essential relation of master and apprentice is disturbed. The teacher and student are brought together in terms of their common interest in a subject. Those other relations which develop between them are a normal and desirable by-product of that mutual interest. The teacher must always put his subject first. This means that in his relations with the student a certain "distance" is preserved. The ideal teacher is one who endeavors to emancipate his students, to enable them to become free and independent inquirers. When, as occasionally happens, that interest is subordinated by the teacher to a preoccupation with the "personality" or the "general welfare" of the student, the educational process is vitiated.

The moral and religious effects a liberal education ought to produce are achieved indirectly. In studying under an able teacher the student becomes informed with that teacher's enthusiasm for his subject. This enthusiasm provides the motive power by means of which the student becomes able of his own will to make the effort to understand that subject. Now the subject begins to master him and the teacher recedes into the background. To the degree that such mastery is achieved, the student emancipates himself from the domination of the instructor and achieves a character of his own in relation to that subject.

To be liberally educated is thus to be freed from ignorance and error in those matters that are of the greatest human concern. For this reason there exists no subject, or none should exist, in our curriculum that is not of supreme human importance. What can be known that is most significant to all men is what is meant by the liberal arts and sciences.

We come now to the practice and teaching of religion in the college. Our recommendations are few and our comments will be brief. We shall discuss the subject under three divisions, religious counseling and religious activities, chapel and church, and courses in religion.

Religious Counseling and Religious Activities

We believe that the present organization is well adapted to its purpose. On this subject we have only one suggestion to make, that the possibility be considered of forming a joint faculty-student organization comprising those members of the faculty who would be interested in associating themselves with the students for the discussion of religious problems and for the practice of religious philanthropy. An organization of this sort might well develop in such a way that it would greatly reinforce the existing provisions for guidance and education in the living practice of religion.

Chapel and Church

Chapel and church were both originally religious services. Chapel was the continuation in college of family prayers. It should not now, however, be considered a service of worship. The two questions of church and chapel are, in our opinion, different ones and therefore should be treated separately.

If chapel is intended to be a service of worship, then it undoubtedly has a bad effect on many students. Compulsory religious worship tends to anesthetize people to religion. It breeds an indifference dangerously close to contempt. It is because the effects of that kind of "exposure" to religion have become shockingly obvious that compulsory chapel has gradually disappeared in most of the private colleges. Almost every Protestant college in New England has abandoned it. The writer of an article in *Fortune* has graphically described the campaign of "passive resistance" to chapel:

> After breakfast comes another dash, usually to classes. In some universities, however, compulsory chapel lingers on, at least for freshmen and sophomores. And in the colleges where the student is still fated to spend ten or fifteen minutes in putative worship, he does it with an air of extreme fatigue. The fatigue is so evident that when the enterprising editor of the *Daily Princetonian* recently assembled a Leica camera portfolio of typical worshippers—some half asleep, some tying shoes and neckties, some reading the *New York Herald Tribune*, some playing Salvo, some doing lessons, and some simply gawking at the rafters—it clinched the case against compulsory chapel with the Board of Trustees. By such persuasive methods has the undergraduate won his case against compulsory institutional religion in many of the universities.[57]

We do not propose to recommend that compulsory chapel be abandoned at Amherst but we do suggest that the distinction be made to the students, as clearly as possible, between a service of worship and a service in traditionally religious form. In view of the deeply rooted Christian tradition of the college it is legitimate to use certain of the forms of a congregational service as a framework for what is essentially a college assembly. Chapel may well be opened with a hymn and

[57] "Youth in College," *Fortune*, 13, no. 6 (1936), 101.

closed with a brief prayer, but it should be emphasized that it is a college meeting, a convocation rather than a religious service. It is "religious" only in the sense that it expresses the corporate unity of the college. On this ground it may well be required.

Changing a thing's name will hardly improve it. If chapel is to survive, every effort must be made to hold the interest of the students. We believe that the chief reason why chapel as at present constituted is too frequently unable to do so is because the meetings are not long enough to be significant. It has been suggested that chapel might be improved by substituting for the present arrangement two regular longer meetings each week. A third period would be allocated for student meetings. These assemblies would be carefully planned, a program of special subjects and speakers being worked out to make them consecutive and, so far as possible, more impressive than the present chapel meetings. While this is an attractive idea, we believe that it would be difficult to schedule two longer chapel periods if the suggestions we have made for the revision of the curriculum were adopted. For this reason alone we do not recommend it. It should still be possible, however, to have a series of programs long enough to possess real significance—if the formal part of chapel were shortened, or, on occasion, omitted altogether if the nature of the subject were unsuitable or the speaker preferred not to have it.

We suggest that a committee consisting of the President, the Dean, and the Director of Religious Activities together with one or two representatives of the faculty and the Student Council might try to plan for each term a series of such meetings in which the subjects discussed would be those which the students themselves consider interesting or important. There should be a maximum degree of participation by the faculty in these chapel meetings, to acquaint the students during the year with a large number of members of the faculty and to help give variety and freshness to the programs.

The argument for compulsory chapel is not, in our opinion, the same as that for compulsory church. A church service is and should be religious in the narrower and fuller sense of the term. It is essentially a service of worship. The arguments for compulsory attendance at church as we understand them are as follows: (1) Amherst College has always been a Christian college requiring church attendance and should continue to do so. (2) To be appreciated, the service of public worship must be experienced, and it is the duty of the college to see to it that every student has this all-important experience. These arguments seem to us to be untenable. They suppose that compulsory exposure to religious services will imbue one with a religious attitude. This was once much more nearly true than it is now and is still perhaps largely true for some religions. It operates effectively, no doubt, with most members of the Catholic faith. When applied, however, to a Protestant community of the present day these arguments confuse the idea of church membership with that of membership in certain other institutions. They depend upon an analogy of this sort: One can no more be religious without attending some church than one can be patriotic without being a citizen of some country. The analogy no longer holds. It was once virtually impossible not to be a member of some church. Since this is not now the case, worship can no longer be compelled. As a result, compulsory attendance at services of worship becomes self-defeating. Moreover, compulsory church attendance contradicts a basic tenet of our society, that of freedom of worship. We even recognize conscientious objection as legitimately excusing a citizen from military service. If the college should have some of the aspects of an ideal community, it should tolerate at least as much freedom of conscience as does the larger society of which it is a part.

For these reasons the committee recommends that attendance at church services be made voluntary.

Courses in Religion

It should be clear from what has been said above that the committee regards the teaching of courses in religion as in no wise different from that of other courses. Religion is an important subject included in our curriculum in the same way and for the same reasons that other subjects, the sciences, history, literature, and philosophy, are included. There is no reason, though it is not likely in the light of Amherst's history and traditions, why courses in religion should not be taught by someone who, though a competent scholar, is himself not a member of any church. It is not a part of the function of a teacher of courses in religion to attempt to convert students to any particular faith. This is a principle which has been observed at Amherst for many years.

The suggestion has been made that a course in religion should be required. We are not in favor of requiring such a course. This is not a theoretical objection but a practical one. The committee has considered carefully and at length what work, if any, might properly be required of all students. A course devoted entirely to religion could not, we agreed, be required without upsetting the balance of the curriculum as a whole.[58]

The suggestion has also been made that religion be separated from philosophy. The committee disapproves of this suggestion. We should like to see the current tendency toward splitting into separate departments arrested. In fact, it might be desirable to unite some departments that are at present separate, e.g., the union of Greek and Latin in a Department of Classical Studies. Some years ago psychology was separated from philosophy. The case of religion, however, is not a parallel one. Psychology is now regarded as an independent experimental science. It has been separated from philosophy for the same reason physics, once called *natural philosophy*, was separated long ago. Philosophy and religion, however, have a certain natural compatibility. Their interests are mutual and complementary and, in our opinion, they belong together.

Finally, it has been suggested that the teaching of religion in the college should be strengthened by a second appointment in this field. This is a question of the balance and distribution of appointments to the faculty in various departments. That distribution is constantly changing. During the last decade the Departments of Political Science, Fine Arts and Music have been greatly developed. Geography has recently been added to the curriculum. The claim for additional courses in religion should be treated on the same basis as any other similar claim. There can be no doubt that it would be desirable to have courses in such subjects as comparative religion and the history of religious thought, but there are other needs which we consider more pressing and which we have referred to elsewhere. An adequate number of courses now exists for the development of a suitable major in religion. We should be opposed, therefore, to the appointment, for the present, of a second teacher in that subject.

Professor Cleland, in his address at the Symposium on Religion

[58] It should be noted that if the two required freshman courses in humanities that we have proposed were adopted, one of them would most probably contain selections from the Bible as a part of its subject matter. It would also be likely to include readings from writers such as St. Augustine, Dante, Milton, and Pascal who have made contributions to religious thought.

(April 18, 1944), said: "My view of the future sees a Department of Religion which will cut across the existing boundaries between Departments very much in the same way that the major in Renaissance Studies does." We thoroughly approve this suggestion for a "horizontal" major. To the extent that students now must elect courses in "related fields" to complete a major, a "horizontal" major in religion now exists.

What we fear most is that the teaching of religion may become segregated, just another set of courses in a separate department taken by a fraction of the student body. Certain subjects such as history, philosophy, and religion should permeate the whole curriculum. Some phases of history and philosophy are, as a matter of course, taught by many members of the faculty not in those departments, since historical and philosophical considerations are relevant to the teaching of almost every subject offered in a liberal arts curriculum. To a lesser degree this is also true of religion, but we should like to see it more fully developed for that subject. A few well placed courses involving various aspects of religion, in different departments of the college, might well do more than additional courses offered in the department itself to bring home to the student body as a whole the vital importance of religion in human experience.

SOME PROBLEMS OF ORGANIZATION AND GOVERNMENT

We have discussed elsewhere a number of problems and have made certain recommendations which might properly have come under this heading. However, we preferred to discuss those in the context where they were most relevant.[59] In this concluding section of the report we wish to discuss briefly the following topics: divisional organization of the faculty; tenure, appointments, and promotions;

[59] These recommendations were: (1) to enlarge the powers of the Curriculum Committee and to change its name to Committee on Educational Policy; (2) to give "departmental status" to general courses and group majors; (3) to appoint an assistant admissions officer who would be concerned primarily with the recruiting of high school students; (4) to establish an advisory committee on admissions and scholarships; (5) to put the orientation program in the charge of the Student-Faculty Conference Committee, the Student Council, and the Dean; (6) to appoint a freshman-sophomore dean, who would assume the responsibility for guidance of the students in the two lower classes.

acceleration of the college course; the size of the college; and the corporate life of the college.

Divisional Organization of the Faculty

It has become fashionable of late to emphasize the divisional mode of organization, particularly as a means of counteracting the excesses of departmentalism. This committee does not believe that such a type of organization should be established at Amherst. While it may be a practical necessity in some institutions, it nevertheless perpetuates on a larger scale the same tendency to segregation of interests and subject matters for which the departmental mode of organization is criticized. In particular, we should dislike to see anything done which might, even implicitly, establish artificial barriers between the three broad fields of the curriculum. If liberal education is to survive, it must do so by breaking down these barriers.

There is no real antagonism between the humanities and the natural and social sciences. One of the group majors in the college is now taught by members of the faculty from more than one division. Several of the general courses and most of the group majors that we are suggesting or recommending in this report should be given by teachers from more than one division. Everything that can be done to establish connections, not disconnections, between all parts of the curriculum should be encouraged. Further, there is no practical need of a formal organization of the faculty in terms of divisions. Our recommendation (in Part II, the section on "The Curriculum") that the general courses and group majors be given departmental status is, we believe, a better alternative. For these reasons we should be opposed to any further strengthening of the divisional organization of the college.

Tenure, Appointments, and Promotions

Some years ago a committee appointed by the Committee of Six made a report recommending that all terminations of appointments and all promotions in the faculty be discussed with the Committee of Six and its opinion ascertained before any final action was taken. This committee would like to see the policy that was then adopted strengthened and developed. A distinguished university president is reported once to have said: "Now that we have academic freedom, we must be careful whom we appoint." To this one might add: "And now that we have academic tenure, it is even more important whom we promote." Perhaps the greatest danger that confronts the administration of any college or university, the danger which must ever be guarded against, is that of accumulating "dead wood" in one's faculty.

There is no panacea for this disease of the academic body, but the faculty can itself, through its representatives, do a great deal to assist in its prevention. Faculty members as a group are conscientious and loyal to the good of the college. They are quick to resent the occasional instances where an individual's merits are unjustly ignored. Equally, they dislike the more frequent instances of laziness and incompetence. On the whole, a faculty committee dealing with questions of new appointments, terminations of appointments, and promotions will exercise its responsibility with the greatest seriousness, since its members know they must justify any decisions that they make to their colleagues.

This committee is in complete agreement with the declaration of principles of the American Association of University Professors. The position of the Association is the following:

> Beginning with appointment to the rank of full-time instructor or a higher rank, the probationary period should not exceed seven years, including within this period full-time service in all institutions of higher education; but subject to the proviso that when, after a term of probationary service of more than three years in one or more institutions, a teacher is called to another institution it may be agreed in writing that his new appointment is for a probationary period of not more than four years, even though thereby the person's total probationary period in the academic profession is extended beyond the normal maximum of seven years. Notices should be given at least one year prior to the expiration of the probationary period, if the teacher is not to be continued in service after the expiration of that period.[60]

If tenure is to be granted after seven years of service as a regular member of the faculty (and we believe it should be), then the only way in which the efficiency of the faculty and with that the educational standards of the college can be maintained is to appraise with the greatest possible care the potentialities of those who are newly

[60] For the full statement of these principles see "Academic Freedom and Tenure," in the *Bulletin* of the American Association of University Professors, 29 (1943), 75-101.

appointed to the faculty and make a decision about them one way or the other before it is too late. Preferably, the decision to terminate an appointment should be made at the earliest possible opportunity and, in any case, there should be a preliminary review at the end of three or four years as well as a final review well before the end of the probationary period. It should be the policy of the college that no younger member of the faculty should ever be retained beyond this probationary period unless it is the considered judgment of a representative committee of the faculty, after they have made careful inquiries of those who should be best qualified to judge his competence, that he gives every promise of being worthy of eventual promotion to a full professorship.

Strictly to enforce this policy would be a service to the individual concerned as well as to the college. The younger member of the faculty who knows at the outset that he cannot hope to have his appointment renewed beyond this probationary period unless he demonstrates unusual competence is more likely to consider his appointment a temporary one and to start looking about for another position well before the probationary period has passed. With such an understanding, it would also be easier and less embarrassing to terminate the appointment of a younger member of the faculty in those cases where it is decided that he should not be retained.

Such a policy would be the more necessary if the suggestions that this committee has made for the institution of courses of a laboratory or seminar type were to be adopted. In that case we should expect a relatively larger proportion of appointments of young men to the rank of instructor. The great majority of these appointments would, perforce, be temporary. There would be openings for permanent appointments for only a few of these younger men, those of the greatest promise, and in those departments where there might be room for advancement within a reasonable time. The majority of them, having received useful training and experience as teachers, would have to seek more permanent positions elsewhere.

A policy of this sort, wisely administered, might, over a sufficiently long period of time, greatly strengthen the faculty. The college would have the opportunity to make the selection of its permanent staff of teachers from among a relatively large group of young men, to some extent competing with one another, who would have been carefully appraised by their older colleagues before they were granted a permanent appointment.

For these reasons we recommend: (1) that in every case appointments to the faculty, terminations of appointments, and promotions within the faculty shall be fully discussed by the Committee of Six and the opinions of its members recorded before any final action is taken; (2) that, well before the end of the probationary period as defined by the American Association of University Professors, the Committee of Six shall carefully study the qualifications of a member of the faculty and record its opinion as to whether or not this appointment should be terminated.

Acceleration of the College Course

The committee has not studied this question in any detail because it seems to be the opinion of a large majority of the faculty that acceleration of the college course, at least in any form similar to that which we have known during the war, should not be continued longer than necessary.

The committee has approved of the earlier admission of students to college, including some students who have completed the equivalent of only three years of secondary school.[61]

The committee is opposed to any other type of acceleration for two good reasons: it is hard on the faculty and it is undesirable for the students. In a small college it is practically impossible to provide the necessary courses the year round and at the same time give the faculty the needed periods for rest and further study. It would require in a small college a reorganization of the curriculum almost wholly on the semester basis, thus shunting certain desirable types of courses out of the curriculum. One of the great advantages of the small college is the community between the students which goes with their organization into classes. This uniformity in the development of the students would be broken up. Finally, a liberal arts course, in contradistinction to certain types of technical training, requires a slow process of growth and maturation. There are no short-cut methods for producing in the students the type of character and attitudes which should be the chief end of a liberal education.

Acceleration of the college course may take different forms. The

[61] Cf. Part II, p. 107.

course may be intensified in such a way that the student does something that looks like the equivalent of four years' work in three. The course may be shortened so that the normal program for the bachelor's degree may be completed in three or even two years. Combined degrees may be given so that a student may again shorten the period of his liberal arts education to three or two years but get a bachelor's degree after completing four years of higher education. All of these types of acceleration have tended to become increasingly common, and the war has greatly stimulated this trend. If universal military service is required, as seems probable, the trend will be further accentuated after the war. Whether the small colleges of Amherst's type may or may not be forced eventually to adopt some of these modes of acceleration depends upon events whose effects cannot now be discerned. There is no need, in our opinion, to make any decision at this time about these contingencies.

The committee realizes that our society has come to demand a longer and longer period of education. Young men going into the professions must spend greater lengths of time in graduate training and in-service training before they can become independent practitioners. This is the result of the higher degrees of specialization demanded of each generation by our increasingly complex society. But the higher the degree of specialization the broader and firmer its foundation must be if we are to achieve what we have called "socialized intelligence." No doubt a relatively larger number of students will, in the future, go on from secondary school to some form of higher education. Of these a greater proportion will go to junior colleges or take combined degrees in order to shorten the time required for them to enter a vocation. But it will still be true, we believe, that the ablest students, those who are headed for the professions or administrative positions in business and government service, should have the equivalent of four years of a liberal arts education if they are to acquire the breadth of understanding that will enable them to comprehend the relation of their work to the good of society as a whole.

The committee is not singular in its belief that the summers of the students should be usefully employed. We should like to see the development of closer relations between business firms and government bureaus and the colleges and universities whereby large numbers of students might be regularly placed during the summers for in-service training. Training of this sort would be educative in itself and would give the student just the type of experience he needs in order to make a reasonable decision about his future vocation. Full development of such a plan or scheme would, of course, have to be on a national scale, probably with the aid of the government. With the increase of the granting of longer vacations for employees of all grades, it might prove easier to arrange for such summer periods of in-service training than has been true in the past. The suggestion has also been made that it would be desirable for a number of the alumni to found scholarships which combine scholarship aid at Amherst with in-service training in their businesses. This is a field in which the alumni can greatly assist the total education of our students during their college course.[62]

Size of the College

As everyone knows, the college has steadily grown, with occasional recessions, since its foundation. During the century 1840-1940 enrollment increased from 169 to 851. It has now reached the point where the question "Is Amherst still a small college?" becomes crucial. President Pease raised this point in his annual report of 1928. His comments are sufficiently important to be quoted at length:

> Many of the faculty and of the student body have felt that the size of the college has become too large, both for the physical and financial resources of the institution, and also for the maintenance of those relations which have characterized it as definitely a small college rather than a large university. . . . It will be noted that since 1900 the size of the college has more than doubled, while in the past seven years there has been an increase of 50 per cent, the situation at Amherst being not unlike that at various other institutions during the same period. There seem indications, if one may judge from the experience of other colleges, that the crest of this sudden increase has passed, and that from now on for some time the pressure of candidates for admission will probably increase, if at all, but slowly, with the gradual increase of the population of the country. In any event, it is clear, however, that the character of a small college cannot but be definitely affected by such increases in the number of its students as Amherst has lately experienced. To make the matter clearer, I may point out that a rough estimate would indicate that

[62] The committee has already made two other suggestions in regard to the use of summers. Cf. Part II, pp. 79-80.

of our living alumni about 50 per cent attended a college of not over 425 students, and that about 80 per cent attended a college of not over 525, while only the classes graduating since 1924 have been familiar with a college of as many as 600. The enrollment of nearly 770 men produces conditions unfamiliar to the experience of the great majority of alumni, and if the claim is still made that Amherst remains a small college it necessitates a revision of their conception of what a small college is.

The problems of administration raised by such an increase in numbers are many and varied. Financially, since the students contribute only 31 per cent of the per capita cost of their education, while the college furnishes 69 per cent, additional students represent an increased burden, necessitating either an increased faculty and a correspondingly increased budget or a diluted type of instruction due to larger and less effective classes. Educationally, the larger groups with more distant relations between instructor and instructed and the increasingly numerous cases in which it is necessary to place restrictions upon admission to certain popular courses of the students' choice cause dissatisfaction and injure the type of education for which Amherst has stood. On the side of social intercourse and college morale, larger numbers of students lend themselves less successfully to intimate relations between the faculty and the student body, while our physical plant itself (with dormitory accommodations for 267, fraternity accommodations for about 300, a college chapel seating 588, a church seating 646, and many class rooms and laboratories too small for our present numbers) finds itself at points unduly stretched by a strain for which it was never planned. In view of these considerations, and authorized by your Board, a Faculty Committee on the Size of the College was selected by the Faculty Committee on Committees, with Professor Harry deForest Smith as chairman, and Professors Beebe, Packard, and Whicher, and myself, as the other members; and this committee, in twenty meetings, has investigated the subject from many aspects, collecting in the course of its studies significant and important data. Its results were reported to the faculty, which, in turn, made to your Board two recommendations: first, that the size of the undergraduate body be eventually set at about 600, and second, that the entering class for 1928-1929 be limited to 200. The latter of these you have already adopted, and it has been put in practice in the fall of 1928. The former you have reserved for later and more detailed study.[63]

The Alumni Committee on Admissions, Scholarships and Secondary Schools in its report in 1934 likewise deprecated any further increase

[63] *Report of the President* (Amherst, 1928), pp. 2-4.

in the size of the college. The committee agreed "with President King in the opinion which he expressed in his annual report to the Trustees on October 13, 1934, that 'the College is now about as large as can be accommodated by our present faculty and our present plant.'" The committee goes on to say:

> The small college, because of its limited enrollment, is able to offer certain advantages, of which, perhaps, the most important is the opportunity for intimacy of friendships of young men as students, with great men as teachers. There can be little doubt that for a certain type of boy there are definite advantages in the small college. In this connection, it is interesting to note that approximately 40 per cent of the reasons given by members of the last four classes for choosing Amherst were, "that it is a small college." We believe that the advantages of the small college, and more particularly the advantages of Amherst as a "small college," are manifest and self-evident. Amherst has a precious heritage to preserve with a rich legacy of memories and traditions. The advantages which have resulted from a small, closely knit undergraduate body should be preserved and, if possible, increased.[64]

This committee concurs in the opinions expressed by President Pease and the alumni committee of 1934. We believe that in no case should the college become any larger and it might well become smaller. This, we think, could best be accomplished, not by reducing the size of the freshman class, but by a more rigorous program of studies in the first two years which would tend to reduce somewhat the number of students remaining in college during the last two years. In other parts of this report we have recommended a more liberal admissions policy together with a more rigorous program of studies for freshmen and sophomores and a greater concentration of effort on the honors students during the last two years. These prior recommendations, it would seem to us, imply that we should continue to admit a freshman class of not over 250 students but select from these underclassmen a smaller number to go on with the work of the upper college.

We recommend that the size of the entering class be limited to not more than 250 students and that the size of the junior and senior classes be regulated by the elimination of the most unsatisfactory students, at least by the end of the sophomore year, in such a way that the total size of the college will be not more than 800 students.

[64] *Alumni Council News*, December, 1934, p. 5.

Conclusion—The Corporate Life of the College

What has impressed us most in preparing this report is the way in which the separate topics we have considered, curriculum, admissions and scholarships, guidance, social life and activities, and the religious life of the college, are all interdependent. To touch one is to affect all. This is more nearly true of Amherst than it might be of many other institutions because Amherst is still a small college and as such a genuine community. In considering our recommendations we have always tried to keep that in mind; we have endeavored to think in terms of the good of the college as a whole.

That good we have defined, in the last section of Part I, as consisting principally in two things: (1) that Amherst should try to become more and more an *honors* college; and (2) that it should (in modern form) maintain boldly the object for which it was founded, "to civilize and evangelize the world by the classical education of indigent young men of piety and talents." How can Amherst College realize this end? We have indicated in this report certain means that would in our opinion help her to do so. Those means are, however, merely means. They are of no value except in so far as they express the *living purposes* of the college as an educational institution.

We look upon the college as a corporate body having a certain historic life extending over many generations. This corporate body contains different elements which have varying functions within the whole. It is essential to the efficient functioning of an institution that each of these elements operate within the whole so as to give the greatest possible freedom and flexibility in the attainment of their mutual purpose. The college should be a free community, freer than any other community except the family can possibly be. The essence of freedom is rational agreement and cooperation in terms of a common end. This is obtainable only by constant communication and a maximum diffusion of responsibility. Every group concerned in the organization and direction of the college as a corporate community should have available to it definite means of expressing its voice in the common affairs of the community. But some of these elements within the community, particularly the alumni and the student body, should exercise influence rather than exert any large measure of direct control. More direct forms of control should of course be exerted by the trustees and by the administrative officers of the college since they have certain financial responsibilities for the management of the college as a corporate affair. But the weight of responsibility for the conduct of the college as an educational institution should rest primarily with the faculty. The college is an organized association where scholars are gathered together for the purpose of carrying on a program of teaching and research. It is, therefore, for them to define the character of this program and to determine in general how it shall be carried out. It is the primary function of the trustees and of the administrative officers of the college to implement this policy. Unless this is the case, there is bound to be perversion of the purposes of the institution. Only those who are actively engaged in the processes of teaching and research are wholly fit to determine what shall be taught, what shall be studied, and by what methods the educational policy of the institution shall be put into effect. This does not mean that the faculty of a college is to be set up as a body which possesses any tyrannical power of determining for itself the course of action of the institution as a whole. It does mean, however, that the entire organization of the community must be in terms of its actual program of education and research, and it is the duty of all other elements in the college to cooperate in achieving this end. An intelligent and cooperative body of alumni and of students will be a stimulus and a support to this purpose. A wise and patriotic Board of Trustees will consider it their duty to realize this purpose so far as they have power to do so. An administration which properly conceives its function will provide to the faculty, to the student body, to the body of alumni, and to the trustees themselves a leadership animated by this purpose. Thus no question which directly or indirectly affects the educational policies of the institution should ever be decided without the advice and concurrence if not upon the initiative of the faculty. Proposed changes and innovations, such as the creation of new courses or new departments, the making of new appointments, questions of tenure and promotion, and proposals for the alteration or revision of methods of instruction may properly be initiated by any group, or any individual, who is connected with the college. But no such proposal should ever be put into effect without the advice and consent of the faculty or its representatives. It is, after all, the quality of the interests and activities of the faculty that primarily determines the character of the college as an educational institution; and it is with the faculty, therefore, that the final decision on any question of policy, which directly or indirectly affects that institution in its educational activities, must lie. It is only in the unusual contingency in which the faculty is so divided within itself that its members can no longer adequately cooperate with one another, and that it can no longer respond to the intellectual and moral suasions of leadership from the administration, that those latent powers which reside in the Board of Trustees should be exercised. But normally a Board of Trustees should reign and not govern.

This would place much greater responsibility and initiative with the faculty than most people are ordinarily willing to allow, but it is, we believe, only when the fundamental responsibility for the educational policy of the college remains with, and is conscientiously assumed by, those who are to do the educating that the primary purpose of the college will be efficiently achieved. It is in this belief that we submit our report to the faculty of Amherst College.

SUMMARY OF RECOMMENDATIONS IN PART II

THE CURRICULUM

1. That the requirements for graduation be redefined in terms of sixteen year-courses or thirty-two semester courses.

2. That each department be asked to reconsider its course offerings and to submit to the Curriculum Committee (or Committee on Educational Policy)[65] its proposals for the new courses to be offered under the four-course program.

3. That all freshmen and sophomores be required to take:

a. A two-year sequence in science.
b. A two-year sequence in history.
c. A two-year sequence in humanities.

4. That the following general courses, *of the laboratory or seminar type*, be established:

a. Science 1-2 and Science 3-4: a two-year course comprising a sequence of topics from the fields of mathematics, physics, astronomy, chemistry, biology, and geology.
b. History 1-2 and History 3-4: two year-courses, one an introduction to Western civilization, the other a course in Problems in American Civilization.
c. Humanities A 1-2 and Humanities B 1-2: the first, a course in which a limited number of classics of the Western world are read in chronological order; the second, a course in the interpretation of texts, intended primarily to give the student training in various kinds of reading experience.
d. Fine Arts, Music and Drama: an introduction to the three arts by a comparative study of their similarities and differences in modes of expression. (Qualified dissent by Professor Funnell.)

5. That the following courses, or choices of courses (with certain

[65] See recommendation 17 below.

exceptions noted below), be required of freshmen and sophomores:

a. Freshmen
   1. Science 1-2
   2. History 1-2
   3. Humanities A 1-2 or Humanities B 1-2
   4. English 1-2
   5. Public Speaking (the present requirement)

b. Sophomores
   1. Science 3-4
   2. History 3-4
   3. Humanities: one full course or two semester-courses, to be chosen from an approved and specific list which should include:
      (a) An introductory course in the arts, such as the course proposed above.
      (b) An introductory course in either fine arts, music, or dramatic arts, similar to the courses given before the war.
      (c) A course in English literature, possibly one, or one of a number, specified by the English Department as fulfilling the requirement.
      (d) A course in the literature of a foreign language, which should be, in the opinion of the department concerned, one in which the student would be sufficiently advanced in his study of the language to be able to give serious consideration to his reading as literature rather than as material for translation.
      (e) An introductory course in philosophy, in which a considerable amount of text would be read, chosen from various writers of different periods.
      (f) A course in classical civilization, in which a large amount of emphasis would be placed on Greek and Latin literature and philosophy and a considerable amount of text read in translation.

6. That the following exceptions to these requirements be allowed:

a. A student planning to major in science may, at the discretion of the department in which he expects to do the work for the major, elect in his sophomore year a parallel course in a science in place of Science 3-4.

b. A student who wishes to take two courses in foreign language, ancient or modern, during his freshman year, and who has passed the College Entrance Board Examinations in English with a sufficiently high score, may take a second course in a foreign language in place of the English 1-2 and Humanities courses, if one of the two courses in foreign language is a course in the *literature* of that language.

7. That the present requirement of a "reading knowledge" of a foreign language be changed as follows:

a. That every student be required, in order to receive a degree, to satisfy a language requirement which, within such practical limits as may be determined by the language departments, will insure a firmer grasp of the language than our present "reading knowledge" requirement.

b. That the list of languages in which the requirement may be satisfied be expanded to include: French, German, ancient Greek, Italian, Latin, Spanish, and any other language which may be approved in an individual case.

c. That the native language of a foreign-born student, educated in a foreign country, be accepted in satisfaction of the requirement.

d. That the departments and divisions give serious consideration to the possibility and advisability of requiring a knowledge of more than one foreign language in connection with advanced work, particularly for honors students.

e. That the teaching of Russian be instituted when possible, and the possibility of satisfying the stated requirement in Russian be studied.

8. That the revised statement of requirements for the major (under the four-course program) be as follows:

A major consists of eight semester-courses pursued under the direction of a department or group. The major cannot begin later than the junior year and may begin in either the freshman or sophomore year; it must be completed in the senior year. No year without a course in the major may intervene between its beginning and its end. Each department decides whether a freshman course in the department shall count toward its major.

The major requirements can be met in accordance with either of two plans:

Plan A: Not less than six of the eight semester-courses must be within a department; not more than two may be in related fields approved by the major department.

Plan B: Combinations of courses not provided for under Plan A, but similar in aim to the established group majors in American Studies and Renaissance Studies, may be made with the consent of the several departments concerned and of the Dean.

9. That the existing requirement that during the junior and senior years the student must elect at least four semester-courses outside of the division in which he is majoring be retained.

10. That when, in the opinion of the department concerned, it is warranted, and with the consent of the Dean, a student whose average is below 80 per cent at the end of sophomore year may be admitted to candidacy for the degree with distinction. Students so admitted would still be required to have a minimum final college average of 80 to be eligible to be considered for the degree *cum laude*, of 86 for the degree *magna cum laude*, and of 90 for the degree *summa cum laude*.

11. That a candidate for the degree with distinction may be permitted, at the discretion of the department in which he is majoring, to substitute in his junior year a conference course or tutorial for one of the four regular courses required, and in his senior year a conference course or tutorial for one or two of the four regular courses required.

12. That the faculty instruct the Curriculum Committee (or Committee on Educational Policy) to make a special study of the possibility of establishing a limited number of additional group majors.

13. That the instructor in any course not open to freshmen be allowed, with the consent of the department concerned and of the Dean, to schedule one two-week reading period or two one-week reading periods each semester at any time during the semester.

14. That the experiment be made of requiring every student to fulfill an assignment of prescribed reading, supplementing the proposed courses in humanities, during the summer between freshman and sophomore years.

15. That a group of scholarships, open to juniors for work on a special honors project during the summer following the completion of the junior year, be established.

16. That a reference librarian be added to the staff.

17. That the title of the Curriculum Committee be changed to Committee on Educational Policy and that the faculty instruct the committee to make an annual report.

18. That general courses and group majors be given independent departmental status.

ADMISSIONS AND SCHOLARSHIPS

19. That the appointment of an assistant admissions officer to work in the high school field be considered.

20. That the established minimum requirement for holders of scholarships be changed to 75 per cent for sophomores and that, *so far as possible*, no scholarships be made available to juniors and seniors who are not candidates for the degree with distinction. (Dissent by Professors Brown and Morgan.)

21. That the admissions requirements proposed in this section be adopted.

22. That a Committee on Admissions and Scholarship Policy, as described in this section, be established.

ORIENTATION AND GUIDANCE

23. That the program of orientation for freshmen described in this section be adopted.

24. That an associate dean be appointed to have charge of the counseling of freshmen and sophomores.

SOCIAL LIFE AND ACTIVITIES

25. That the faculty pass a resolution advising the trustees that it is to the best interests of the college that fraternities be abolished at Amherst. (Dissent by Professor Brown.)

26. That the program of physical education described in this section be adopted.

THE RELIGIOUS LIFE OF THE COLLEGE

27. That attendance at church services be made voluntary. (General dissent to this section by Professor Beebe.)

SOME PROBLEMS OF ORGANIZATION AND GOVERNMENT

28. That in respect to questions of tenure, appointments, and promotions the following procedure be adopted:

a. In every case appointments to the faculty, terminations of appointments, and promotions within the faculty shall be fully discussed by the Committee of Six and the opinions of its members recorded before any final action is taken.

b. Well before the end of the probationary period, as defined by the American Association of University Professors, the Committee of Six shall carefully study the qualifications of a member of the faculty and record its opinion as to whether or not this appointment should be terminated.

29. That the size of the entering class be limited to not more than 250 students, and that the size of the junior and senior classes be regulated by the elimination of the most unsatisfactory students, at least by the end of the sophomore year, in such a way that the total size of the college will be not more than 800 students.

APPENDIX TO PART II

A Memorandum from President King on Costs of Operation of the College, Scholarship Funds, Etc.

July 5, 1944

The following memorandum is prepared for the Long Range Policy Committee. It deals specifically with questions 17, 20, and 21 of their memorandum submitted to me with Professor Kennedy's letter of June 19, 1944. All of the financial figures in this memorandum prior to 1933 are to be taken with caution. The College installed a modern accounting system in 1932-33. The accounts before that date were kept on what we should call today a very informal basis and comparative statistics taken from the Treasurer's books covering the early periods are of little value.

For example:

a. Administrative officers were paid a small salary for administration but the bulk of their salary was charged to instruction.

b. In the earlier records only the expenditures for books are charged to the library.

c. In the earlier records a great many items are charged to Miscellaneous which it is impossible now to analyze.

d. Certain charges which have nothing to do with the educational program of the College were included in certain categories and cannot now be segregated.

The figures in this report have been taken from the following sources:

Number of Students—from the catalogues.

Tuition—from the catalogues.

All other figures—from the printed Treasurer's Reports of the College where such are available. No printed Treasurer's Report was issued by the College for the year 1920-21. Such figures as I have submitted for this year were taken from the Auditor's Report. Some of the figures for 1900-01 were taken from the Auditor's Report and some from the printed Treasurer's Report.

Figures indicating cost per student are based upon rough computations and are approximate.

	1900-01	1910-11	1920-21	1930-31	1940-41
Plant account		$1,029,000	$1,752,000	$3,442,000	$ 5,297,000
Endowment	$1,675,000	2,620,000	4,610,000	8,615,000	12,163,000
Students	393	494	498	670	851
Gross expense	129,000	166,000	392,000	857,000	1,044,000
Student fees	47,000	67,000		330,000	475,000
Net expense	82,000	99,000		527,000	569,000
Instruction	72,000	106,000		378,000	448,000
Administration	14,000	? {14,700 16,000		123,000 ?	157,000
Library	5,600	5,000		18,000	50,000
Buildings and grounds	18,000	23,000		148,000	182,000

	Scholarships	Loans	Enroll-ment	Tuition	Endowment
1940-41	$89,915.51[a]	$3,957.04	851	$450	$12,163,000
1930-31	73,342.00	6,274.83	670	400	8,615,000
1920-21	26,182.90	1,875.00	498	200	4,610,000
1910-11	17,677.84	460.00	494	110	2,620,000
1900-01	14,557.50		393	110	1,675,000

[a] Note: Includes $3,300 Student Aid Employment

	1900	1910	1920	1930	1940
Endowment per student	$4,260	$5,250	$9,200	$12,800	$14,300
Plant account per student		2,050	3,400	5,100	6,200
Gross expense per student	330	325	780	1,280	1,200
Net expense per student	220	198		780	660
Instruction per student	180	212		560	520
Administration per student	35	60		180	180
Library per student	14	10		26	58
Buildings and grounds per student	45	46		220	210

REPORT OF THE REVIEW COMMITTEE ON THE NEW PROGRAM, 1954

PART III

A REVIEW OF THE NEW PROGRAM

When the report of the Faculty Committee on Long Range Policy was issued, no one knew what would become of it. The usual fate of such documents is to become pathetic reminders of impossible hopes. In this case, that did not occur. Our purpose in Part III is to tell what did happen. Taken as a whole, this book is the record of a successful attempt to change radically the pattern of education in one college. It has, then, the value of a case history, an example of how in one instance something important was done.

Since the recommendations of the committee were adopted by the faculty, they have become a part of the official educational policy of the college. In the account which follows we have included comments and recommendations which represent, of course, merely our own opinions. No attempt has been made to undertake a formal evaluation of the new program because we believe that it is impossible. Our opinions on that subject are stated in the final section, "On 'Evaluation.'"

FORMULATING THE REPORT

In the Introduction to their report the committee stated: "Here at Amherst we are attempting something that has rarely if ever been done, to secure through the democratic processes of study, report, and discussion the cooperative agreement of the whole faculty upon a comprehensive long term policy for the college." Because what was attempted was achieved, achieved in a short time and with a minimum of confusion and conflict, we believe that it is worth while to say something more than properly could be related in the report itself about the way in which the report was composed. Any person who has participated in the work of committees knows that much of what is essential to their success is often apparently inconsequential and that a large part of the most important work of such committees never appears in the record. To be understood such documents must be read between the lines. That this report was not merely written but almost wholly adopted is largely due, we believe, to the way in which it was done.

What, then, were some of the factors contributing to the committee's success, and how were some of the basic difficulties with which they were confronted resolved? As the committee themselves noted in their preface, the war period was a most opportune occasion for initiating any radical change. Being abruptly thrown out of one's customary routine usually generates fluidity of mind coupled with a heightened sense of responsibility for the future. This was the mood of almost everyone involved.

Within this setting the most important single factor was the personnel of the committee itself. Appointed by the President in consultation with the executive committee of the faculty, the Committee of Six, its members were all chosen from the middle age group of the faculty. All of them could anticipate that they would have to live with and be heavily responsible for what was done during many years to come. Moreover, it was a group who were personally congenial, who had seen common service on other faculty committees and were accustomed to working with one another. Shortly after the committee began its task, it was decided that the regular Curriculum Committee of the faculty should meet with this group on matters concerning the curriculum. However, the Long Range Policy Committee invited the Curriculum Committee to attend all of their meetings. Thus three more members of the faculty were added to the group. The two committees functioned as a unit, though in coming to final decisions the members of the Curriculum Committee did not have a formal vote. This group of ten was compact enough to be efficient yet collectively was large enough to be, in an institution as small as Amherst, highly influential. It was certain that if this group could unanimously agree upon any recommendation the faculty would give it serious consideration, and it was probable that each of the individual members of the group had enough personal following within the faculty to secure its adoption. Thus the members of the committee could feel that if their recommendations made good sense and were persuasively presented they could institute real reforms.

Their confidence was enhanced by the attitude of the administration. President King's mandate to the committee had emphasized the probable need for radical changes. Moreover, during the deliberations of the committee, having given this complete freedom, he assisted them in any way that was within his power; he freely expressed his opinions on any matter when they were asked for but made no effort to "influence" their conclusions. Similarly, the committee was not subjected to any sort of pressure by the alumni. On such touchy points as athletics, chapel and church, and the fraternities (particularly the latter), there was concern among alumni groups about the possible recommendations. But here again no one interfered. Some members of the Long Range Policy Committee were not even aware that during their consideration of the fraternity question the President had protected them from the interference of certain local alumni groups to whom he suggested that it was not for them to do anything until after the faculty report had been completed.

The meetings of the committee were kept as informal as possible. Unless it was meeting with some large group of the faculty, these were held, usually twice a week, from four to six, at the house of the chairman. They resembled rather the coffee hour at the faculty club, with a more persistent sticking to the present subject of conversation, than anything usually thought of as formal procedure. Not all members were able to attend regularly, but a sufficient confidence was soon generated to make possible effective meetings on important topics when only four or five members of the whole group could be present, topics sometimes not even recurred to. Between fifty and sixty meetings were held. Subjects were not taken up in any predetermined order, but to suit the occasion—such as the availability of certain outside guests and meetings with the subcommittees of the parallel alumni group. The usual procedure was to discuss an agenda prepared in outline by the chairman or by some other member of the committee. Each topic in the outline would be talked over until apparently everyone had said what he wished to say. Brief informal minutes summarizing discussions were kept by the secretary, Professor Funnell. No formal motions were made, and practically no votes were taken. Straw votes were asked for, however, in meetings with outside groups, to determine group sentiments. It was agreed at the outset that each member of the committee might dissent on any point whatever. Little or no effort was made to secure agreement by compromises which would sacrifice the real opinion of any individual. The process was essentially one of self-education through mutual discussion.

The committee avoided one of the greatest hazards confronting such a group by neglecting the explicit discussion of educational "objectives." There are only two references to them in the secretary's minutes of the meetings. For the tenth meeting there is the pregnant remark, "Odegard raised the question of *ends*. There was agreement that they could be postponed and perhaps reached *via* means"; and in the minutes of the thirty-eighth meeting there is the laconic statement, "Discussion of objectives of a liberal education." From the remainder of the minutes, it is apparent that much of the time during this meeting was taken up with other matters. It is, indeed, true that objectives were reached *via* a discussion of means. As the preface to the Report says:

> On the central question of the curriculum, the members of the committee found themselves, somewhat unexpectedly, in more substantial agreement than they had supposed. They were therefore able to send out to the faculty as early as June 12th a memorandum making a number of concrete proposals, particularly for the freshman and sophomore years.

The proposed curriculum outlined in this memorandum is almost exactly the one which was subsequently recommended in the report. One paragraph in this memorandum states "some of the assumptions underlining the type of curriculum here proposed for discussion," assumptions later defended in some detail in the report itself. But these assumptions were never the subject of extended discussion. Part I of the report, "Objectives of the Liberal College in a Changing Society," was written by the chairman *after* the detailed recommendations in Part II had been agreed upon, and when submitted to the committee was accepted with only a few unimportant changes.

Though there was basic harmony within the committee and with the administration, the earlier conferences with various groups of the faculty were not equally propitious. The tentative proposals for a new curriculum sketched out in a five-page memorandum and distributed to the faculty as a basis for opening these discussions did not fare well. For a good while it seemed as though the committee's trial balloon would never get off the ground.

In these initial meetings all sorts of objections were raised. One curious impediment, though it sounds trivial, actually proved most troublesome. The committee had suggested that in each of the required courses which it proposed for the first two years at least some provision should be made for a "laboratory" type of teaching. In outlining the assumptions underlying the type of curriculum suggested it was summarily stated "that one learns by doing something about it when confronted with a problem. The 'laboratory' is intended to supply for freshmen and sophomores in an elementary way a greater opportunity for that kind of education." The use of this word "laboratory," perhaps because the context in which it was employed had something of the aura of "progressive" education, involved the committee in difficulties which one cannot easily imagine would arise merely from the use of a certain word. It was objected, particularly by some members of the social science group, that the term cannot be properly used except for the natural sciences. When the word "seminar" was suggested as a substitute, the objection then was that this word can be applied only to graduate or advanced undergraduate work. Unfortunately, there is no third word in the English language which would meet the committee's need, and they finally resorted to speaking of "courses of the 'laboratory' or 'seminar' type," hoping by such use to obviate the semantic difficulty.

A second objection was to the committee's advocacy of cooperative courses. Many members of the faculty were suspicious of this proposal because they felt that, if it were applied, some one might be telling the teachers how to teach their courses. Such initial apprehensions and suspicions were inevitable but not, hopefully, too important. However, the committee encountered more serious opposition within two groups, the teachers of the freshman composition course and the teachers of mathematics and natural science.

Shortly after their meeting with the English Department the instructors in English 1-2 sent a letter to the committee stating that the committee's proposal for a humanities course in the freshman year which would run parallel to the existing course in English composition was unnnecessary. Their reasons were as follows:

> We, the instructors in English 1-2, have worked out an "orientation" of the Freshman mind and an "integration" of Freshman knowledge which we believe is a workable, teachable answer to the needs which the Humanities Course proposes to fill. We have developed our methods of orientation and integration by actual class-room teaching, and we use these methods every day that we teach. English 1-2, therefore, might well be officially designated as the Introduction to the Liberal Arts which it in fact is for those who take it now.
>
> The instructors in English 1-2 are prepared to plan such a course and to administer it by enlisting other members of the Faculty, as we do now, to teach an expanded English 1-2.

A discussion of this difference went on without resolution of the disagreement until Professor Brower of the English 1-2 group proposed a third course, to be called Humanities B. This course they suggested should be added to the committee's proposals, the plan being that all students would be required to take English 1-2 and that they might choose one of the humanities offerings, Humanities A or Humanities B.[1]

The suggestion in this initial communication of a required two-year sequence in general science was also received with hostile comment. At the initial meeting with the science group, the agenda prepared for the discussion began with the question: Is a general science course desirable? And to this a large number of those present answered with an emphatic *no*.[2] Subsequently, the two members of the Long Range Policy Committee who belonged to the science division were commissioned to carry on discussions with the science group in the hope that eventual agreement might be reached on a two-year sequence which would have some resemblance to what the committee had proposed. These discussions went on and on without arriving at any definite conclusion. One of the key points involved was the place, if any, that mathematics should have in a general course, and one of the alternatives seriously considered was that students intend-

[1] For a description of the two types of humanities courses see below, p. 229.

[2] The straw vote on whether a general science course "might be" desirable was 7 for, 8 against, 4 abstaining.

ing to major in science might elect regular courses in mathematics and the sciences instead of a general science sequence.

In September the Department of Mathematics informed the committee that they were unanimously in favor of requiring mathematics for all freshmen and were not in favor of a general science course (Professor Brown dissenting) which would include mathematics. By November Professor Brown and Professor Beebe were able to report that a number of the science group now approved a course of the type the committee had proposed, and a good many were not really against it. The Department of Mathematics by now had said that, though not in favor of including mathematics in such a course, they would be willing to cooperate if they were needed in teaching whatever course was agreed upon by a majority. The committee decided, therefore, that they might recommend their original proposal for a two-year sequence in the sciences, including mathematics, with the hope that continuing discussions within the science division would in time produce a consensus in their favor.

Meanwhile, the committee had become concerned with another problem, one that they came to designate as "curricular arithmetic." General outlines were all very well, but, as they began to plan the new program in more detail, it became obvious to them that the greatest obstacle to education is lack of time. After all, *could* students do and do well everything they were so confidently demanding? The problem of curricular arithmetic took two forms—"contact hours" in the first two years, and the satisfaction of requirements imposed from without on students intending to prepare for graduate work in physics and chemistry, to take the Amherst-M.I.T. combined five-year program, or to go to medical school.

In the endeavor to solve the first problem one schedule after another of contact hours in the freshman year was proposed. How could the three sequence courses and the foreign language courses *all* be of the "laboratory" or "seminar" type and still take up only a reasonable number of hours? Every schedule suggested looked burdensome, yet the committee finally decided to go ahead with its recommendations in the belief that this difficulty could be gotten over, if the new program were put into effect, through a process of mutual concessions by the faculty groups concerned. Really, what the committee was recommending was that each faculty group should have at its disposal one-fourth of the student's time and could decide in its wisdom how that time was to be employed.

The other problem of curricular arithmetic proved easier to deal with. It soon became apparent that premedical students could meet both the requirements of the new program and those of the medical schools. To take care of the needs of students majoring in science and of the M.I.T. group an "escape clause" was provided, enabling them to substitute in their sophomore year a parallel course in a science for the second year of the required sequence in general science. But the prescriptions of the American Chemical Society for students planning to do graduate work in chemistry remained an obstacle until Professor Beebe showed that by an ingenious reshuffling of the contents of certain courses even these requirements could be met. When the time came for writing the report, a draft incorporating statements on particular topics by those members of the committee who were especially competent to do them was prepared by the chairman. This draft, with only minor changes, was adopted. There were a few dissents on specific points.

The activities of the committee had extended over a period of ten months, from March to December, 1944. The total cost of preparing the report had been a leave from teaching duties of one semester for the chairman and the expenditure of approximately $500 for clerical assistance and for travel. Fifteen hundred copies of the report were printed for distribution to members of the faculty, trustees, and any other person who might request one. It was issued in January, 1945. Upon delivery of the report to the President for distribution, the committee was discharged, its members free to participate as individuals in subsequent faculty actions in any way they might choose.

Meanwhile the parallel Alumni Committee on the Postwar College was also at work. This committee had been appointed by the Alumni Council in the fall of 1943. Charles W. Cole, who was to succeed Mr. King as president of the college, was designated its chairman. Associated with him were Walter F. Downey, Ordway Tead, J. Seelye Bixler, Theodore M. Greene, and Eugene S. Wilson. Four members of this group, Walter Downey, Ordway Tead, Seelye Bixler, and Theodore Greene, were in turn designated chairmen of subcommittees, each having five to eight members chosen from the alumni, on Admissions and Scholarship, Student Activities, Religion, and Curriculum. In addition to circulating a questionnaire among the alumni and faculty, each subcommittee held a week-end symposium at Amherst in the spring of 1944 to discuss with faculty, alumni, and officers of the administration the problems assigned it. On these occasions the alumni committees met with the Long Range Policy Committee for an informal interchange of opinions. For the most part this liaison with the alumni subcommittees was maintained—with the result that with one exception, the recommendations regarding church and chapel, there was a broad general agreement in the two reports, though the alumni report was necessarily in some of its recommendations, particularly in the section on the curriculum, less specific than the faculty report. This alumni report was published as a number of the *Alumni Council News* under the title "Amherst Tomorrow."[3]

PUTTING THE PROGRAM INTO EFFECT

The faculty report having been delivered, it was distributed to the members of the faculty in February with a covering letter from the President stating that the "responsibility for the post war program of the College now rests with the faculty."

The members of the Long Range Policy Committee had gradually come to realize that their job was much more one of propaganda for the faith than solely one of writing a report. By the time the report was completed so many individuals had become actively involved in discussions of the problems with which the committee had dealt that enough impetus had been generated within the faculty to make certain further study and planning. Looking back upon it now, one cannot but consider remarkable the way in which the faculty took up the responsibility which was passed on to it—the efficiency with which they carried on the subsequent discussions and decisions respecting the recommendations in the report and the way that, the decisions having been made, the organization and planning necessary to carry them out were accomplished. Of course there were difficulties. Every faculty has its share of mavericks and prima donnas, and there were always those who remained in opposition. But when it came time

[3] Some of the recommendations of this alumni report, particularly where they differ from the report of the faculty committee, are discussed at appropriate points later in this review.

to make a decision, there existed a body of faculty opinion of sufficient weight to insure that the new program would be put into operation.

When President King delivered copies of the report to the members of the faculty, he referred it also to the executive committee of the faculty, the Committee of Six, who in turn referred the first fourteen recommendations, those concerned with the curriculum, and recommendation 17, that a Committee on Educational Policy be established, to the Curriculum Committee for further study. In May, the Curriculum Committee having reported in favor of these resolutions, the Committee of Six voted that their report be brought before the faculty for special consideration at a meeting to be held the following year.

It was desirable to have an interval for the members of the faculty in which to consider the report. An additional reason for delay was that it came out when the college was still on a wartime year-round basis. Members of the faculty were preoccupied with administration and teaching in military units. There had been many temporary appointments of faculty members for the instruction of these units, and a considerable number of the regular faculty were away on war service.

Meanwhile, since it looked as though the war were drawing to a close, one of the important recommendations of the report was brought up for immediate consideration. In March the recommendation, "That the faculty pass a resolution advising the trustees that it is to the best interests of the college that *fraternities be abolished at Amherst*," was presented to the faculty for a roll-call vote. Members who could not be present at the meeting were polled by mail. The resolution was passed by a large majority.[4]

In June the trustees, after study of the faculty and alumni reports, and after additional investigations of their own, reached the following conclusion: "That the interests of the College can best be served at this time by a program of radical reform rather than by one of abolition, with its inevitable untried substitutes."

During the following academic year the college was still on a wartime basis, though many students were returning from the armed services and civilians were again beginning to apply for admission.

[4] The fraternity question is treated in the section on "Social Life and Activities."

Regular members of the faculty were also returning from their wartime occupations. A third United States Military Academy Preparatory Unit necessitated the appointment of thirty-nine additional teachers, and the college was still planning to operate on a year-round basis for the benefit of the returning G.I.'s. It was also a year during which there were many resignations and new appointments of regular members of the faculty. And, finally, Mr. King had made known his decision that this would be his last year as president.

Nevertheless, progress with recommendations of the report went forward rapidly. The first question to be settled was that of church and chapel. At an October meeting of the faculty, it was voted to approve recommendation 27, "That attendance at church services be made voluntary." This meant, in effect, that college church services would not be continued. In April it was voted that, in accordance with the recommendation of the Long Range Policy Report, daily chapel services should be resumed in the year 1946-1947.[5]

In October the Committee of Six prepared a resolution recommending to the faculty the adoption of the new curriculum. At the faculty meeting there was virtually no discussion of educational policy as such. The whole of the debate centered on certain motions intended to postpone or amend the recommendations. The motion to postpone was to the effect that a final vote be delayed until the members of the faculty on leave for war service could be present at a meeting and the new president of the college, when he was chosen, should have had an opportunity to study the Long Range Policy Report. After extended discussion this motion was lost. Two other amendments were then offered:

> [1] A student planning to major in science or social science may at the discretion of the department in which he expects to do the work for the major elect in his sophomore year a parallel course in a science or a social science in place of Science 3-4 or History 3-4 respectively.
>
> [2] That Article 3a of Section 1 be amended to read, "A year course in Mathematics, Physics, and Astronomy."

Together, these two amendments would have limited required courses to the freshman year. Both were defeated.

[5] For a discussion of the church and chapel question, see the section on "The Religious Life of the College."

It was then moved that the question be divided and the first three recommendations be considered together. Another amendment was offered, to the effect that the new curriculum be organized on an experimental basis for a small selected portion of the freshman class. This amendment was also defeated. The faculty then voted to approve recommendations 1, 2, and 3, of the report, which covered the curriculum for the freshman year. This was a voice vote and was apparently carried by a large majority.

The next motion was that the faculty approve in principle recommendations 4-14, which covered the upper three years. After a brief discussion this motion was passed unanimously. Thus the whole business of adopting a new curriculum was transacted at one faculty meeting—in fact, with time left over for a vote on the recommendations concerning compulsory church at the end, and in an atmosphere of remarkably cooperative discussion. The debate was keen, but it became increasingly apparent from the tenor of the meeting that nearly the whole of the faculty present were in favor of the new curriculum, and the fact that after the adoption of the first three recommendations the approval in principle of the group dealing with the upper three years was voted unanimously shows that those members of the faculty who were opposed to the report as a whole or in part, or who wished to postpone its consideration, were loyally acquiescing in the decision of the majority. Happily, there were no record votes—and therefore there was no identifiable opposition to the adoption of the new curriculum.

The Committee of Six and the Curriculum Committee now had a mandate from the faculty to proceed with plans for adoption of the new curriculum. Early in the next month they appointed committees to be in charge of the planning of the two-year sequences for freshmen and sophomores. They also appointed two members of the faculty, Professors George Taylor and Anthony Scenna, to a "Stimulating Committee" to coordinate and expedite plans for these curricular changes.

In January the trustees elected Professor Charles W. Cole of Columbia, who had been the chairman of the Alumni Committee on Postwar Amherst College, as president. At a special meeting of the faculty the President-Elect made a speech in which among other things he expressed personal enthusiasm for the new curriculum which the faculty had adopted. Thus with a faculty and administration fully united the college entered upon the planning of the new curriculum.

In February the Stimulating Committee submitted a report of progress in which they made recommendations on a number of problems. Of these the most important was that the freshman curriculum should not be introduced until September, 1947. Since planning had begun in October, this would allow practically two years in which the college could get back onto a normal basis, new members of the faculty could be recruited, and the planning of the courses themselves could be carried out in detail. Thus the new program, when it was introduced, would be well planned and well taught.

As it turned out, this decision was doubly fortunate. All of the planning had been done on the basis of a freshman class of approximately 250 students, but the officer who was then in charge of admissions admitted nearly a normal class of students from secondary schools and at the same time (as he should) a large number of returning veterans, with the result that the freshman class entering in the fall of 1946 contained slightly more than 400 students. The presence of this class, nearly twice our normal size, because of the excessive teaching load it imposed on the faculty, was a severe handicap throughout the first three years of the new program.

By the beginning of April the Stimulating Committee was able to get reports from the chairmen of the various sequence courses in which they outlined the progress to date of the planning for those courses and submitted estimates of the teaching force which would be required. These reports showed that detailed plans had by now been well developed except in the case of the science sequence. Here, the chairman stated that for a number of reasons, the preoccupation of some members with heavy teaching duties, the continued absence of one or two persons in government service, and "the very evident loss of interest in the New Curriculum by the science members of the faculty—never dominantly enthusiastic—since it was voted not to introduce it until the fall of 1947," little or no progress had been made. However, he added: "Members of the faculty in the science departments may dislike the effects of the plan on their own work; but they are committed, like those in other fields, to working out and developing to the fullest extent the possibilities of general education courses." The great impediment to the successful planning of the science sequence was that no consensus could be arrived at within the group as between a number of alternative plans, each of which was unacceptable to some faction.

Another committee composed of President-Elect Cole and two members of the faculty was appointed to make a special report on the problem of administration and organization of the freshman-sophomore courses. It recommended that each sequence course should have a chairman and a special budget, and in this respect should function as a department, but that the staff in these courses should be recruited from the departments. The members of the groups teaching sequence courses should cooperate with the departments in appointing members who would participate in them, and independent appointments to the staff of a sequence course should be made only after all the possibilities of a joint appointment had been carefully explored. This recommendation for the organization and administration of the sequence courses were adopted. No independent appointment to the staff of these courses was made until 1954.

At their first meeting in September, 1946, the faculty established a Committee on Educational Policy with the powers and duties recommended for it in the report. The members of this committee the first year were Gail Kennedy, chairman, Ralph Beebe, Bailey Brown, Lester Chandler, and Reginald French. Professors Beebe and Chandler were succeeded on the committee by John Hall and Anthony Scenna in the second year. The Committee on Educational Policy had a heavy mandate. Theirs was the difficult function of acting as a steering committee to expedite the planning and institution of the new program, and to mediate, sometimes with the aid of the Committee of Six, the Dean, and the President, in the occasional conflicts which arose.

The three major difficulties which had confronted the Long Range Policy Committee were, as we have noted, those of the organization of the humanities sequence course for the freshman year, the organization of the science sequence, and the question of "contact hours." The first of these had been resolved by the compromise arrangement of two parallel humanities courses in the freshman year. In December Professor Brower, chairman of the group planning the Humanities B course, informed the Committee on Educational Policy that his group had decided it would be inadvisable to offer Humanities B in 1947-1948. The explanation, as stated in a letter to the committee, was as follows:

The principal reasons for not offering Humanities B are our strong desire to continue English 19-20 and our obligation to provide English work for some two hundred Sophomores during 1947-1948. We also believe that it is not consistent with the aims of the new curriculum to divide the Freshmen into two groups taking the two proposed Humanities courses. They will not have the advantage of a common educational experience, nor will they be able to see, as was hoped, the relation between their work in Humanities and their work in history and English.[6]

The committee accepted this decision.

Trouble in organizing the science sequence was due to a number of factors. Perhaps the most important was the legitimate claim of six groups to a place in the sequence courses. These were mathematics, physics, chemistry, biology, astronomy, and geology. To fit these six blocks of subject matter into four semesters and at the same time provide an adequate training in the first two years for students planning to enter medical schools, take the Amherst-M.I.T. program, or major in one of the physical sciences seemed impossible. It was like trying to put six cars on a siding that would hold only four. Planning on this basis would result in a contraction of all these subjects which would leave everyone dissatisfied, and the only alternative seemed to be that, if only two courses were to be included in the sequence, something would have to be "bumped off," at one end or the other.

By this time the discussions of the science sequence had narrowed down to a consideration of these alternatives:

1. A combined course in mathematics and physics for the freshman year in which many of the topics in mathematics would be selected expressly for their value in the solution of certain problems in physics. In the sophomore year, the student could choose between
   a. A course in chemistry and biology (it is hoped that these two units would be closely tied together) and
   b. A course in "evolution" that would incorporate materials from astronomy, geology, biology, anthropology, etc.

[6] For a description of the course referred to, now called English 21-22, see the section entitled "The New Curriculum." No attempt has since been made to revive Humanities B.

2. A combined course in physics and chemistry for the freshman year.[7] In the sophomore year the student could choose between
   a. A semester course in biology to be followed by the election of any one of a number of semester courses in the sciences, e.g., astronomy, geology, geography, etc., and
   b. The course in "evolution" described above.

The Committee on Educational Policy and many members of the science group were strongly opposed to the second of these alternatives since they were convinced that the omission of mathematics from the required sequence would make it necessary for a large number of the students majoring in mathematics and the natural sciences to be exempted from some part of the general requirements for the first two years. They were afraid that if this type of science sequence were adopted it would be only a matter of time before this defect would lead to an abandonment of all attempts to establish a required science sequence and cause a reversion to the old group requirement—a choice among several conventional year courses in mathematics and the natural sciences. The conflict over these alternatives was sharp. After a long series of discussions it was finally decided that the first of the alternatives was closer to the recommendations which the faculty had approved and that if these courses were properly organized the needs of students majoring in mathematics and science could be met.

In all cases except that of science, planning of the sequence courses proceeded so smoothly that the Committee on Educational Policy had little to do but receive and transmit the results, so far as the character of the courses themselves was concerned. But when the final plans of the various groups were received, it became clear that the Long Range Policy Committee had been justified in their concern with "curricular arithmetic." In all, plans for the freshman courses, as they were submitted, called for a total, including beginning courses in foreign languages and the one-hour course in public speaking, of twenty-six contact hours each semester. Professor Chandler declared the views of the committee when he stated in a memorandum on this subject:

[7] A small experimental course for freshmen attempting to combine physics and chemistry was given by Professor Ralph A. Beebe and Professor Theodore Soller during 1946-1947.

> The recommended program would tend to emphasize too much the work that a student does or has done for him in the classroom, and it would do this at the expense of work done independently by the student outside the classroom. I believe this is a step in the wrong direction. The essential point of the Long Range Policy Report was not, it seems to me, to increase the amount of time spent by the student in a classroom but rather "to learn by doing," or "to acquire and learn to use skills through the solution of problems." This purpose cannot be achieved unless the student is required to do a large amount of independent work outside the classroom.

Accordingly, the committee proposed a *quid pro quo* type of reduction in the number of contact hours; but the beliefs of the committee were apparently not so strongly held by the teachers responsible for the conduct of these courses. The best the committee could do was to get the contact hours, including public speaking, reduced to twenty-three and a half hours each semester. The following year they attempted again to deal with this problem, but the only permanent result was the elimination of one hour each semester by moving the required course in public speaking to the sophomore year where the number of contact hours was not a problem. That the views of the committee could not prevail has now become evident. The freshmen who enter Amherst have proved their ability to carry this load without undue strain, even, in the great majority of cases, those who are also (at the present time) taking in addition the R.O.T.C. course. Today the number of contact hours in the freshman year, excluding the R.O.T.C. course, is twenty-two the first semester and twenty-three the second for students taking one of the introductory courses in a modern language.

By February this task was completed. At that time the Committee on Educational Policy was able to submit for the faculty's approval the entire program for the freshman year, including revised statements of the requirements in ancient and foreign languages and of the admissions requirement, according to the recommendations of the Long Range Policy Report.

When the "guinea pig" class entered in the fall of 1947, enrollment was nearing its postwar peak. It was up to 1163 that year, a considerable expansion for an institution which had about 850 students before the war. And the college remained oversize during the progress of this class; in their senior year Amherst still numbered over a thousand students. Yet the faculty were able to carry this burden of larger classes and also make the transition to the new curriculum without too much strain.

Everyone wondered, of course, how the freshmen would "take hold" of the new curriculum. Their position was in some respects a disadvantageous one. First, these hard-pressed youngsters, who seemed to be always either in a class or preparing for the next one, were juxtaposed with a body of sophomores on a three-hour, five-course schedule who always seemed to have time for bridge, the "flicks," or a date. School friends who had gone to other colleges brought back on their vacations no such reports of ceaseless labor. Perhaps our students heard that some alumni were concerned lest all work and no play (meaning lack of time for freshman teams to get in a sufficient amount of practice) might make Jack a dull boy and that, with apparent inconsistency, these alumni seemed to be equally afraid that the college would have to admit too many "bright boys" who were not "all-round" youths with a healthy interest in games and of sound character. These apprehensions, as the sports records show, were unfounded, but at the time they may have affected morale. Certainly the freshman year, by contrast, was too hard and the freshmen felt it. A member of the class, reviewing that year, probably expressed the typical opinion when he said:

That is about all I have to report about the new curriculum in operation except one other criticism which, I believe, should not be left out. This, I say again, is not merely my opinion, but a gripe I have heard expressed most frequently and most bitterly by my fellow classmates. Most students, whether they have need to or not, complain that they have too much studying to do. In the case of the '47-'48 frosh I think this complaint is reasonable. I have talked with many friends from other colleges, and the only ones who spent as much time in the classroom and in study after class were attending technical brain mills—Rensselaer or M. I. T. I personally do not believe in too much study or in too much extracurricular activities—dramatics, sports, etc. Moderation is the key to success in many things and in this case the balance needs a little shifting away from the study side. Amherst has wonderful facilities for athletics, wonderful opportunities for work in the glee club, dramatics, the newspaper and magazine. Why not provide the chance to grasp these opportunities without losing ground in studies? Perhaps to this year's frosh that chance will be presented.[8]

Yet the academic standing of the class at the end of the year was 78.6 per cent while that of the preceding class in their first year was 79.44. Of the freshmen in the new program only 13.7 per cent were in some sort of academic difficulty as compared with 15.9 per cent for the preceding freshmen. Of the 248 freshmen in this class taking the first year of the new curriculum, only seven students were dropped from college.[9]

The work was hard, but the students did it. They did it because they had the ability, were challenged by the difficulty, and took a self-conscious pride in themselves as the "guinea pigs" who would show they could meet that challenge. This attitude was soon to die out. As the whole college gradually went over to the new program, freshman year seemed comparatively less difficult and the student body came to take a matter-of-course attitude toward the harder work.

In their first annual report, the Committee on Educational Policy outlined the problems for the coming year. Of these the two most important were the final organization of the sophomore courses and the transition for the entire college from the five- to the four-course plan.

The former was so effectively carried out by the various groups involved in the planning of the new sophomore courses that action by the committee was limited to approving their final proposals and recommending them to the faculty. As was anticipated, the really difficult problem was the reformulation of the course offerings of

[8] Danny D. Gustafson, "A Freshman Looks at the New Curriculum," *Amherst Graduates Quarterly*, 38 (1948), 4.

[9] In his annual report for 1948-1949, President Cole states:

"Enrollment of undergraduate students during 1948-49 reached what may well prove to be the all-time high for Amherst College. The fall semester opened with 1201 students present on the campus, as against 1163 in 1947-48 and 1154 in 1946-47. The second semester started with 1145 students, the decrease being the result largely of graduations at midyear time. The attrition rate for all causes reached an all-time low, since it was only 1.3% for the first semester and .7% for the second semester, or a total for the year of about 2%; as against 6.9% in 1939-40, 8.2% in 1940-41, 6.4% in 1946-47, and 2.9% in 1947-48.

"The low attrition rate has forced an upward revision of our estimates for future enrollment. While the drop will be sharp in 1950-51, the College may well be as large as 1035 that year."

each department and interdepartmental group under the four-course plan. In requesting each department and group to submit its course offerings, the committee urged that each department or group should plan, in so far as possible, in terms of semester units in the interests of flexibility and in terms of a college of 850 students, and that the total number of courses to be offered in any given year should be reduced by at least 20 per cent.

A number of the proposals received were clearly out of line with the committee's request. In advising that such a reduction should be attempted, the Long Range Policy Committee had in mind that the transition from a five- to a four-course plan, where each course was to take a fourth instead of a fifth of the student's time, should logically entail a reduction of this order, and that, in any case, the number of courses in the old curriculum was too large and ought to be reduced. That committee had bequeathed the problem with its blessing to the new Committee on Educational Policy. The blessing was needed, for this proved to be the most trying and delicate assignment yet undertaken. First of all, how could one determine a norm on the basis of which a justifiable estimate could be made as to what constituted a 20 per cent reduction? Departments are constantly changing in size and in the number of courses which they offer. After a good deal of deliberation the committee finally succeeded in arriving at a set of rules by means of which they could determine the typical course offerings in each department and group of departments during a sequence of prewar years. By comparing these trends with the postwar offerings and with the proposals before them, they were able to arrive at what they considered a defensible judgment as to the actual reduction in number of courses contained in the present proposals of the various departments and groups. In making this analysis, the committee did not confine itself to merely statistical criteria but also scrutinized the contents of the courses proposed. After all, the Committee on Educational Policy was an elected and representative group of the faculty who were in a position to survey the whole curriculum in a way in which those making their plans for some particular part of it could not.

There ensued a series of seemingly interminable meetings with many departments in which the Committee on Educational Policy tried to get reductions and changes voluntarily effected, even attempting in one or two instances to secure the deletion of certain courses which had been offered in the past and which, though perfectly justifiable in themselves, were not, in the committee's opinion, what should properly be included in an undergraduate liberal arts program. In this last respect they had, as one might expect, no success, but they did manage to secure in most cases a reorganization of certain courses and a reduction in the number of courses proposed. However, there still remained instances in which the departments concerned were reluctant to accede to the 20 per cent reduction. At this juncture the committee requested a joint meeting with the President, the Dean, and the Committee of Six. During this meeting, the committee submitted for their consideration the new announcement of courses as it stood at that time and presented for their consideration and advice a number of specific comments and questions concerning the course proposals of some departments. As a result, the Committee on Educational Policy was enabled to send out letters renewing their requests with the backing of the President, the Dean, and the Committee of Six. In this way the reduction of courses by a little over 20 per cent was attained—with the qualification that in a number of cases it was achieved by giving certain courses in alternate years rather than by deleting them.[10]

By February the organization of the upper three years was ready for submission to the faculty. The report of the committee was a mimeographed pamphlet of fifty-four pages, the greater part of which was the new Announcement of Courses under the four-course plan. At this time the faculty approved, with one deletion (the recommendation that there be a program of required reading during the summer between the freshman and sophomore years), one omission (that a group of scholarships open to juniors for work on special honors projects during the summer be established), and a few minor amendments, all of the recommendations of the Long Range Policy

[10] Though the natural tendency for the number of courses to expand immediately set in again, a recent estimate by the Committee on Educational Policy shows that there has been an increase, in terms of semester hours, of less than 10 per cent since 1948-1949. This is a better record than might have been expected when it is recalled that the original request was to plan for a college of 850 students while the present enrollment is still about a thousand—and when one considers how numerous, elusive, and persistent are the forces acting to produce a gradual increase.

Committee dealing with the curriculum which had not been previously voted.[11] The faculty then took under consideration the proposed Announcement of Courses. It was moved that all the courses should be approved. The faculty voted unanimously to approve the new curriculum.

Everyone knows that it is the usual history of a new model that many subsequent modifications and alterations are required to take care of inadequately apprehended or unforeseen consequences. Yet there have been surprisingly few changes made in the new program, and those have been of a relatively minor character. A discussion of the modifications in the sequence courses will be found in the next section. Here we shall briefly summarize the other changes which have been made.

At least two of the probable difficulties inherent in the new program had been foreseen and discussed at the time of its formulation. One of these was that the four-course plan when put into operation would, by eliminating the fifth course, place a severe limitation upon the student's freedom of election of courses outside the field of his major. This might well increase the natural tendency of students to major in the larger departments, thus making big departments bigger and small departments smaller. Another factor operating in this direction was the severe limitation upon the student's opportunities during his sophomore year to sample subjects which he had not previously taken. Ignorance and inertia combined might thus incline him to major in subjects which had a privileged position in being required for the first two years. Furthermore, the requirement for a major with honors would in many cases impose a concentration of the student's work in the last two years which would impel him to elect a large number of courses within a comparatively narrow field of study, especially where the student could not begin his major until the junior year. These were some of the considerations which induced the Long Range Policy Committee to retain the previous requirement that during the junior and senior years the student must elect

[11] The three remaining recommendations in this section of the Long Range Policy Report were those concerning the establishment of a Committee on Educational Policy, the departmental status of group courses and group majors, and the addition of a reference librarian to the staff. The first two of these had been dealt with previously. A reference librarian was appointed in 1950. The proposal for summer scholarships was never brought before the faculty.

at least one-fourth of his courses outside of the division in which he is majoring.

It was also recognized that the bias of the new curriculum was definitely in favor of the honors student as against the *rite* student, and it was hoped by those formulating the report that one effect of the new curriculum would be to stimulate a greatly increased interest in honors work among the student body.

Actually, these are two of the three major problems which since the institution of the new curriculum have come before the Committee on Educational Policy, the third being the accommodation of an R.O.T.C. program.

The first of these problems to come up was that of the four-course plan. One aspect of this problem had been unforeseen. In proposing a four-course plan for the whole college, members of the Long Range Policy Committee had supposed that courses could be reconstructed in such a way that each one would take a fourth instead of a fifth of the student's time. The committee had also insisted, quite properly, that course credits should not be equated with contact hours, but they failed to take account of the effects of long-established custom. The result was that, while some courses met four hours a week, and others met three hours a week, and both received the same amount of course credit, the opinion began to prevail that some of the three-hour courses were "unreconstructed." An invidious distinction between "three"- and "four"-hour courses was prevalent, sometimes unjustly, in the minds of the students. (The fact that the fourth hour was nearly always at 7:50 may have had something to do with this.) There seemed to be no other alternative than a change in the four-course plan. Consequently, the faculty adopted in 1949-1950 a proposal whereby the graduation requirement was stated in terms of semester hours, not of courses. At the same time a more flexible system was adopted whereby the student would have greater freedom of election than he could have under a rigid four-course plan by allowing for courses with a variation of from one to four credit hours. However, in the case of advanced courses meeting certain criteria and of honors courses, credit hours were not tied to contact hours, and for the tutorial or conference courses given to honors students as much as eight hours of credit might be allowed.[12]

[12] The distribution in semester units for 1950-1951 was: 155 four-credit courses, 82 three-credit courses, 16 two-credit courses, and 8 one-credit courses.

It also became clear that the requirements for honors[13] made impractical for some students the stipulation that one-fourth of the upperclassman's work must be outside the division of his major. Accordingly, the faculty voted that departmental representatives be empowered to waive a portion of this requirement. The following year this permission was extended to *rite* students.

The Committee on Educational Policy also became concerned with the fact that a number of students whose scholastic attainments made them eligible were not taking honors. In the senior class for 1948-1949, of 108 seniors with the requisite general average, only 66 were candidates for honors. With the idea that greater publicity might be a help, more adequate and attractive descriptions of honors in each department were included in course announcements, and a special booklet, *Honors at Amherst,* was printed for distribution to students and faculty. In addition, the academic average necessary to be eligible for honors was slightly relaxed. For whatever reason, nearly half of the seniors were taking honors in 1952-1953, 102 out of a class of 217. In 1953-1954, out of a senior class of 239 the number eligible was 135 and all but 22 of these were in the honors program.

A correlative problem was that of the *rite* student. Many members of the faculty came increasingly to feel that on the whole the *rite* group of students were not working as hard as they could during their last two years and that something should be done to make the major without honors more of a challenge to their abilities. An editorial in the *Student* expressed the same opinion. Accordingly, a detailed study of this question was made by the Committee on Educational Policy. They came to two conclusions: that the proportion of under-achievers in the *rite* group was much smaller than had been commonly supposed—probably not more than a fourth to a fifth of this group, or approximately 10 per cent of the two upper classes, were genuine "gut hoppers"—and that none of the several proposals, comprehensive examinations, conference courses, senior theses, and the like, which would make available to *rite* students some of the honors type of educational experience were acceptable to the faculty as a whole. The committee was able to make only the general recommendations that stricter standards be applied in the upper-class courses open to *rite* students, that an effort be made to stimulate

[13] Called "degree with distinction" in the Long Range Policy Report. The name was subsequently changed to "degree with honors."

participation of a more active sort, through the assignment of reports, papers, etc., in these courses, and that it be made as easy as possible for the marginal student to take honors work, even though there might be a good chance that he would not actually qualify for an honors degree.

The final problem considered in these years was imposed from without. The Korean crisis forced at Amherst, as it did in many other colleges, consideration of the desirability of applying for an R.O.T.C. unit. There was, naturally, a good deal of concern about the impact of an R.O.T.C. program upon the new curriculum, especially that of the first two years. Surely something would have to give ground and that would not be the armed forces. The new curriculum had been framed in accordance with Aristotle's dictum that business is to make leisure possible and war is for the sake of peace. It was planned as a *post*war program and did not allow for mobilization on the campus. Despite these apprehensions, the faculty approved the installation of an R.O.T.C. unit. The apprehension, it turned out, was largely unfounded. A vast majority of the underclassmen enrolled carried this handicap with ease. While there is a provision allowing students taking the R.O.T.C. course to postpone a part of the required work in freshman year, little use has been made of it and, in the Dean's opinion, under present conditions few exceptions of this sort need be made. Indeed, since two hours of credit were granted for each semester of R.O.T.C. work in the first two years and three semester hour credits for each semester of the last two, the handicap seemed to work in reverse. *Rite* students taking R.O.T.C. courses might actually have an easier program in the last two years. In order to effect a better all-round balance between the R.O.T.C. and non-R.O.T.C. groups and also between lower-class and upper-class years the faculty voted that "The total number of credit-hours to be required for graduation should be increased from 120 to 128 with 64 credit-hours to be completed during the first two years and the same number during the last two years."

Except for a proposal intended to improve academic guidance for freshmen and sophomores in the choice of their electives, these are all of the defects in what might be called the regulatory mechanism of the curriculum during the seven years it has been in operation. That the defects inherent in the program itself had been partially foreseen and were dealt with only as it gradually became apparent that modifications should be made is evidence that they were imperfections, not radical faults in the structure.

THE NEW CURRICULUM

We come now to a review of the new curriculum. The questions we shall try to answer are these: What problems arose as the courses in the three required two-year sequences and the new type of foreign language courses were put into effect? To what degree have these problems been solved? What, in some detail, does the new program for the whole four years look like as it stands today? And, finally, what are some possible emendations or improvements which are suggested by this review?

In 1948-1949 the Committee on Educational Policy undertook a review of the new freshman curriculum as it was organized and taught in its first year of operation. They asked each of the groups responsible for these courses to give them information on:

1. Changes made from the original plan of the course during the giving of the course in 1947-1948 and for the year 1948-1949.
2. The effectiveness of the course from the point of view of the faculty (problems of administration, personnel, teaching, etc.).
3. The effectiveness of the course from the point of view of the students (problems of assignments, active participation, interest, attrition, etc.).
4. An appraisal of the two Big Ideas of the new curriculum: the laboratory method and the integration of previously separate subjects in one course.

The following year similar reports on the sophomore courses were requested. These reports showed that, with the exception of the science sequence, no outstanding difficulties had been encountered. The principal complaints were that in several of the courses sections were too large, that in some cases there were not enough contact hours for the most efficient teaching of the subject, that the teaching was arduous and time consuming (since a great deal of work had to be done at this stage on detailed planning of assignments), and that securing a competent staff for some of the courses would be a continuing problem. These troubles were largely incidental to the inauguration of a new program. The chairmen of the various groups had shown administrative skill, and with few exceptions the cooperation of all members of the various groups was excellent. Morale was generally high, and there appeared to be no disposition whatever to give up or seriously modify the venture. In reporting to the faculty on the results of the first year, the Committee on Educational Policy summed up their comments as follows:

> It can hardly be expected that such a novel venture as the new curriculum could at once spring into being full-grown and perfect. The original plans must be modified in the light of actual practice and during this period of readjustment and growth certain growing pains will appear. The teachers engaged in the new courses are well aware of this and are in general willing to undertake revisions of their plans and practices to fit actual situations. The realization that the students are part of the experiment and the practice of seeking their reactions are evidence of an open-minded attitude that is commendable. We as a Committee are highly pleased with the achievements that have been attained in one single year's operation.

Whatever modifications and improvements might be necessary could, it seemed, be made by the groups concerned without the need of intervention by the Committee on Educational Policy or the whole faculty. And this has been the case. Each of the groups responsible for these courses, with one possible exception, has maintained an experimental attitude toward its work. There has been no tendency toward falling into a routine merely because the courses are required. This is due to a number of reasons: The original enthusiasm of the participants has, in nearly all cases, been maintained; new personnel with fresh ideas have been entering the staffs;[14] and there has been within each group a strong sense of responsibility to the college as a whole for the effective teaching of these courses.

How, then, has each of the sequences developed, and what are they like at the present time? In the following account varying amounts of space are given to the description of these courses. While they are all presumably of equal importance for the education of our students, some of them are more unconventional than others. Hence, our exposition of them varies in degrees of particularity.

[14] Continuity is maintained in each of these courses by frequent staff meetings, usually once a week. It is in these meetings that the planning is done. The discussion in great detail of plans naturally generates a flow of suggestions for improvements and experiments.

The Two-Year Sequence in Science

In the earlier sections of this review we have described the controversy over the proposal by the Long Range Policy Committee of a two-year sequence in science based upon a series of topics from mathematics, physics, astronomy, chemistry, biology, and geology. The question raised by this proposal was: How can the two seemingly incompatible objectives be realized—a course which will be a *general* one as defined in the report and at the same time provide an *adequate* foundation for a subsequent major in mathematics or one of the natural sciences. The result was an uneasy compromise: a course in mathematics and physics required of all students in the freshman year in which it was hoped some real integration between the two subjects would be achieved, and a choice between two parallel courses in the sophomore year, a two-semester sequence of chemistry and biology or a year course in Evolution of the Earth and Man. It was expected the latter would be elected by nearly all of the sophomores who did not intend to major in science.

During the first year of the freshman course a number of faults in it became apparent. It was not too well taught, partly because it was new but also because there was a persistent difference of opinion within the group as to method, content, and objectives. In attempting to be a course for everyone which would also cover as much as possible of the usual first year's work in mathematics and physics it was at once too easy for some students and too difficult for a much larger number. Some integration of mathematics and physics was achieved in the first semester, but in the second the two subjects were taught in such a way that they were practically independent of each other.

As a consequence of this first year's experience, it was decided that the course should be split into two divisions. Students would be assigned to one or the other in accordance with their ability and preparation as evidenced by school records. The two sections would cover the same material, but the first group would study the topics assigned more intensively and make greater use of mathematics in the physics part of the course. It was proposed to introduce a certain amount of historical material into the work of the lower division, and in general its content and organization would approach somewhat more closely the intentions of the Long Range Policy Committee's recommendation. The work of the two sections was to be correlated in such a way that it would be possible for the abler students in the lower division to take further courses in mathematics or physics.

In examining this reorganization of the course, the Committee on Educational Policy made the following comment:

> This proposal represents a double compromise dictated by the great differences in ability and aptitude among the students and by the imposition of requirements *from above* that students entering the subsequent courses in mathematics and in physics must have attained a certain predetermined standard of proficiency in those subjects.
>
> The members of the Committee have approved this compromise with reluctance as, under the circumstances that exist, the most feasible proposal for next year. We believe that, difficult though this may be, it is possible and desirable to develop a freshman course in mathematics and physical science that conforms more closely to the recommendation of the *Long Range Policy Report*. Ideally, such a course would be organized and taught in a way that would make it interesting and stimulating to every student regardless of his aptitude and previous training in science. If in the present proposal as described below it is possible for the students in Division B, the division for those less well qualified in science, to elect the subsequent courses in mathematics and in physics, then, *a fortiori*, it should be possible for the students who next year will be in Division A to take a course similar to the one described in the *Long Range Policy Report* and still proceed to the subsequent courses in mathematics and in physics.
>
> We hope, therefore, that in another year the means will be found to reorganize Division A along the lines of Division B and that both sections will eventually develop into the sort of course that was originally proposed. Students who are prospective science majors, many of whom have a life-time of intensive specialization before them, need and should receive a broad and cultural introduction to their chosen subject.

In reply, a member of the science division who had a good deal of the responsibility for the conduct of the course stated an opinion with which many of his colleagues, but not all, would have agreed at that time:

> On page 2 of the June 2, 1948, report of The Committee on Educational Policy, the statement is made that the committee approved the compromise plan for the course as given this year with reluctance, and indi-

cates its desire that a freshman course in mathematics and physical science be developed that conforms more closely to the recommendation of the Long Range Policy Report. I have grave doubts that it will be possible within the foreseeable future to achieve this ideal. I am firmly opposed to giving a strictly pre-professional or technical course to our science majors, but, on the other hand, I feel quite strongly that the spread in scientific interest and aptitude on the part of our incoming freshmen is so vast that a *single approach and treatment* for the entire class would be a mistake. For this reason, it is my feeling that it would be far better to recognize that native interest and previous training have a greater significance in the matter of science courses than in history, for example. In languages, previous experience and aptitude is recognized, and it should be so in science. If this is done, there must necessarily be two divisions, perhaps even two completely separate courses. The approach to science in these two should not necessarily be the same, and the pace would certainly be different. For the faster group, which would presumably include most of those intending to major in science, the approach can and should be no less a "broad and cultural introduction to their chosen subject" than is the course designed to take into account the attitudes and capabilities of the larger group of freshmen whose interests are not mainly scientific.

This division of the students worked better, without doubt, for the type of course being given and was continued during the next two years. Then an overly large freshman class was admitted as a hedge against the draft. This necessitated dividing the class into three groups in order to avoid overcrowding of the lecture room and laboratory facilities and gave the opportunity for those who believed in the feasibility of the Long Range Policy Committee's original proposal to organize a separate course, the C division. But the students assigned to this course were those who had definitely decided not to major in mathematics or physics.

What the Long Range Policy Committee had asked for, however, was a course to be given for *all* students. Freshmen enrolled in the C division could not qualify for the subsequent courses in mathematics and physics. Once under way, this splitting off of a large fraction of the freshmen as a *definitely* "nonscience group" in the freshman year might well have created a reaction in which, eventually, two entirely separate groups of courses would have been set up, courses for the nonscience majors and for the science majors. This consequence would have been entirely inconsistent with the original recommendations.

Fortunately, Professor Arnold B. Arons was appointed a professor of physics for the next year and made cochairman with Professor Bailey LeF. Brown of the freshman course. Professor Arons was convinced that it was possible to go between the horns of the dilemma, general education *vs.* technical training, and he had workable ideas as to how it could be done. Science 1-2 was completely reorganized. It is again *one* course to be taken by all freshmen. The mathematics and physics are now fully integrated. And the course does achieve both of the desired objectives. The problem has been solved. How, then, was it done?[15]

Despite the common belief that these objectives are mutually antagonistic, or at least that it is not feasible to combine science majors and others in the same course, the personnel now teaching Science 1-2 are satisfied that this double objective *can* be achieved in a single course required of all students. The difficulty is not with the subject matter but is centered in the attitudes and points of view adopted by the teachers and on the kind of performance required of the student. A more detailed definition of what is involved here will be given after a description of the structure of Science 1-2.

As parent sciences, requiring a certain minimum of initial factual knowledge, mathematics and physics offer themselves as logical choices for a freshman course. Science 1-2 is based on a selection of subject matter from physics to illustrate the growth and development of certain important concepts in physical science, while at the same time mathematics is being treated in a way that will show its rise as an independent discipline and how it also became an integral part of physics.

Since the available lecture room can accommodate only one-half of the freshmen, the class is separated into two divisions of equal size. There are some differences between these two sections. Most of the students who have indicated a prior interest in science, engineering, and medicine are placed in the A division, regardless of previous scholastic record or aptitude scores. To the A division are also assigned some men who have good scholastic records and aptitude

[15] This account of the present Science 1-2 is composed from two memoranda by Professor Arons.

scores, but who may not have had either physics or trigonometry in secondary school. Care is taken not to debilitate the B division by removing all the able students, but in general the average entrance scores of the B group are significantly lower than those of the A group. The two divisions do identical work in physics, having the same lectures, assignments, examinations, and laboratory experiments, but the B division adopts a slightly slower pace in mathematics, leading to a lag of about two weeks behind the A division at the end of the first semester.

In mathematics, the first semester is devoted principally to basic concepts of differential and integral calculus as applied to the simplest mathematical functions (principally polynomials), emphasis being placed on the conceptual scheme rather than on facility with complex manipulations. The second semester continues with the development of some more fundamental theorems in the calculus.

In physics, the first semester is devoted to mechanics. The kinematics of uniformly accelerated linear motion is introduced first without calculus. However, immediate use is made of the analytical geometry of the straight line, concurrently being studied in the mathematics classes. Newton's laws of motion are then introduced and the static equilibrium of forces is treated as a special case of the second law. By the time rotational motion is considered (about the middle of the semester), the concepts of derivative and antiderivative are available from mathematics, and kinematics is redeveloped in terms of the calculus. The concepts of impulse, momentum, work, and energy are introduced directly in terms of the definite integral, which has by now been dealt with in the mathematics sections. The semester concludes with a brief discussion of the growth of planetary theories, intended to indicate the impact on our culture of the Newtonian synthesis of the laws of motion and the theory of gravitation. In the first half of the second semester, material is selected from the fields of wave motion, electricity, and optics. It is chosen in order to pave the way for devoting the second half of the semester to an analysis of the growth of our concepts of the structure of matter.

Two textbooks are used in the physics work: Holton's *Introduction to Concepts and Theories in Physical Science* and White's *Modern College Physics*. Holton's basic pattern is followed in the course, but the emphasis is frequently changed, much less time being spent on the growth of the planetary theories and considerably more time on fundamental concepts in both electricity and optics. Every possible advantage is taken of the fact that the student has these two texts. Parallel assignments are given and it is pointed out to the student how much more efficiently an understanding of concepts can be attained if more than one source of information is used in routine study. A conscious effort is made to arouse in the student an awareness that the printed word is not beyond criticism. He is frequently asked to compare and criticize parallel treatments in the two books.

This description of the physics course reveals the large gaps which have been left. Nothing is said about fluid mechanics, elasticity, thermodynamics, or alternating currents. Very little is said about sound, gases, and electric circuits. The science majors and premedical students take in their sophomore year a one-semester physics course which is designed to fill these gaps.

Throughout the freshman course every effort is made to focus the attention of the students on the *ideas* which are involved—the language, the concepts, and the inferences. It is explicitly pointed out that problems are simply the *means* to an end, not *ends* in themselves. In the final analysis, a student will consider important not what his teachers tell him but only what he is actually asked to do. He may hear repeated expressions of the wisest and most mature view of science and its ideas, but if he is then asked only to obtain the "answers" to trivial problems without a word of analysis or explanation drawn from within himself, he will naturally regard this performance—that for which he is being rewarded—as the only important thing, and will lightheartedly disregard all the significant ideas.

It is, therefore, the policy in this course to require the students to explain what they are doing on all quizzes and examinations. They are required to define terms, to translate algebraic statements into words, to identify the starting points in lines of reasoning, to recognize and distinguish between defined concepts and deduced information, to explain all the steps of a problem, and to interpret the results. At the same time every opportunity is taken to show them how the growth and use of language in science is a special application of the general concepts which are concurrently being developed in the freshman English course. The student is required (in parallel with the

English Department) to formulate statements entirely on his own in precise words which will make sense to other individuals. The English course is frequently referred to during our classes, and mention of the science course arises with increasing frequency in the English section meetings. This carry-over has produced clearly visible effects in student morale and attitude toward both courses and is proving to be a powerful educational force.

When a real understanding of concepts and lines of reasoning—as opposed to superficial facility at problem solving—is insisted on, it is found that all the freshmen are at virtually the same level regardless of their previous background. An approach of this sort not only makes possible but actually *necessitates* the treatment of the freshman class as a unit, without separation into advanced and beginner groups. This fact is a serious indictment of a secondary educational system which stuffs the minds of our youth with what Whitehead has called "inert ideas" instead of stimulating in them a comprehension of what precedes the end results on which they are drilled.

The tone adopted in the laboratory work is similar to that described in connection with class and lecture.[16] The student is expected to make his own verbal formulations. He writes up all experiments in a blank notebook. The experiments comprise simple situations with a minimum of "set" or elaborate apparatus. At every possible opportunity he is required to state his problem and then to investigate it. Virtually no specific instructions as to procedure are given. For example, in an experiment on magnetism each pair of students is given a needle and cup of water for making a crude compass, a couple of unmarked bar magnets, a battery, and a length of fine wire. Their instructions are to determine the polarity of the magnets and then to construct an experiment in which they study (in accordance with concepts previously discussed in class) the direction of torque on a current-carrying coil in a magnetic field. It is indicated that they should first write out a plan of experiment, execute it, and, since that will probably be a false start, amend the plan and continue until the experiment is successful—carefully writing up *everything*, including all failures and the reasons therefor. In an experiment in geometrical optics the students are given an optical bench and some simple lenses and told to construct experiments of their own, aimed

[16] A specimen laboratory assignment is given in Appendix I.

at investigating the concepts of real and virtual images as well as the validity of the simple lens equation.

All the ideas discussed above are *explicitly* called to the student's attention not once but many times. They are not ideas which are simply *implied* in the course of the work. This taking of the students into one's confidence in adult fashion, while being strict and demanding at the same time, has been principally responsible for the gratifying response in the course. Naturally, there is a wide range of performance with respect to these stringent requirements in both class and laboratory work, but about 90 per cent of the freshmen survive. The abler students visibly gain in strength and confidence. Nearly all of the students sense that they are undergoing a valuable educational experience; their attitude toward the course is good and morale is high.

In the sophomore year the students choose between a sequence of two semesters in Chemistry-Biology (Science 21-22) and the year course entitled Evolution of the Earth and Man (Science 23-24).[17] The original purpose of the Chemistry-Biology sequence was to serve as an introduction to those fields for students who intended to major in science. However, this sequence is taken by many who do not plan to major in science since, on the average, registrations in that course are only a little below those in Evolution of the Earth and Man. In the first semester a good deal of integration with the previous year is achieved by applying the knowledge of atomic structure gained in the physical sciences to chemical phenomena. This portion of the sequence leads through inorganic chemistry into the fundamentals of organic chemistry. Integration between the chemistry and the biology is brought about by this incorporation of organic chemistry. The organic chemistry is of great value in the biology course.

The students in the Chemistry-Biology sequence have already acquired a general familiarity with the language and methods of physical science and know something about atomic structure and the electrical properties of matter. With these advantages the time involved in presenting general chemistry can be shortened to an appreciable extent. The present one-semester course in chemistry, requiring as it does one-quarter of the student's time as opposed to one-fifth of his

[17] The discussion of these two courses is based on memoranda prepared by Professor George W. Kidder.

time under the old curriculum, is able to acquaint him with approximately 80 per cent of the material formerly covered in the year course, and there is a similar saving of time in the semester of biology.

The course in biology takes advantage of this background in chemistry and physics and relates those subjects to the study of living organisms. Biological material is considered as composed of chemical and physical units, and the student is encouraged to think of the various functions of living organisms in those terms. In particular, there is an integration with the first semester's work by a continuation of the discussion of the organic molecules important to metabolism. The first three weeks of Science 22 are concerned with the chemical reactions which yield energy for movement, synthesis, secretion, and so forth, in animal and plant organisms. Next, lecture and laboratory time is devoted to observations and discussions of the kinds of organisms present on the earth. A portion of the course is devoted to the physiology of organs and organ systems in plants and animals and to the major principles of biology. This sequence has been successful in giving preprofessional students (biology, biochemistry, chemistry) a grounding which enables them to proceed to more advanced courses during the second half of their sophomore year or during the first semester of their junior year.

The alternative, Evolution of the Earth and Man, was originally designed as an interdepartmental course for students not majoring in science. It is a cooperative course, the staff being drawn from the departments of astronomy, geology, and biology. The purpose of this course is to present the more important data upon which the generally accepted ideas of the evolution of the earth and man are based. The theory of evolution is an important unifying principle, which runs through the physical sciences, the earth sciences, and the biological sciences. It is a generalization which changed man's thoughts about the stars and the solar system and gradually overturned his ideas about his own origin, his relationship to other animals, his languages, customs, and institutions.

One of the members of the group who participated in its organization has described the course as follows:

> In many respects Evolution of the Earth and Man is the most distinctive course in the required curriculum in science. It combines a short discus-

sion of cosmic evolution, a review of the forces and processes which have molded the earth, a study of the changes in plants and animals through geologic time, a more detailed history of the vertebrates and especially those leading up to the ancestors of man, and a detailed study of the succession of men before and since the Ice Age. Genetics and especially the processes involved in heredity in man are discussed, and theories and causes of organic evolution are studied. The final month of the course is concerned with primitive human cultures, and evidences for the evolution of cultures are developed.[18]

Instead, then, of allowing the student to get these facts bit by bit from different sciences, this course attempts to collect the evidences of evolution in nature, whether on the earth, in the plant or animal kingdom, or in man and his cultures. The method of presenting the material in the course involves an integrated series of lectures, required reading, and laboratory exercises.[19] The different subdivisions are planned by a specialist in each of the scientific fields represented, and he gives the lectures in that part of the course. However, the presentation is unified, since each lecturer continues as a member of the staff throughout the entire year. Each of the two-hour laboratory periods has two staff members in charge. There are about twenty students in each laboratory section.

The Evolution of the Earth and Man is, in principle, the sort of course that was recommended by the Long Range Policy Committee. Since a successful course of this type had been given in prewar years by the late Professor Loomis, no one, we believe, anticipated the difficulties that arose in organizing and teaching it. Certain failures in this respect aroused an increasing discontent on the part of the students which came to a head in 1951-1952. Then, criticisms, with the replies by members of the staff, were aired in the *Amherst Student* and at a forum held under the auspices of a student organization. It was not the subject matter of the course but the manner of its presentation and some features of its administration which provoked this reaction.

Not all of the students who had taken the course were in agreement, but the criticisms subscribed to by many were that the course

[18] Harold H. Plough, "Science in the New Curriculum," *Amherst Alumni News*, 2 (1950), 138.

[19] A specimen laboratory assignment is given in Appendix I.

was crowded with so much detail that students often lost sight of the generalizations which these facts were supposed to support; that the examinations laid so much emphasis upon a precise mastery of these masses of detail that grades were excessively low and out of line with the general college average; that there was a lack of synchronization between lectures, readings, and laboratories; that the instructors often failed to explain adequately how materials drawn from diverse fields were related; and that the teaching was poor in some of the laboratory sections. It is easy to surmise that of these defects the low grades were most important to many students. For the teaching staff, the main difficulties with the course were the lack of a real interest in science on the part of many students, who appeared to be taking it as the easier way out of an onerous requirement; an excessive turnover in the staff—with the result that some of the teachers had an insufficient opportunity to accustom themselves to the type of instruction needed and to master the materials involved; disagreements among the members of the staff themselves as to methods which should be employed in the organization of the course; and, most important of all, the lack of adequately trained personnel.

All of these difficulties but one were extrinsic to the plan of the course and are now being remedied. A new feature meeting one of these criticisms is the introduction of transition lectures between each new phase of evolution to be presented, pointing out as clearly as possible the relation of new material to that which has already been treated. Yet the principal difficulty may well persist. With such a wide spread in disciplines, it is not surprising that inequalities in instruction are present. It is as impossible to expect a classical geologist to be familiar with biological details as it is to expect someone trained as a biologist to be familiar with geological details. This defect will continue, to a degree at least, until the course is manned by a staff for whom teaching it is their chief duty. In spite of this basic difficulty, there is no disposition among the staff to abandon the course and there is good reason to believe that in the future it can be far more successful than it has been in the past.

Amherst College has for many years been strong in science. Our account of this period of trial and error, inevitably perhaps, emphasizes the errors, for this has been, as could be expected, by far the most troublesome part of the new program. In fact, however, the successes have far outweighed the errors and have been cumulative. Today the situation is more favorable than it has ever been, and it seems certain that continuing improvement will occur.

One of the chief doubts regarding the science sequence has been resolved. It has been shown that for our students an introductory course in science for everyone *is* feasible. And there has been no need for students majoring in science to postpone some required course of freshman year in order to take additional work in that field. Moreover, little use has been made of the "escape clause" provided in the Long Range Policy Report: that a student planning to major in science may, at the discretion of the department in which he expects to do the work for the major, elect in his sophomore year a parallel course in a science in place of the required course. We are informed by the Dean that,

> . . . on the average, each year ten sophomores have been allowed to substitute Chemistry 24 in place of Science 22 because they were enrolled in the M. I. T. Program. As a general rule, all other students have been required to complete either Science 21-22 or Science 23-24. I do not think that more than three other exceptions have been made since the program has been in operation.

During this period the number of undergraduates interested in science has definitely increased. In part this may be due to the preselective influence of our science requirement: students lacking an interest in or a facility for science and knowing about this requirement may be more prone to apply elsewhere. In any event, more students are going on to graduate work in science, the number of students entering medical schools has nearly doubled since the war,[20]

[20] The figures are:

Amherst students who have *graduated* from medical schools:

Year	Number of Students
1938	14
1939	18
1940	10
1941	15
1942	27
1948	16
1949	15

Amherst students *admitted* to medical schools:

Year	Number of Students
1951	17
1952	25
1953	24
1954	33

and the number of students majoring in science has grown. In three recent senior classes the percentage of students majoring in science was: for 1951, 24.8 per cent; for 1952, 26.6 per cent; and for 1953, 31.6 per cent.[21] Our new curriculum appears to have fostered an increasing interest in mathematics and the natural sciences.

A Two-Year Sequence in History and Social Sciences

The social studies sequence in the new curriculum consists of two courses: The Development of Western Civilization (History 1-2), which is required of all freshmen, and Problems in American Civilization (American Studies 21-22), which is required of all sophomores.

The first of these courses, The Development of Western Civilization, is taught by the History Department. It is the continuation of an unusually successful course which had been given for many years. In fact, it was so popular that, though an elective, it was taken by almost all the freshmen. What the Long Range Policy Committee recommended was that the course be retained, but modified in a way that would make it more consistent with the schema of the new curriculum. This is not quite what happened. When the Committee on Educational Policy called for a review of the freshman year in 1948-1949, the report of the History 1-2 staff revealed a considerable discrepancy between the ideal and the reality. We quote at some length from this report:

Herewith please find our reply to your inquiry about the working of the "new" History 1. It is arranged under the topical headings which you suggest.

Changes made from the original plan of the course, as worked out during 1946-1947.

(a) 1947-1948. History 1 as planned, and History 1 as carried out, a) in 1947-1948, and, b) in 1948-1949, are three quite different things. The differences, in each case, arise from changes affecting the *laboratory* or *section* portions of the course.

In accordance with the aims of the Long Range Policy Committee, History 1 was planned as a five hour course: three hours for lectures and two for sections. In these section hours, not more than 15 students were to participate. The original plans, therefore, stressed the following

[21] These figures *exclude* psychology, which was shifted from the Division of Social Studies to the Division of Mathematics and the Natural Sciences in 1952-1953. Combined majors in which one-half is in a science are credited as a half.

objectives: a) study of the problems of sources, method, and analysis; b) presentation of individual, oral reports several times each semester; c) performance of some written projects; and, d) ample opportunity for discussion and questioning on all phases of the course: lectures, reading, and section assignments.

The dropping of one-half hour from the sections at the beginning of the course, led, necessarily, to the curtailing of projects and a reduction of the amount of material with which we could deal. Further reduction was necessary when it became evident that the over-all freshman load was too great. In most sections, consequently, only one oral report was possible, per semester, and even that had to be crowded in. The number of problems assigned was also reduced. . . .

(b) 1948-1949. The second year of the new course began with the further reduction of section periods by 30 minutes. This loss was rendered doubly effective by the increase of the over-all size of the course by numbers equivalent to two sections. At the same time, the staff was reduced by one member. Thus the number of sections was reduced by two, and the number of students per section was increased by three to nine individuals. Our sections now include from 18 to 24 men; the average is slightly over 21. During the second semester, due to sabbatic leave of one staff member, the number of students in each section will be still more enlarged. The result is, that the work of the sections is now down to routine crowding of efforts to "cover" or "get around" the group.

In replying to the committee's request for an appraisal in terms of what they called the two Big Ideas of the new curriculum, the "laboratory or seminar" method and the integration of previously separate subjects in one course, the staff of History 1-2 stated:

(a) Sections. We feel that the original plan cannot be assessed because it has not been applied. The value of the idea has been greatly decreased in application by the limitations of staff and the pressure of numbers, as well as by the reduction in time.

(b) Integration of previously separate subjects in one course. Not as much has been achieved in this connection as we had hoped. What we have done has been chiefly through the means of the lectures. Here, with our increased time, the equivalent of one-half hour per week, we have added a week's survey of the heritage of antiquity, a brief reference to the constitutional and legal heritage of the English Middle Ages, and a new emphasis on 19th century intellectual developments. In the sections we have added an introductory survey of the other "social sciences," and illustrative material of the medieval and modern periods.

History 1-2 as it is now given is concerned with a brief introduction to the nature and scope of the social sciences and a general survey of the development of Western (European) civilization from the Roman synthesis to the present time.[22] During the first semester the work deals with that period of European history between the disintegration of Roman civilization and the Revolutionary and Napoleonic era—terminating in 1815. The second semester is concerned with the nineteenth and the first half of the twentieth centuries.

There are three lectures per week, one-half of the third lecture hour being devoted to a written test which is uniform for all members of the course. The test "covers" the lectures of the preceding week and the so-called general reading. This general reading, about 100 pages—sometimes in several books—is concerned with a major topic: as, e.g., Mohammed and the Rise of Islam, the Medieval Church, the Commercial Revolution, the Enlightenment of the Eighteenth Century. The lectures are also concerned with major subjects, often chronologically, but not topically, related to those in the reading, such, for example, as the effort to explain the Disintegration of the Roman Civilization, Feudalism, or the Intellectual Revolution of the Seventeenth Century. The lectures also make an effort to supply something of historical continuity. A weekly map is given in addition to the reading.

There is one sixty-minute section meeting per week. It was originally planned that these sections should have a membership of not more than fifteen students. The increase in size of the sections has necessarily changed the character of the work originally planned for them—especially individual oral reports. For each weekly meeting of the section there is assigned, in addition to the general reading, a brief selection from one or more books dealing with an elaboration of topics treated in either the lectures or the general reading, or with some subject of contemporaneous importance not otherwise treated—such as Shaw's *St. Joan* (for the week dealing with medieval intellectual development); *Song of Roland* (the week dealing with the rise of feudalism); selections from Cellini's *Memoirs* and Machiavelli's

[22] The first three paragraphs of this section are from a memorandum by Laurence B. Packard.

Prince (the Renaissance week); selections from Condorcet and Rousseau (for the period of the Enlightenment). These section assignments vary widely in numbers of pages (from the whole of *St. Joan* to only fifteen or twenty pages from Hobbes' *Leviathan* and Locke's *Essays*)—depending on the nature of the reading. The assignments are discussed in the section meetings, where the procedure is normally: (a) review of the previous week's written test, which is returned, graded, for question and discussion; (b) explanation of the ensuing week's general reading assignment; (c) discussion of the specific section assignment; (d) general questions on lectures and reading.

So far as the attempt to achieve an integration with subject matter usually given in other courses is concerned, there have been changes, some of them of importance, since the adoption of the new curriculum. History 1-2 now incorporates material which would be normally associated with the social sciences, and the students become acquainted, at least, with their scope and general point of view. The general concept of these subjects as social studies, their interrelations, and their common use of historical material are examined—superficially, perhaps, but in a way that is instructive to most freshman. In particular, the section assignments frequently make use of readings which connect history with other fields. Instances besides those mentioned in the description of the course are selections from Lewis Mumford, *Technics and Civilization*, in dealing with the Industrial Revolution, and from the *Communist Manifesto* to illustrate the development of socialism, and a case study of the conflict between science and religion in the nineteenth century based on Thomas Le Duc's *Piety and Intellect at Amherst College, 1865-1912.*

However, there has been little effort to introduce the "laboratory or seminar" method into the work of the sections. Assignments for the sections are usually treated in the same way as the other readings for the course. Most of them are discussed in about the same way as in the usual "quiz sections" employed in many large courses. Scant attempt is made to introduce students to the methods of the historian, to examine the nature of historical data and to raise questions concerning the validity of historical evidence. Of course, individual instructors occasionally bring up some of these questions, but there is no uniform or sustained effort to do so.

Now there is no intrinsic reason why the course could not be so organized as to make use of the section periods in the way recommended in the Long Range Policy Report. If a sixty-minute section is too short, more time could be found by giving fewer lectures, say three one week and two the next, or by having section meetings only once in two weeks for a longer period. It should also be possible to plan the assignments for most of these section meetings as "problems" on which the members of the group would be required to prepare oral and written reports. To do this effectively the sections should not be larger than a maximum of fifteen (in 1954-1955 they had an average of nineteen students), and it would be necessary for the staff to plan the assignments and to follow a fairly uniform procedure in the section periods in a way similar to that employed in the sophomore course in American Civilization. There are, we repeat, no important *intrinsic* difficulties involved in a reorganization of this kind. We believe that it would improve the course, good though it now is, and we hope that a reform of this sort may be put into effect.

The second part of the required social studies sequence, the sophomore course called Problems in American Civilization, was developed as an entirely new offering in accordance with the recommendation of the report of the Faculty Committee on Long Range Policy.[23] Planned by representatives of several departments (economics, history, English, philosophy, and political science), emphasis was placed on the laboratory or problem approach. Certain assumptions were made in planning the course. The most important of these were: first, that the students had already acquired considerable factual knowledge in European and American history as a result of taking earlier courses in these subjects; second, that the general-survey type of course in which the instructor and textbook writer do most of the thinking and organizing and the students memorize the facts and take the notes was not desired; third, that the course should be centered on significant problems which required the student to work out his own solutions; fourth, that the attempt at an integration of the various social sciences should not be sought by separating the work in the various fields (for example, economics, English, history, philosophy, political science, and sociology) but by applying all of these approaches

[23] See above, pp. 53-55. This discussion of Problems in American Civilization is taken from an article by Professor George R. Taylor, "Meeting the Social Studies Where They Are," *Journal of Higher Education*, 23 (1952), 68-74.

in so far as they were applicable to the solution of each problem, thus promoting a natural synthesis which arises out of the problem itself; fifth, that all the members of the class should have a common reading assignment and a common day for reporting their conclusions to the end that a community of interest and of discussion would be created; and sixth, that the heart of the course should be in the seminars or laboratories—that is, small discussion groups led by a teacher.

On the basis of these assumptions the course has been developed each year around twelve problems in American civilization, eight historical and four contemporary.[24] The topics are chosen with an eye to securing significant problems—those which have given rise to public controversy and honest disagreement. Even relatively small problems have been deemed acceptable if they have large implications. New problems (at least half of those used) have been prepared each year. This has several advantages. It permits the discovery by actual trial of those problems which are most suitable, and it keeps the staff alert and interested. It does necessitate the preparation each year of new lectures by members of the staff—not a bad provision in a world in which wine improves with age but lectures rarely do.

A typical year's program of twelve problems follows:

Historical Problems

1. Puritanism in Early America
2. The Declaration of Independence and the Constitution
3. The Transcendentalist Revolt Against Materialism
4. Slavery as a Cause of the Civil War
5. John D. Rockefeller: Robber Baron or Industrial Statesman?
6. The Turner Thesis concerning the Role of the Frontier in American History
7. Pragmatism and American Culture
8. The New Deal: Revolution or Evolution?

Contemporary Problems

9. The Place of Loyalty Tests in Our Democracy
10. Industry-Wide Collective Bargaining
11. National Health Insurance
12. American Aid to Western Europe

[24] In some instances only five problems have been assigned during a semester.

Great care has gone into the selection of the readings on the various assignments. Materials are chosen which will introduce the student to the issues and place before him contrasting points of view. For this purpose items are garnered from books, periodicals, newspapers, government documents, pamphlets, speeches, and letters. Though in part descriptive, the readings are largely analytical and interpretative.[25]

Each problem constitutes a two weeks' (sometime a three weeks') assignment. In connection with each problem the student attends about five lectures. These lectures, which are given before the whole class of about 250 students, are used for various purposes. Often they provide supplementary information not furnished by the readings. Occasionally they present technical analysis. Thus on the problem "Roosevelt, Wilson, and the Trusts," two lectures of this character were included in 1949-1950—one on competitive theory and one on monopoly theory. The lectures given in connection with the historical problems are rarely designed to defend a point of view. The assigned readings adequately perform that function. However, for the current problems, outside speakers are often secured who are prepared to urge particular solutions. In such cases care is taken to make sure that a reasonable balance is maintained among the varying viewpoints represented. Occasionally the lecture period has been used for a panel discussion of the problem. The chairman of the forum is a member of the teaching staff. The speakers may be members of the staff or, as has been more frequently the case, students chosen from the class who represent differing viewpoints. The first twenty minutes of the forum are devoted to formal statements by the speakers; during the last part of the hour students raise questions from the floor. These sessions have been successful in stimulating student interest before groups which are, of course, much larger than the discussion sessions. At times, movies and phonograph records have been used during part of the lecture period.

The program on each problem culminates in a two-hour seminar or laboratory period. Two days before this meeting each student turns in to his seminar teacher a three-page analytical paper in which he

[25] Twenty-two volumes of these readings have been published by D. C. Heath & Company. For a list of these and other problems that have been used in the course see Appendix I.

states his conclusion on the problem and attempts to defend it. The student is not asked to prepare a summary of the facts or of the arguments in the readings. Instead he is expected to express at least a tentative conclusion on the problem and to defend the point of view adopted. In doing this he is encouraged to show an awareness of his assumptions, to deal with essential matters of definition, to weigh alternative solutions, and to reason logically to his conclusion.

Having read the students' papers, the teacher meets with thirteen to seventeen students in the seminar session for discussion of the issues. The conduct of these sessions varies with the individual instructor and the subject, but their essential purpose is to provide open discussion in which the students actively participate. The function of the teacher is not to lead the students to any particular conclusion. It is rather to make sure that in the clash of opinions premises are recognized and alternative assumptions considered, that meanings are clarified, that use is made of pertinent factual materials and analytical methods, and that conclusions are reasonably and logically derived.

An important procedural aspect of the plan is that all papers are due at the same time and that all laboratory sessions are held on the same day and as nearly as possible at the same hour. Thus the whole sophomore class, roughly one-fourth of the college, is directly concerned with the same problem during the same two-weeks period. Indirectly, of course, many students from outside the course are drawn into the discussions. As a result, a great deal of self-education goes on in fraternity houses, dormitories, and dining halls.

The plan and the procedures of this course are perhaps best understood by examining an assignment for a two-weeks period. The following is such a program:

THE GOSPEL OF DEMOCRACY AND OF WEALTH

	Lecture Topics
Friday	Laissez faire: Theory and Practice
Monday	The Supreme Court and Capitalism
Wednesday	Politics after the Civil War
Friday	The Coming of Evolution
Monday	Democracy and Culture: Whitman and Arnold (papers due)
Wednesday	Seminars
Friday	Forum led by members of the class

Assignment

A. Both Whitman and Carnegie raise the question as to the future of democracy in this country. Write a paper of not more than 750 words in which you show: . . . in what each of these two men chiefly placed his hope of the future and . . . why you are more nearly in agreement with one or the other of these two authors.

B. Read Gail Kennedy (editor), *Democracy and the Gospel of Wealth* (Boston: D. C. Heath & Company, 1950).

C. Supplementary reading: (Six to eight books or articles are usually suggested for optional reading.)

The essential purposes of this course are: first, to lead the student to become interested in and to think about the problems of modern society, and second, to encourage him to form relevant and conscious judgments as to issues and policies.

Perhaps not much need be said about the first of these objectives, for the use of the problem method has been so effective in arousing the student's interest and in stimulating his thinking that it seems unnecessary to labor this point. But it should be noted that, since the course serves as a general introduction to the social sciences, its chief emphasis is on those aspects of living together which are called economic, political, and sociological. Obviously, this does not preclude the consideration of other aspects such as the aesthetic or the religious, or mean that they are not given careful attention. Actually, the aspects to which attention is directed tend to grow out of the problem chosen.

The second purpose—to lead the student to reach relevant value judgments—is peculiarly important, especially because it is so often neglected or even deliberately avoided in courses in the social sciences. "Relevant judgments" are understood to mean those which grow out of recognized assumptions, in which alternative assumptions or values are considered, in which there is a reasonable familiarity with the facts, and in which the conclusions follow logically. It is, of course, obvious that nearly every word in this definition cries out for further explanation, but we shall have to leave it as it stands in the hope that it is sufficiently meaningful. Let it be added merely that by a "reasonable familiarity with the facts" we mean what is feasible and practicable under the circumstances—a difficult quantitative decision which has to be made by the instructor in connection with each problem. It is in the nature of the case that all of the facts are never in. Most decisions which we must make as individuals and as citizens are customarily and necessarily made on the basis of a very limited acquaintance with the facts. Furthermore, as emphasized later, the question is not merely a matter of how many facts but also of whose facts. For this reason, if for no other, we subject the students to facts as summarized by authorities who are in fundamental disagreement concerning the solution of the problem.

Since the unusual nature of this course has led to many questions, an attempt is made in what follows to state two of the more important of these and to try to answer them.

In abandoning the attempt at a broad survey do you not also sacrifice continuity? Do not your problems occur in a vacuum? The background for the problems, which is provided to some extent in the lectures and readings, appears to be merely ancillary to the problems. Should not students be shown how problems really emerge only from their background?

The program does largely sacrifice chronological continuity, for, although the historical problems ordinarily follow each other in chronological order, there are often large time gaps between them. On the other hand, there are other kinds of continuity or unity besides the merely chronological. The unity provided by this course is primarily one of method and of purpose.

As to the statement that "problems really emerge only from their background," we suggest that backgrounds emerge from problems. In fact, the writer or student of history faced with the almost endless welter of facts selects those which he regards as important to the problem or problems he wishes to solve. These factual materials thus become background. In a sense, the problem determines its own background. Why deprive the student of the advantage of seeing the problem first and then studying the background, which thus becomes meaningful in the light of the problem? The question of how much background should be included becomes a matter of coverage. Complete examination of background is never attained. A fair case can be made for the contention that the students acquire a better background of knowledge from a study of the twelve problems which they make in this course than is usually secured in courses of other types.

How can the student be expected to deal with such difficult problems before he has learned the techniques of analysis provided by the various social sciences? Should not discussion of such problems be postponed until the students have been trained in the techniques employed in economic theory, comparative government, statistics, historical research, and so on?

This is a thorny question which has had varying answers in the social studies. Ideally, neither the student nor the citizen should have to make important decisions until he has mastered many difficult techniques. However, three observations may be made in this connection: In the teaching of mathematics and the natural sciences, there is often a logical, sequential order in which problems must be approached. Thus, understanding of the binomial theorem rests upon previous mastery of a whole series of algebraic operations in which the student proceeds from the simple to the complex. By analogy, it is often assumed that teaching in the social studies should follow a similar logical pattern. This conclusion is seriously questioned. The nature of the materials for the social studies is fundamentally different from that of the mathematical. Neither chronological sequences nor syllogistic systems provide a satisfactory approach to the social studies. Parenthetically it may be noted that even in the study of mathematics and foreign languages there has been a movement toward presenting the student in the first instance with the complex problem. For example, in foreign language teaching, the older method of starting with general rules and drill in grammar is being largely abandoned, at least as the exclusive approach to the acquisition of a reading and speaking knowledge.

Without belittling the tools of analysis which have been developed in the social sciences it may be noted that there has been a growing tendency to teach the social studies not in the abstract but in connection with concrete problems. Thus the older notion that the student should not study economic problems before he has secured a thorough grounding in economic theory has largely given way to an approach in which theory and practice have been mingled.

Many students never have an opportunity for advanced work in the social studies or a special study of the techniques of analysis used in connection with them, although as citizens they will have to deal with these and similar problems. This course, although it cannot give the student a mastery of the formal studies, can at least give him some appreciation of the need for careful analysis and of the importance of exposing and considering assumptions. On the one hand, he will gain an appreciation of the contribution which the expert may make toward analyzing certain aspects of experience; on the other, he may acquire a healthy skepticism of the competence of such experts to select the values or assumptions from which their chains of reasoning seem to follow.

It is not contended that the program described provides a final answer to the problem of the introductory social studies course in all institutions and under all conditions. But it can be reported that it has proved an exciting adventure in genuine education for both students and teachers.

A Two-Year Sequence in Humanities.[26]

As adopted, the Humanities sequence in the first two years follows closely the recommendations in the report (pp. 55-65). A half-course in humanities, or in directed general reading, shares one-fourth of the freshman program with a half-course in writing, given in the English Department. The two courses are taken concurrently throughout the year; English 1-2 meets three hours a week the first semester and two the second while for Humanities the hours are two in the first and three in the second semester.

Of the two reading courses proposed in the report, Humanities A and Humanities B, the second proved to present difficulties of staffing which led to its being withdrawn from consideration. The first of the two proposed courses, now called Humanities 1-2, was instituted as described in the report. It is of a familiar type, perhaps best known through the course given for many years at Columbia College, and therefore needs little description here. Since at Amherst, however, it is a half-course, the amount of reading that can be assigned and discussed is more limited than is usual in such courses elsewhere.

The reading list has varied somewhat from year to year, but in

[26] This section incorporates, with some additions, contributions by the following: Humanities 1-2, Professor George B. Funnell; English 1-2, Professor Theodore Baird; Humanities 21-22, Professor Vincent Morgan; and English 21-22, Professor Reuben A. Brower and Professor César L. Barber.

general the first semester is given over to Greek literature and to the Bible and the second semester to a few books selected from the medieval, Renaissance, and modern periods.[27] It is not a course in world literature or in the history of ideas; time limitations make such ambitions impossible. Little attempt is made at "coverage." Each book is read for whatever can be got out of it, with the hope that by the end of the year some sense of a kind of continuity will have been acquired.

The success of a particular book clearly depends to some extent on the quality of the translation used, and finding the right translation is a persistent problem. But the number of good ones available has been increasing and this problem is not a serious one.

The procedures of the course can be dealt with briefly. The work is carried on entirely in sections, theoretically in "small" sections. Their average size varies from twenty to twenty-five. There is a strong feeling among the teachers that more satisfactory results would be obtained if this number could be kept down to about fifteen. In principle the class is a discussion, and twenty is often too many for a good discussion. Doubtless some teachers do much, perhaps even too much, of the talking themselves, but there are no formal lectures. Short tests are frequent, particularly in the early stages. Since the inception of the course there has been increasing latitude in the various sections as to what form such tests take and when they are given. The longer examinations, however, are the same for all sections. As to classroom method, none is imposed. Each teacher finds his own. This problem is sometimes discussed in staff meetings, but on the whole, considering the nature of the subject matter and the character of the teaching group, such freedom seems to offer the best prospect of good results.

The teaching group has included members of the Departments of the Classics, English, French, German, Italian, Spanish, History, Philosophy, and Religion. The staff holds regularly weekly meetings, and the variety of professional background among its members has made for a good deal of both enjoyable and fruitful discussion. It has been customary for teachers to take turns in preparing background

[27] A list of the readings used in 1952-1953 and the responses of students in the course to a questionnaire on the readings assigned in 1948-1949 are given in Appendix I.

material in the planning of assignments and in making up tests. The whole group participates in preparing the longer examinations.

The maintenance of a wholly satisfactory teaching group has, however, become more rather than less difficult. The course is not an easy one to teach; many who have taught in it, and who seem to have enjoyed doing so, on the whole, have admitted that they found it the most difficult part of their teaching assignment. It forces everyone to go outside the limits of his particular professional interest, of his "subject," and while this is probably a good thing it is not always easy. To do it successfully involves a willingness to submerge at least some of one's personal enthusiasms or prejudices in the common enterprise of a fairly large group, and this necessitates a real belief in the value of the common enterprise. If such can be assumed, then the inevitable compromises can be cheerfully accepted. If an individual cannot achieve this, he will be unhappy in the course, and an unhappy teacher makes for bad results. It is clearly a mistake to assume that this course can be well taught by anyone with time available. Interest and fundamental belief in it, and a willingness to cooperate, are essential.

Even more is needed. Many who are well prepared to teach the conventional "subject matter" type of course are not adept at participation in one of this kind. Here, and in the sophomore course in Music, Fine Arts and Drama—and in a different way in the sophomore American Studies course—the "instructor," because he is for a great part of the time operating outside of the boundaries of his professional field, is put on a par with an unusually resourceful and intelligent student who is making the most of his inadequate knowledge. The teacher's only claim to superiority must lie in his greater range and superior depth of culture. He has to be, in the best sense of the term, a "gentleman amateur." If the student is asked to learn in most of his courses what people *do* in those specific fields, as historians, physicists, and the like, here he is confronted with a situation in which he is expected to acquire a more general pattern of behavior—that of the cultivated man dealing with elements of our cultural heritage and with matters of common social concern.

In this all-important matter of staff a few trends may be noted, not so much by way of adverse criticism as to provoke reflection. In the first year the course was given, 1947-1948, of the nine teachers working in it only one was an instructor. In 1953-1954 fifteen men were concerned with the course in at least one semester, and of these seven were instructors. The figure fifteen itself deserves comment: six of these men taught in the course for one semester only. Although sabbatical leaves and departmental commitments make such an arrangement necessary, it is possible that there is a loss when the same teacher cannot carry the whole project through.

There has also been a change, though a less marked one, in the professional interests represented in the staff. In its first year the group included only one man whose primary professional interest was neither literary nor philosophical. In the current year the number of such men has risen to four. These differences in age, in experience, and in first loyalties, so to speak, affect the nature of the teaching group and would appear to make the achievement of a satisfactory unanimity on some basic points somewhat more difficult than it was five years ago.

To maintain for such a course an adequate teaching staff, drawn *in toto* from members of other academic departments, becomes a college enterprise and one that requires careful planning and constant watching. Easy solutions, here even more than elsewhere, are to be avoided.

In many ways the course seems to have worked out well. Students accept it, on the whole, with few complaints; they do the work with only occasional lapses; in many cases they give evidence of enjoying it, although, since it is a required course, there are inevitably some students with little natural inclination for reading of this kind who find it dull. Yet many of those who seldom participate in class discussion show in their written work that they have not only done the reading but also done quite a little thinking about it. Freshman Humanities forms, it seems clear, a kind of general background for more advanced work of various sorts in literature and in philosophy. On the other hand, the freshman course appears to have had little or no effect in increasing upperclass registration in such advanced courses, which, in general, are smaller than in the prewar period. This may be due, of course, partly to the "four-course" system and partly to the climate of opinion in these times.

So far as long-range results are concerned, it is probably too early to form a judgment. What the alumni committee referred to as a contribution to "serious leisure" in adult life remains a hope.

The other required freshman course in the Humanities sequence has been described for us by Professor Theodore Baird as follows:

"What is now known as English 1-2, described in the college catalogue by the word 'Composition,' has a history which goes back some ten years before the new curriculum. It first appeared in 1938-1939 as one of three English courses open to freshmen, the other two being literary history and appreciation. With the beginning of the new curriculum in 1947-1948 English 1-2 was required of all freshmen. It had by that time become entirely a writing course, and the responsibility for a freshman's literary education was taken over by Humanities 1-2.

"In English 1c, as the course was originally called, we began with several purposes: to teach grammar, to read books as material for writing, to analyze passages somewhat in the manner of the early I. A. Richards. With further experience we limited and defined our aims and methods, discovering what we could do, learning about ourselves as teachers by learning something about students. For example, under pressure of the various army programs (we taught English to about 1600 soldiers) we proved to ourselves that we could conduct a course under almost the worst possible conditions; we could create an English course we believed in out of nothing. Or almost nothing. We found that we could operate effectively when we had nothing more to work with than a classroom full of students, when, in other words, we could not count on the students doing any work for us outside our classroom. This was a revelation, for we proved that we could confidently teach writing to almost any group of people so long as we could catch their attention for but a moment. All we had to do was tell them to go ahead and write, and when asked what about, all we had to say was, tell us what you know.

"English 1-2 is conducted entirely in sections—we have come to regard twenty-five as a small class—and for each meeting the student writes a paper on an assigned subject. The course is entirely self-supporting, as there is neither textbook nor outside reading. We make constant use of the mimeographing machine, regularly bringing to class examples of the student's work for comment and reconstruction. Our usual procedure is to go over the next assignment, consider the examples of the last paper and reconstruct them, and ask what this shows about doing the next assignment. We correct but do not grade individual papers.

"The assignments are our leading questions, our instruments for putting the student in a special position to answer a question, yet a list of them does not give an adequate idea of what goes on until it is made plain what function they serve. They are our means of locating that situation in which the student knows what he is talking about, in which he feels the desire to express what he knows. When we make an assignment we do not say 'Discuss ——' or 'Write a paper about ——,' but give such explicit directions that once they are followed the student will find himself saying something he did not know he could say. Hence our assignments are like a scenario rather than a syllabus, an argument of the play rather than the play itself, and to be understood a particular assignment should always be placed in the context of a classroom (where emphasis varies from section to section) and read in terms of the student's actual performance. For the teacher the assignments are his means of controlling conversation, of saying over and over again and always more particularly, tell us what you know. They are stimuli, springboards, invitations to stand on the edge of an abyss, bear traps, land mines, and often enough they don't work.

"The following assignments are taken from a sequence dealing with the common phrase 'on the spot' and making use of maps and a photograph:

1. Here is a map of the Amherst Campus.
   a. Let us assume you are now within the area contained in this map and you recognize this as a map of the spot you are now on. What did you do to recognize this?
   b. Define in the context of (a) "the spot you are now on."
2. Here is a photograph, an air view of Amherst College.
   a. Let us assume you are now in the middle of the area contained in the photograph and you recognize this as a photograph of the spot you are now on. What did you do to recognize this?
   b. Define in the context of (a) "the spot you are now on."
   c. What difference do you see between this spot and the one in the above assignment?
3. Here is a road map of southern New England.
   a. What did you do to recognize that this is a map of the spot you are now on?
   b. Define in the context of (a) "the spot you are now on."

   c. What differences do you see between this spot and the ones in assignments above?
   d. What does it mean to be on a particular spot?
4. What spot do you take it you are now on?
   a. Give three different labels, all new, all fair enough, to locate the spot you are now on.
   b. Now tell what you are doing and then define your location, the spot you are now on, in terms of what you are doing.
   c. Express in general terms and in a coherent paragraph the difference in the act of defining in (a) and (b).
5. "The spot in the phrase 'on the spot' can be described as both anywhere and nowhere."

   Tell what this sentence means by (a) explaining what it means when the spot in the phrase "on the spot" is anywhere, (b) when the spot in the phrase "on the spot" is nowhere.

"In planning assignments we first make a rough distinction in order to conform to the shape of the college year and say that we shall devote the first term to considering a student's knowledge as derived from his experience outside the classroom, the second term to what he has learned from teachers in school. And beginning wherever our best judgment at the moment suggests, we break into the subject of extracurricular activities by marking off some area as a promising subject for writing. Thus one term we looked at games and asked the student a great number of particular questions about what he did and how he did it. Other years we have concentrated on the student's experience with machines, examined the situation of the apprentice who learns by imitating another's actions, the feeling of being in conflict with another person, the peculiar uncertainty when faced with a mystery or a puzzle, the process of finding where you are by reading a map. The second term we ask questions about the student's formal education, that part of his life which always seems to him so unphysical, so purely mental, inviting him to tell us what he does as a historian and as a scientist. What does he do when, turning the pages of his required reading, he isolates an Important Fact? What does he do when, running upstairs or rolling a ball down an incline, he takes a Measurement? I must emphasize at this point that in directing the student's attention to football or mathematics or what not the teachers of English 1-2 are constantly aware of their own position. We are not teaching games or how to work problems, and if in the classroom a dispute arises over some technique the student must settle it for himself. We are teachers of composition. We can tell the student that we do not understand something he has written, perhaps what it is we do not understand, but the burden of knowledge is his.

"By means of our many assignments ever shifting the approach to the problem of the writer we try to put the student in the position where he can see for himself what his subject may be. For example, when the student writes about his activities as a historian he may begin with something as apparently remote as his memories of his own grandfather; then by taking describable steps he translates his personal recollections into statements about American history. Or he may begin his account of his activities as a scientist by reading the instruments in the campus weather station and again by taking describable steps make a larger statement which might be called sciēntific. Our art as teachers lies in finding examples so simple that when we talk about them we are reasonably sure that we are all talking about the same action.

"Of course we try to do many things during the hours spent in the classrooms and in the written comments on particular papers besides isolate in a particular action the element of order. As we go along we try to define necessary words so that the student makes for himself a rhetorical vocabulary by which he is able to talk about the act of writing. We try to arouse in the writer an awareness of his relation to his subject and his audience, asking the devastating question: Who—besides his English teacher—could possibly be interested in what he writes? We consider the meaning of technical vocabulary in general and train the student in asking what a word in a given context points at. But most important of all, I think, is our effort in encouraging a student to see his subject so that he knows what he is writing about. And always in the back of the teacher's mind is the desire to put the student in that position where he feels he is speaking from his own experience. The student's motivation, as always, eludes us.

"This, then, tells something about English 1-2. No account can convey what the course is like day by day and in the student's papers. It is probably both better and worse than you think. Certainly its existence lies in what the student actually, finally does, not in what the teacher plans and contrives. It is a drama, each year a new plot takes shape, and like the drama it has its lively and its dull moments. There are always some members of the audience who are bored, who wish they were somewhere else, and this seems understandable. Must all students in a college like all their courses all the time? Then there are a few students who never recover from the shock of discovering that this is not like the usual freshman English course, and they tell us with perfect regularity two or three times a week throughout the year that they do not understand—that and no more, they do not understand. Still others detect a philosophy and in arguing with us use hard words like "pragmatism" and ask us to take the example $2+2=5$. This is perplexing, for then the teacher may well feel he has lost the thread of discourse. He sees himself not as an instructor issuing instructions about how to write but as someone who picks up the pieces wherever they may be found and tries to see how they can be put together in some kind of shape, any kind of shape. It is this act of going together which is his concern, and he is a teacher, as the catalogue says, of Composition.

"Let it also be added that during the year some decent writing does get done, and the student sees it happen. He may even say, as one surprised, 'Why, I know what I am talking about.' And there may be by-products. The student may come to respect good writing, however plain. He may even recognize as the marvel it is the human being's power of making order out of chaos."

Although the possibility of a single required humanities course for all sophomores was considered, to institute such a course under present conditions seemed neither practicable nor advisable. With the field so large, and with individual tastes or inclinations so varied, it was thought better to make possible a choice, though the requirement as it stands insures that all students will have the *experience* of a second year in the general field.

The choice, though considerable, is not wholly free. In literature, in the narrower sense, a student may elect an approved course in any of various foreign literatures or in English: in practice the sophomore course, English 21-22, is each year elected by a sufficiently large number to be for many students a part of their "core" curriculum. Introductory courses in philosophy and religion, and the course in the History Department called Classical Civilization, are also approved; in all of these a considerable amount of reading in primary texts is the rule.

In the field of the "nonverbal" arts an entirely new course has been established, which to a large extent replaces the previous introductory courses in the separate subjects.

This new course, Humanities 21-22, An Introduction to Fine Arts, Music and Drama, is a creation of, and has been developed by, the members of the Departments of Fine Arts, Music, and Dramatic Arts. As in all new courses, and perhaps more than in many, it has changed with repetition, and it will doubtless change further. But in the main its development has been in line with the general purposes of such a course as expressed in the report (pp. 63-64): first, to acquaint the students with the vocabulary, materials, and methods peculiar to each of the three fields, without regard to chronology and with no attempt at interrelation, and second, to proceed to a consideration, through selected examples, of the relation of the arts to each other and to the times that produced them, with no pretense, however, of historical "coverage." These two aims became the basis of the work of the two semesters. Since the course is, so far as we are aware, without parallel, it should be described in some detail.

In the first semester each of the three fields is given an approximately equal share of the available time for an introduction to its materials and methods, its "vocabulary and grammar." This leads to a consideration: in the fine arts, of line, form, color, composition, and technique in drawing, painting, sculpture, and architecture; in music, of notation, rhythm, melody, texture, harmony, forms, timbre, and interpretation; in the dramatic field, of types of drama, dramatic structure and values, stage composition and movement, setting and lighting.

Illustrative material is drawn from any useful source, since there is no historical emphasis.[28] The guiding principle is to train the eye, the ear, and the mind. Occasionally material that illustrates a specific problem under consideration may be useful also as a preparation for the work of the second semester, e.g., Michelangelo's "Creation of Man" or Sophocles' *Oedipus the King*. Except for the drama, outside reading is replaced by direct contact with works of art, through originals, reproductions, photographs, and recorded music; in the case of drama, study of photographs and scene designs and attendance at productions support the reading of the plays.

[28] A listing of typical materials studied in this course is given in Appendix I.

Along with lectures and demonstrations to the entire class, weekly laboratory sections (average size twenty) give an opportunity for discussion, questions, and active demonstration. In the fine arts and in drama considerable use is made of problems for solution outside of class, to serve as background for discussion in the sections. For example, sections in fine arts may be asked to observe, and to list in order, "all the ways in which the Doric order as used on the Chapel differs from the correct Greek Doric order which was its inspiration." An assignment in drama may ask the students to determine the most expressive arrangement of the characters on the stage at particular moments in Maxwell Anderson's *Winterset*, and to comment on the basic geometrical forms, emphatic figures, and compositional balance in a series of photographs of scenes from other plays. In music the lack of "literacy" makes this kind of problem almost useless: the considerable technical knowledge necessary for significant comment on musical matters tends to rule out any extended discussion. The laboratory periods in music are given over largely to practice in reading a score or in listening to specific compositions, for which directional notes are provided, with opportunity for questions and answers.

After this foundation, the principal objective of the second semester is to illustrate the relation of the arts to each other and to the intellectual and social conditions which foster them. The main work of the semester is planned around five epochs—the age of Pericles, the age of the Church, the period of humanism, the Romantic period, and the twentieth century. Between the last two epochs is interjected an analysis of the significance of three artists of the late nineteenth century, Ibsen, Rodin, and Wagner, as bridges from the nineteenth to the twentieth century.

This has been the more difficult section of the course from the point of view of the teachers, and its problems are perhaps not yet entirely solved. The material is integrated in various ways: through the lectures, by rapid alternation and juxtaposition of illustrative material from the different media, and by test questions requiring correlation on the part of the student.

The course is taught by the Departments of Fine Arts, Music, and Dramatic Arts. All members of these departments participate, at one time or another, in section work, and new members of the staff attend all the lectures. The enrollment rose from 75 in 1948-1949, the first year, to over 130 for 1951-1952.[29] There is commonly a considerable falling off in the second semester, which may be partially due to the fact that the first semester's work is of necessity somewhat technical and that some students may not realize that their investment is due to pay its dividends in the second semester. As the course becomes better known, realization of this may spread. In the meantime, the large majority who complete the course would seem to constitute a contribution to that "larger and more aware audience for the artists" which the report hoped for.

During the six years that Humanities 21-22 has been given there have been many minor changes and adjustments in procedure and in content. Some of these have come about through suggestions from students in the course, criticisms which were required of all students in late May of the first four years. Minor revisions will probably go on indefinitely. The staff feels at this time that the course is in good shape and there is genuine enthusiasm for it among those students who take both semesters. We believe that it is providing a better than adequate introduction to important areas in man's nonverbal experience.

We feel, however, that under existing circumstances it is not truly fulfilling the purpose for which the course was designed: to give the major portion of the sophomore class an experience of the discipline and artistic meaning of the arts. The variety of elective counter-attractions in the sophomore humanities area, most of which are no more than extensions of disciplines introduced in the freshman year, produces most unfortunate results. Faced with the opportunity of coasting on in familiar fields, too many students fail to rise to the challenge of something which is new and which has the reputation of being difficult.[29a]

English 21-22, Introduction to Literature, has become the largest

[29] Enrollment, fall 1952, 137; enrollment, fall 1953, 98.

[29a] In the spring of 1955 (after this book was completed), the Humanities 21-22 staff decided to omit the course for the time being and to try as an alternative separate introductory courses in the three departments involved. After the seven years' trial most members of the staff felt that the attempt to integrate the diverse techniques, styles, and histories of the three arts into a cohesive interdepartmental course was not altogether satisfactory. The separate presentations were too brief and hurried, integration at this stage was often superficial, and the course was so broad that it prepared inadequately for advanced work in the three departments.

of the courses in the sophomore humanities group. In recent years it has been taken by about a half of the sophomore class. For this reason, and because it is one of the more original courses in the Amherst curriculum, we include the following account.[30]

The aim of English 21-22 is to help students enjoy the fullest and yet most precise experience of a particular piece of writing. The method might be described as "slow motion," slowing down the process of reading so as to attend closely to the words, both their meanings and sounds. To teach this kind of reading is to develop one of the fundamental skills of general application in the humanities. When the new curriculum was established, the course became one of the humanities group from which sophomores elect the equivalent of six semester hours. It has become the largest of these courses.

The course is taught in sections, with weekly staff meetings to prepare common assignments, discuss the works taught, and compare notes on classroom experiences. There is no single sacred technique, but the teacher does have some ways of reading that he sets out to demonstrate to his students. Obviously, what can be demonstrated is never equivalent to the full experience of reading a work of literature. Each teacher starts from his own excitement and does everything he can to infect his students with it. But he cannot hand over his feelings to his students. He can, however, direct their attention to words on the printed pages which he and they have in common, moving constantly back and forth from evoking meaning by paraphrase and summary to demonstrating relationships between one place in the text and other places.

For example: When Othello, just before Desdemona's death, says, "Put out the light, and then put out the light," we feel not only the horror of his intention, but also a remarkable concentration of much that has gone on before, the moving history of the relations between the lovers and between them and Iago, the echoed presence of earlier moments of "lightness" and "darkness." In considering this speech the teacher may begin by asking what the words mean in terms of stage

[30] This account of English 21-22 is an abbreviated version, prepared by Professor César L. Barber, of an essay on the course written for the *Amherst Alumni News*, July, 1953, by Professor Reuben A. Brower, who was chairman of the course from its inception in 1941 until he left Amherst in 1953 to become professor of English at Harvard.

business. He may then call for a paraphrase: for "put out the light" someone may offer "bring darkness," or "put an end to." The class can next be asked to connect this expression with others used elsewhere in the play. Someone may recall Othello's earlier line associating Desdemona with darkness and death: ". . . when I love thee not, Chaos is come again." Any reader will now appreciate better the poignancy and the irony of Othello's picturing his action as "putting out the light." So by directing his students to words and relationships, the teacher may put them in a position where they too must feel the pity and terror of this moment in the play.

English 21 might be described as a "mutual demonstration society." After a series of exploratory classes on each new work, the students are given directions for a paper, a carefully planned series of questions designed to lead them to practice in an essay the sort of interpretation they have been attempting in class. An example of such an exercise, used in 1952 when studying *Othello*, is included in Appendix I. English 21-22 develops through a succession of such exercises, assigned at intervals of about two weeks. Each semester ends with a paper on material read without guidance during a two-week reading period.

The year normally begins with short poems, no more than one or two for a class. Gradually each section builds up a small critical vocabulary, but throughout the course emphasis is placed, not on using the word "metaphor," or some other term, but on detecting a particular use of words and on grasping what it expresses. Following a period of reading poetry, the course moves on usually to a poetic drama, so that the student can see at once that the way in which he reads poems "works" also for a play and that there are some basic similarities between the structure of different types of literature. He may see, for example, that the "man speaking" in a poem corresponds to the "character" in a play, that Shakespeare has his large metaphors, just as Keats has his smaller ones. From dramas the course may go on to a novel or two, and from there to a work of "ideas," such as *The Education of Henry Adams* or Arnold's *Culture and Anarchy*.

Frequently the course ends with the study of a major poet, one object being to give the students experience in interpreting and evaluating the whole body of a writer's work. In recent years during the second half of the course various experiments have been made in historical interpretation of literature. After reading a number of more or less contemporary works, the question has become: "What do these works have in common as expressions of the life of a particular era?" For example, "What kinds of experience in Henry Adams and Henry James and W. B. Yeats do we recognize as belonging distinctly to the twentieth century?"

The teachers in the course have aimed not to be the victims of their methods, whether analytical or historical. In approaching each book and in working out the exercises, the staff are always asking, "What is the best way to get into *this* literary experience?" Old ways have to be dropped or cut to fit new cloth. The result is sometimes baffling for students who want to go blindly ahead with a rule-of-thumb method that they can apply to all authors alike. But their bafflement is usually educational: they have really encountered a new mind or a new form of literary experience. At the same time, they have had occasion to acquire a habit of mind which is alert to recognize unexpected relationships, to see structure and so find meaning after particular conclusions arrived at in English 21-22 may have been forgotten.

Referring to the sophomore "group requirement" in humanities, the Committee on Educational Policy said in their fourth annual report:

> It might be argued, we believe, that this list of courses implies a definition of "humanities" so elastic as to be downright vague. While no faculty committee can arrive at a rigorous definition of the term, it nevertheless does seem possible to specify characteristics of study more homogeneous than the above list would assume. The CEP proposes, therefore, to consider this problem more closely next year.

However, they were diverted from this project by more pressing issues, the introduction of an R.O.T.C. program, and the planning of a possible summer school if the Korean crisis required it, and no subsequent committee has taken up the problem. We suggest that the Committee on Educational Policy seriously consider the feasibility of putting into effect a restriction upon sophomore elections in the humanities sequence which would impel students to *widen* their acquaintance within this diverse field and would, therefore, conduce to an improvement in our program of *general* education. This is a modification of the present curriculum which would be wholly in accord with the tenor of the Long Range Policy Report.[30a]

Ancient and Foreign Languages

The Long Range Policy Committee, after some preliminary discussion of the subject, made five recommendations with regard to the study of foreign languages (pp. 69-70). These will be taken up in order, with some remarks on what has happened in each case. Other general remarks and some evaluations and opinions will follow.

1. That every student be required, in order to receive a degree, to satisfy a language requirement which, within such practical limits as may be determined by the language departments, will insure a firmer grasp of the language than our present "reading knowledge" requirement.

It should be said at the outset that what follows concerns largely the modern languages. To permit satisfaction of the requirement in the ancient languages was a wholly new departure, of course, but in this field the requirement remains necessarily a "reading knowledge" requirement, and the determination of what is satisfactory is necessarily the responsibility of the teachers of these languages.

So far as the modern languages are concerned, the important words in the proposal quoted above are "firmer grasp." If it could be assumed that in the past most students had been given a respectable "reading knowledge," it was clear that something was to be added. The first thought that occurs to most persons is that of speaking ability. But it did not and does not seem possible to *require* anything that might be considered an adequate speaking ability of all students, at least with American language-training in the schools what it is, and in the time available. It was therefore decided not to include this ability in the "firmer grasp" aimed at.

[30a] In the spring of 1955 (after this book was completed), the faculty voted two changes in the sequence requirement in Humanities. The first is quantitative: a student must now elect, beyond the required freshman courses (Humanities 1-2), three semester courses in this division for a total of at least nine credit hours. The second change is distributional. Approved courses are now grouped: (a) philosophy, religion, classical civilization; (b) music, fine arts, dramatic arts; (c) English or foreign literature. The student may elect *either* one semester course from each group or two semester courses from one group and one semester course from either of the other two groups. Two of these semester courses must be completed by the end of the sophomore year; many students will doubtless, as is now the case, anticipate a part of this requirement in the freshman year through electives.

It should be remarked in passing, however, that a number of students do acquire, as a sort of by-product, some ability at speaking; some acquire a considerable ability. More do so than under the old system. There is a good deal of evidence that young alumni, or undergraduates, who find themselves in a situation which invites the use of a foreign language—whether as members of the armed forces, as students in foreign universities, or simply as tourists—now are rather quick at picking up some speaking facility. Since these are the usual circumstances in which speaking ability assumes importance, the foreign language group is not dissatisfied.

The members of the staff believed, however, that in an American liberal arts college the primary purpose of foreign language study is to develop reading ability to the point where it may be used for the study of significant literature. They also believed that this ability could be strengthened, and its acquisition speeded up, by trying to develop in the student the ability to *hear* what he reads. They believed that it should be possible so to train a student as to create in his mind a "sound track," and that the existence of this sound track should not only diminish the amount of two-language thinking that goes on but also increase, even subconsciously, the student's awareness that the language he is reading is alive.

Accordingly, it was proposed to include in the college language requirement a certain *aural* ability, a capacity to comprehend the spoken language, along with the normally expected reading ability; and the departments proceeded to alter the lower-level language courses so as to achieve this purpose. In doing this it was possible to draw on their experience during the war with the A.S.T.P. program—though naturally the amount of time available in a normal college course is much less than in a specialized program, and sights had to be set lower.

There was established, for these reasons, in 1947-48, a new type of course for students at the elementary, intermediate, and advanced language levels (courses 1, 3, and 5). Entering freshmen were placed in these courses as carefully as possible. All students with a CEEB achievement score of 550 or over[31] are informed that they are eligible to take, when they enter in September, an aural-comprehension test. If they pass this test they are considered to have satisfied the college language requirement—the CEEB score being taken to

[31] This figure is not published.

indicate an adequate reading knowledge. For them further language work is voluntary. Those who do not pass this test, and all the others not eligible for it, are placed, on the basis of whatever information is available, where it is thought they should go. This is done at a long conference, during the summer, between representatives of the language departments and the admissions office; members of the language group consider the student's CEEB score (if there is one), how long he has studied the language, whether there has been a gap since he last studied it and if so how great a gap, whatever knowledge they have of the school he attended, and their judgment of his general ability. Errors sometimes occur, of course, but they are not numerous.

In the three courses into which these students go (together with real beginners and others progressing normally) the procedure now involves two separate things: (1) a meeting three times a week, in a large group (sometimes too large), with the professor in charge; and (2) a meeting three times a week (four in course 1), in a small group, with an assistant to whom the language is native.[32] In the large class meeting it is the professor's business to introduce, to explain, to demonstrate, in general to "teach," the progressively new material. In the section meetings, the work of which is, of course, carefully planned and directed by the professor in charge, the time is used for drill of all sorts, repetition, variation, dictation, and what not, with the intention of so increasing familiarity that many things will come to seem merely normal, even automatic. These sections average ten students or fewer, and, although they are not intended to develop speaking ability as a primary aim, they undoubtedly do develop it in some students with a flair for language.

This work is supplemented to some extent, and more in some languages than in others, by the use of recording and playback apparatus, which is useful for helping an interested student to make progress. Some departments make regular use of sound films as further ear training, though such films have proved far from uniformly satisfactory.

No student satisfies the requirement at the end of course 1. Some do so at the end of course 3, where an aural-comprehension test is included as a part of the course examination. At the end of course 5,

[32] Except in Italian, where the small number of students involved makes it necessary for the professor to do this work also.

a passing grade in the course is taken as evidence that the college requirement has been satisfied—though in occasional instances this is perhaps unjustified.

As a consequence of this sort of work in the lower courses it has become possible to use the language more in advanced courses than was formerly the case—though here the practice varies from course to course and from department to department. The staff does not attempt, as some institutions claim to do, never to use English in the classroom. They consider it more important that the student always understand clearly what is being discussed.

It seems fair to say that on the whole this method has produced as much as was produced before in the way of reading knowledge and, in addition, in many students at least, another sort of awareness that was not produced before, which may perhaps be termed, loosely, a "firmer grasp" of the language.

2. That the list of languages in which the requirement may be satisfied be expanded to include: French, German, ancient Greek, Italian, Latin, Spanish, and any other language which may be approved in an individual case.

This has been done, and few if any complaints have been heard. In the case of the ancient languages, of course, the requirement is satisfied by a reading knowledge only; in the modern languages the aural comprehension has become a part of the requirement.

3. That the native language of a foreign-born student, educated in a foreign country, be accepted in satisfaction of the requirement.

This is done. Few students are affected, but we no longer require a Korean, say, who already knows enough English to be a student here, to study another language. If he does so he does it voluntarily. For our purposes, his knowledge of English constitutes adequate foreign language experience.

4. That the departments and divisions give serious consideration to the possibility and advisability of requiring a knowledge of more than one foreign language in connection with advanced work, particularly for honors students.

Here little if anything appears to have been done. So far as is known, no department or division *requires* such a thing. Some departments presumably advise advanced students who intend to enter graduate school to acquire some German or French as a second language before leaving Amherst, but perhaps not many do so with much conviction. The English Department has apparently been responsible for a certain number of registrations in Greek or, less often, Latin on the part of its honors candidates. But many departments would seem not to believe that a year of pregraduate German, say, is important—or at least as important as more courses in the student's field of concentration. The French and German departments are continuing to offer courses (two semesters each) that are known, not too precisely, as "reading courses." Their purpose is to allow a student who has already satisfied the college requirement in another language to acquire a reading knowledge at a fairly rapid pace. These courses are elected by a certain number of students, usually upperclassmen, who have their eye on graduate school, but the registrations in them are not what one might expect them to be. It seems clear that the responsibility on this point rests with other departments or divisions and not with the language departments themselves.

5. That the teaching of Russian be instituted when possible, and the possibility of satisfying the stated requirement in Russian be studied.

In accordance with this proposal a course in Russian, taught by a native Russian then a member of the Mount Holyoke faculty, was established in 1948-1949. In the elementary course in the first semester twelve students were enrolled. Of these nine continued in the second semester and four in a third semester the following year. But in that year, 1949-1950, only two new students registered for the elementary course, and after that year Russian disappeared from the catalogue. Since then a few students have done work for credit in Russian, either here with Professor Peppard or at neighboring institutions.

In connection with the first recommendation and its implications there is more to be said than merely to state that in general the desired "firmer grasp" has been achieved.

In the faculty discussions when the new curriculum was being considered the matter of student load in the first two years loomed large. To insure that the student should get everything it was felt he should get in these two years, and at the same time have a certain amount of elbow room for elective courses and for exploration, seemed in some ways quite difficult. The teachers of language were, in effect, asked to assure the faculty that the attainment of the desired objective in language study would not take too long. It seems fair to say on this point that the new courses have accomplished their aim, in general, more rapidly than the older-type courses did. A student who *begins* a language in the fall of his freshman year now normally satisfies the requirement in three semesters, and a respectable number do so in two semesters. Under the old system four semesters were a normal minimum. Progress from other starting points has become correspondingly faster than it used to be.[33]

These aims—"firmer grasp," faster progress—have, however, been attained only at a cost, literally. This type of teaching is expensive. The President is fond of telling the modern language departments that they are the most expensive, per student, in the college, "except possibly the classics." (In mitigation it should be said that the modern languages are contributing something like one and two-thirds men to the freshman Humanities course.) The use of assistants, for what they help to attain, costs money. Whether it costs more money than the additional faculty-rank instructors who would be needed if Amherst were still offering the prewar type of course, at the prewar rate of speed, is an unanswered question.

With respect to the assistants, there is another point worth mentioning. In bringing such people to the campus it was not the main purpose to provide the college with a small group of non-Americans, or to offer foreign students the opportunity to spend some time in an American college. But both these things are worth doing, and should perhaps be reckoned in what the money is buying. In the years since the present program was begun there have been more than a score of young Frenchmen, Latin Americans, and Germans at Amherst, most of whom would not have come here otherwise. Almost all of them profited by their stay here, and the association with them has been educative to our own students.

In another respect the results of the new methods have been disappointing. The number of registrations in the more advanced courses, as well as the number of majors and honors candidates, is

[33] For example, the rate at which the language requirements were satisfied by the class of 1953 was:

At entrance	22 %	At end of third semester	7½%
At end of first semester	37½%	At end of fourth semester	1 %
At end of second semester	30 %	Remainder	2 %

smaller, sometimes markedly so, than before the war. These relatively low registrations are to some extent connected with the increased speed achieved in the lower courses. In many colleges comparable to Amherst the language work that here occupies one semester requires two. This naturally makes the total registration figures in such institutions larger than in ours. It is difficult, however, to believe that this trend can be explained by, or attributed to, the new-type lower courses only. The situation is by no means unique at Amherst. Among possible reasons the following may be involved: (1) the effect of the "four-course" program, with the expected disappearance of what used to be known often as the "fifth course"; (2) at least in the first two years, the number of required courses, which limits the possible electives; (3) what appears to be a larger number of students concentrating in the general field of science; (4) the powerful impact of the English Department, which takes by far the greater number of students with a primary interest in literature; (5) the appearance as strong competitors of one or two new subjects—for example, psychology; (6) an apparently somewhat general feeling that a requirement is something to be passed off and then forgotten—a feeling which, it is possible to suspect, is sometimes fostered by advice given in deans' offices; and (7) a general national attitude toward foreign languages, which has markedly affected their position in the schools and which is so widespread as to need no emphasis here, no matter how much it may be regretted.

Forced to make some attempt at rendering their subject more attractive—perhaps we should say more available—and in the face of administrative distress at low registrations, the various departments have tried offering "short courses," meeting once or twice a week for one or two credit hours. These seem to have attracted some students, concentrating elsewhere, who might not have been able to include a four-credit course in their program. To this degree they have swelled registration figures, for whatever that may be worth. The fact remains that some basic courses are still extremely small. It is regrettable that such a large number of students stop the subject just at the point where they are ready to draw dividends on their investment. The adoption of the recommendation we made in discussing the Humanities sequence, that the group elective in sophomore year be further restricted, might help to remedy this situation.

The Junior-Senior Years

The Long Range Policy Committee considered reform of the first two years of crucial importance. Beyond recommending the changes necessary to accommodate the work of the upper classes to the four-course plan they made no major recommendations for the junior-senior years. Those alterations which have been made since the inauguration of the new curriculum have been concerned: (1) with a redefinition of the major and the major with honors in accordance with subsequent changes of the requirements for graduation; (2) with a relaxation of the minimum requirements for eligibility to take honors similar to that which had been previously recommended in the Long Range Policy Report; and (3) with permission to waive a part or all of the requirement that in each of the last two years the student must take at least one-fourth of his work outside of the division in which he majors. The Committee on Educational Policy also studied various suggestions as to ways in which the *rite* degree might be made more meaningful, more like honors work. All of these changes have been briefly described in the preceding section, "Putting the Program into Effect."

It is our opinion that the Long Range Policy Committee's approval of the previously existing provisions for the work of the upper two years, and in particular the honors program, has been more than justified during the subsequent years. Since 1951, at least, the success of the honors program has been extraordinary. Nearly all the students who are eligible to do so now take honors work. In the class of 1954, 113 students (46 per cent) out of the graduating class of 242 received the degree with honors.[34] This result is, we believe, in large part due to the intellectual atmosphere created by the new curriculum for the first two years. One way in which the committee stated the objective of the new program they were proposing was that it should give students both the training and the knowledge to provide a basis for specialization in any field of the curriculum that they might choose, and that it should stimulate all students who proved capable of it to undertake the honors program. This objective has been realized.

Since we agree with the previous committees that the present pro-

[34] A list of these honors projects as printed in the commencement program is given in Appendix I.

visions for the major and major with honors are highly satisfactory, we have comments to make on only two points, the requirements for work outside the division and the attempt to make the work of *rite* students more significant.

No doubt it was desirable to waive a part of the requirement of some diversification in the last two years for honors students. However, it is not so clear that there is any such necessity for those taking an ordinary major. While no precise figures concerning present practice are available, the possibility remains that extensive use of this permission might be made by students in the *rite* group. We believe that the Committee on Educational Policy should continue to watch the situation and, if the privilege is used in such a way as to result in an excessively intensive program for many students, should see that, at least so far as the *rite* student is concerned, it is curtailed.

The second point is making the *rite* degree more significant. The Committee on Educational Policy which recently studied this question found that such proposals as comprehensive examinations, conference courses, etc., tending to make the work of the *rite* student similar to that of the honors student, were not acceptable to the majority of the faculty. We should go further and say that for the same reasons as those given in the Long Range Policy Report they are not desirable as well.[35] Nevertheless, there is a relatively small group of students with averages above 80, or near to it, who may not be getting what they deserve. The only resource we know of, which we believe to be feasible, is the recent proposal of a seminar on the senior level, intended primarily for this group, similar to the colloquium given at Columbia—a "great books" course meeting once a week for two hours and conducted jointly by members of two departments. This course, already approved by the Committee on Educational Policy, cannot at present, owing to unforeseen circumstances, be offered, but we hope that the proposal will soon be put into effect.[36]

There are two recommendations of the Long Range Policy Committee which should be briefly considered here.

The first of these, which was approved by the faculty at the time

[35] See pp. 76-78.

[36] It should be added that students not eligible for honors may apply for admission to honors courses. A considerable number of the students in the borderline group take advantage of the opportunity.

the new curriculum was enacted, is: "That the faculty instruct the Curriculum Committee (or Committee on Educational Policy) to make a special study of the possibility of establishing a limited number of additional group majors." One Committee on Educational Policy mentioned this topic in an annual report as on their agenda for future study, but the study was not made. Perhaps it is not feasible in a college of Amherst's size to offer other group majors than American Studies.[37] Yet the reasons given in the report (pp. 78-79) are, we believe, of sufficient weight to warrant a study of the question. In particular, we think that it would be desirable to consider the possibility of inaugurating a group major in European Studies (or perhaps in the more restricted field, nineteenth-century Europe) to complement the American Studies major. The latter has become one of the larger departments in numbers of students who major and take honors in it and has proved to be an important addition to the curriculum as a type of concentration organized in contrast to the patterns of regular departments.

One other minor proposal for the curriculum made by the Long Range Policy Committee was never, so far as we are aware, brought up for consideration. This was: "That a group of scholarships, open to juniors for work on a special honors project during the summer following the completion of the junior year, be established." For the past four years there has been a Summer Intern Program in Washington for Amherst students. The Department of Political Science would like to establish a group of scholarships which would enable students who could not otherwise afford it to spend a summer as an intern in Washington or engage in directed study of political party activities in their own communities. There are many other equally profitable ways in which honors students might spend a summer in study and research. We hope that the Committee on Educational Policy will consider this neglected recommendation.

As we look back on this review of the new curriculum, considering what it was intended to *do*, the balance of success appears to be large. All the changes which have been made since it was begun and the few suggestions that we have made for its possible improvement

[37] A group major in Renaissance Studies is on the books, so to speak, but is taken only by an occasional student.

have been concerned with matters of detail. Taking it for what it is, it has worked well. Nor has the new curriculum created any perceptible body of dissent. Such unanimity was natural in the earlier days when everyone's loyal support for the new venture was tacitly expected, but now the new curriculum is no longer really "new," and if discontent or the desire to do something else exists, it should have appeared. We must conclude that those concerned, the faculty, students, and administration, are satisfied. Here lies the risk of gradually subsiding into a complacent routine. For this reason we make one final recommendation: that there should occasionally be a drastic review of the whole program. If it is still, for us, the best, enthusiasm for it will be revived; if not, something better, we hope, may take its place. What the Long Range Policy Committee said of Amherst is still true: "The real danger is that it will survive merely as 'another good college.' "

ADMISSIONS AND SCHOLARSHIPS[38]

The presumption which controlled the discussion of this topic in the report was: "We believe that Amherst's best chance for a bright future lies in trying to become predominantly an *honors college*, offering a general education preparatory to the professions of such excellence that it can command nation-wide recognition. All of the comments on the various problems of admissions and scholarships which follow are based on this presumption."

In discussing admissions during the decade 1931-1941 the Long Range Policy Committee found that (1) there was a large increase in the number of applications and that the percentage of applicants rejected also rose, despite a concomitant growth in the size of the college; (2) there was an increase in the percentage of students admitted from private secondary schools as against those admitted from high schools; (3) the number of sons and relatives of Amherst alumni tended to increase; and (4) the geographical distribution of the students remained about the same.

Comparing these trends with the postwar years, we find that (1) the number of applications has continued to increase; (2) there

[38] We are indebted to Deans C. Scott Porter, Eugene S. Wilson, and Theodore S. Bacon and to the Comptroller, Herbert G. Johnson, for data presented in this section.

has been a *decrease* in the percentage of students admitted from private schools; (3) the percentage of sons of Amherst alumni (figures on relatives are no longer available) has increased slightly (from an average of 12 to an average of 13 per cent in a class); and (4) the geographical distribution of our students is somewhat wider.

Precisely comparable statistics for the postwar period are not available. However, the accompanying tables should be of interest.

APPLICATIONS AND ADMISSIONS FOR THE PERIOD 1951-57

Year	Total Applications	Total Accepted	Came	Per Cent Actually Admitted
1947-1948	1050	—	250	24
1948-1949	900	—	275	30
1949-1950	803	333	264	33
1950-1951	792	315	267	34
1951-1952	957	505	299	31
1952-1953	1100	425	263	24
1953-1954	1300	478	271	20

NOTE: No figures on "total accepted" were available for the years 1947-48 and 1948-49. The large increase in the number of students accepted since 1951-52 is due to the deletion from the college board test report forms of the applicant's choice of a college. Before the elimination of this specification of choices Amherst was getting about 85 per cent of the students accepted. Currently, the college is getting less than 60 per cent of the students it accepts.

More important than this positive increase in the actual number of applicants is the great increase in the number of qualified applicants. Thus in 1953-1954, of the 1300 applicants, 1100 were in the opinion of our Director of Admissions able to do the work at Amherst. What has happened is revealed in the following college board scores:

COLLEGE BOARD SCORES OF STUDENTS ADMITTED

Class	Verbal Aptitude	Mathematical Aptitude
1945	504	519
1954	578	596
1955	581	597
1956	563	611
1957	583	626

By comparison with the class of 1945, postwar classes are, in terms of these scores, far superior. The average student now at Amherst is in the top 20 per cent of the whole group of students taking the college board tests.[39]

ADMISSIONS FROM HIGH SCHOOLS AND PREPARATORY SCHOOLS, 1947-54

Year	Number Admitted	Per Cent Admitted from High School	Preparatory School	Both
1947-48	250	41	42	17
1948-49	275	42	35	23
1949-50	264	48	44	8
1950-51	267	43	46	11
1951-52	299	49	35	16
1952-53	263	45	34	21
1953-54	271	53	30	17

In 1953-1954 for the first time, at least since 1933, the number of high school students admitted is a majority of the freshman class. And this class has the highest average scores on the college board tests of any admitted to Amherst. Since there is no discrimination as between applicants from high schools and from private schools, all candidates being judged by their apparent qualifications, this increase in the percentage of high school students admitted means that we are now receiving a larger number of applications from well-qualified high school students.

ADMISSIONS OF SONS OF AMHERST ALUMNI

Year	Students	Sons	Percentage
1947-48	250	53	21
1948-49	275	45	17
1949-50	264	31	12
1950-51	267	35	13
1951-52	299	29	10
1952-53	263	28	11
1953-54	271	40	15

[39] The average student in Amherst ranks at the eighty-second percentile in verbal aptitude and at the eighty-sixth percentile in mathematical aptitude on these tests.

GEOGRAPHICAL DISTRIBUTION OF THE CLASS OF 1957

New York	75	New Hampshire	1
Massachusetts	43	Maine	1
New Jersey	31	Rhode Island	1
Pennsylvania	28	Indiana	1
Connecticut	27	Kentucky	1
Illinois	11	Colorado	1
Ohio	9	West Virgina	1
District of Columbia	5	Virginia	1
Missouri	4	Tennessee	1
Maryland	4	Idaho	1
Minnesota	4	New Mexico	1
Michigan	3	Louisiana	1
California	3	Arizona	1
Iowa	3	Canada	2
Vermont	2	Belgium	1
Wisconsin	2	Korea	1

Typically, the great majority of an Amherst class comes from the first seven states in this list. That there has been some increase, however, in geographical distribution is shown by comparing the number of states and areas represented in a series of classes:

Class	Number of States and Areas
1941	16
1945	20
1951	27
1952	29
1953	31
1954	26
1955	28
1956	31
1957	32

Despite these substantial gains in the number of applicants, particularly from high schools, and an increase in geographical distribution, the student body remains overwhelmingly middle class; it is still, in the words of the report, "too narrowly homogeneous a student body." The staff of the *Amherst Student*, in making a survey of the state of the college in 1951, took this fact to be an explanation of much in the prevailing attitude among the undergraduates.[40] They say:

As far as geographic distribution is concerned, Amherst has successfully increased the diversity of its student body. However, as it may well be pointed out, a suburb of Detroit and a suburb of New York City are not really very different. And so the important consideration is the social and economic distribution of Amherst students.

The recent *Student* poll shows that the majority of those answering tend to think of themselves as coming from the upper middle class. And practically all others rate themselves as coming from the middle class with only a few in either the lower or the upper class.

As to family income the recent Sabrina poll is extremely interesting. It shows that more than half of the students' families have incomes of more than $10,000 per year. Only 10.7 per cent of the student body comes from families with less than $5,000 income per year. Four-fifths of the nation's families have incomes less than $5,000. . . .

Amherst, then, by omission if not by commission, effectively solicits the applications of a particular socio-economic class as well as of an extremely high intellectual class. . . . Amherst is the kind of place it is because its student body is of a certain nature. As one professor has pointed out there are very few "mavericks," men who do not fit into the near-homogeneous student group at Amherst. This does not mean that Amherst men are all of a mold. They are strongly individualistic. But nevertheless, socially at least, they conform to a particular pattern of sophisticated behaviour. And the benefit of such an arrangement is that the Amherst campus is relatively quiet, well-adjusted and not torn apart by problems of tolerance of other groups—since there is one general group into which most seem to fit.[41]

The result, then, is what the staff of the *Student* refers to elsewhere in their survey as "high-level mediocrity." Or, as the authors of the study of education in relation to the class structure of our society, *Who Shall Be Educated?*, put it:

The old-established eastern colleges and universities draw from the upper-middle and upper classes, with a sprinkling of mobile lower-middle class youth. These are the "Ivy League" institutions—Yale, Harvard, Prince-

[40] For a discussion of this prevailing attitude see the section on "Social Life and Activities."

[41] *Amherst Student,* April 30, 1951.

ton, Dartmouth, Amherst, Williams, Hamilton, Haverford, etc. Like them are a few colleges and universities west of the Alleghenies, of which Stanford is the outstanding example.[42]

Now the major question raised by the Long Range Policy Committee was "How can we enlarge our social basis?" They suggested that means should be found for increasing the number of applications by good students from the public high schools.

> When one recalls [they said] that there are some 25,000 public high schools in the United States, 3500 of them in the northeastern section of the country, and that one recent Amherst class drew its members from only 62 of these 25,000 schools, it becomes clear how highly restricted are the sources of our student body.[43]

The committee proposed four major ways in which the total number of applications from good students might be increased. These were

> (a) the provision of funds adequate for the establishment of a more complete system of regional scholarships; (b) the appointment of an assistant admissions officer to develop relations with secondary schools and in areas from which we are not at present drawing any significant number of students; (c) a greater use of the alumni to assist us in obtaining able students; (d) the adoption of admissions requirements which would make it easier, particularly for high school students, to meet the *formal* conditions of admission.[44]

These are undoubtedly effective means of increasing the total number of well-qualified applicants, but it does not now seem at all certain that their employment will materially widen the social base of our student body. It appears, after the lapse of nearly a decade, that the committee was too optimistic in one respect and too pessimistic in another; too pessimistic in believing that the college would find it increasingly difficult to get a sufficient number of well-qualified students from the relatively small reservoir of boys in private schools and certain large urban or suburban high schools with increasing

[42] W. Lloyd Warner, Robert J. Havighurst, and Martin B. Loeb, *Who Shall Be Educated?* (New York, 1944), pp. 71-72.

[43] See p. 93.

[44] See p. 93. Though not equally specific on some of these points, the recommendations of the alumni committee were in general agreement with those made by the faculty committee. See "Amherst Tomorrow," *Alumni Council News*, 18 (1945), 58-69.

competition for them, and too optimistic in believing that "by turning to new fields and new methods" we could *substantially* increase the number of students coming from other social classes. Apparently the reservoir was larger than they thought, and Amherst has more than held her position in the intense competition for the better students in this group. With this caveat in mind, we shall comment briefly on each of these four recommendations.

Of these means, the most important in the opinion of the committee was the "effective use of our scholarship funds and an increase in these funds." They recommended (a) an increase in the minimum scholastic requirements for scholarships, "That the established minimum requirement for holders of scholarships be changed to 75 per cent for sophomores and that, *so far as possible*, no scholarships be made available to juniors and seniors who are not candidates for the degree with distinction" (dissent by Professors Brown and Morgan), and (b) "a consolidation of scholarship funds that will enable us to offer a number of large regional scholarships strategically placed in such a way as to draw more students from remoter areas and at the same time positively to increase the quality of our student body by obtaining more top-ranking students."[45]

In respect to the first of these recommendations the opinion of the Long Range Policy Committee prevailed. The official stipulation is: "Scholarship awards are competitive and are made to candidates with the best records of achievement who can clearly demonstrate their financial need. They are seldom made to students who barely meet the minimum requirement of a seventy-five average." The second recommendation, that a system of regional scholarships be established, was tried out on a small scale and then abandoned. After presenting the basic facts concerning scholarships at the present time we shall state our opinion of these two recommendations.

1. In 1953-1954 the college planned to spend approximately $2710 per student. The total of all charges for tuition, room, board, etc., was $1296. In 1940-1941 the college spent $1261 per student and the total

[45] The subcommittee on admissions and scholarships of the alumni committee made no specific recommendation regarding standards of eligibility for scholarships but strongly advocated the establishment of a system of national scholarships similar to the one in effect at Harvard. In a subsequent poll the alumni voted as follows on the question: Do you favor the establishment of national scholarships? Yes, 620. No, 71. See *ibid.*, pp. 65-68.

charges were about $900.[46] Thus the "invisible" scholarship given to *all* students in the college was in 1940-1941 about $360, while in 1953-1954 it was over $1400.[47] The subsidy given each student, regardless of ability to pay, has increased about 400 per cent.

2. At present 22 per cent of the students at Amherst are receiving scholarship aid. Beginning in September, 1954, awards varying in value from $300 to $1500 and totaling more than $180,000 per year will be made to over 225 undergraduates. The average scholarship amounts to approximately $750. More than fifty of these scholarships are awarded each year to freshmen.

3. Awards of scholarships in 1953-1954 were as follows:

	Upperclassmen	Freshmen
Undergraduate enrollment	775	272
Total number of scholarships awarded this year	173	65
Per cent receiving scholarships	22.3%	23.8%
Total amount of scholarships awarded	$111,385	$43,000
Last year's scholastic average of all undergraduates	81.30%	77.61%
Last year's scholastic average of all scholarship holders	83.06%	79.11%

4. The scholastic standing of upperclassmen receiving scholarships in 1953-1954 was as follows:

Class of 1954—55 scholarships awarded
41 students (74.6%) had averages above 80.
14 students (25.4%) had averages below 80.
Class of 1955—57 scholarships awarded
38 students (66.6%) had averages above 80.
19 students (33.4%) had averages below 80.
Class of 1956—49 scholarships awarded
32 students (65.3%) had averages above 80.
17 students (34.7%) had averages below 80.

5. The relative number of scholarship students receiving full tuition or more was as follows:

[46] Amherst now charges uniform fees to all students for the various services.
[47] These figures taken from a letter sent by the President to parents announcing an increase in tuition are more accurate than the estimate made on p. 95.

Class of 1954
  44 students (80.0%) received full tuition or above.
  11 students (20.0%) received less than full tuition.
Class of 1955
  51 students (89.4%) received full tuition or above.
  6 students (10.6%) received less than full tuition.
Class of 1956
  41 students (83.6%) received full tuition or above.
  8 students (16.4%) received less than full tuition.

6. The relative number of scholarship awards to upperclassmen coming from high schools was as follows:

Class of 1954
  39 students (71.0%) are from high schools.
  10 students (18.2%) are from private schools.
  6 students (10.9%) are from high schools *and* private schools.
Class of 1955
  32 students (56.0%) are from high schools.
  14 students (24.5%) are from private schools.
  11 students (19.3%) are from high schools *and* private schools
Class of 1956
  36 students (73.4%) are from high schools.
  8 students (16.3%) are from private schools.
  5 students (10.2%) are from high schools *and* private schools.

From a comparison of these data with those given in the Long Range Policy Report the following facts have become evident: (1) The distance between the usual minimum requirement for a scholarship and the college average has *increased*. Thus in 1935-1936, when the minimum average grade for sophomores was 72 per cent, the college average for five recent classes was 75.87 per cent; now the usual minimum average is 75 per cent but the college average has for the past several years been over 80 per cent. (2) The percentage of students receiving scholarships has slightly declined. (3) The number of scholarships awarded to students with averages below the college average has substantially increased. In 1940-1941, 25 per cent of the awards were made to students whose average was below that of the college as a whole, while in 1953-1954, of awards to students in the three upper classes alone, *at least* 31 per cent went to students with averages below the college average. (Note that our figures are for averages below 80 per cent whereas the college average for 1952-1953 was 81.3 per cent.) (4) The proportion of scholarship students receiving full tuition or more has markedly increased—since fewer than half the scholarship holders received full tuition or more in the prewar years. And (5) a somewhat higher percentage of the scholarships (67 per cent for the three upper classes in 1953-1954) now goes to students who come from high schools.

The committee also compared expenditures for scholarships to those of Williams and Wesleyan. We are able to present a more comprehensive comparison in the following table. The figures are for the year 1952-1953:[48]

College	Student Costs[a]	Number of Scholarships	Per Cent of Students	Average Amount	Range	Total Amount
Amherst	$1296	222	22	$658	$300-1300	$146,000
Bowdoin	1318	148	20	425	200- 700	63,000
Brown	1530	580	29	450	100- 800	263,000
Dartmouth	1360-1620	499	18	740	300-1700	370,000
Hamilton	1355	126	22.5	430	100-1275	54,000
Harvard	1355-1655	1071	24	588	100-1600	630,000
Princeton	1500-1620	825	31	590	200-1300	480,000
Wesleyan	1278-1378	217	29	640	50-1200	139,000
Williams	1301-1495	186	18	600	300-1500	119,000
Yale	1600	1200	30	645	100-1600	770,000

[a] "Student Costs" includes tuition, room, board, and miscellaneous fees.

Finally, the Long Range Policy Committee in its consideration of the facts about scholarships looked into the relation between endowment, gross expenditures by the college, and scholarships. On the financial aspects of the scholarship program for the postwar years we present the following brief summary on the basis of the data made available to us.

The absolute amount disbursed by the college for scholarships and student aid was relatively small in the immediate postwar years because many students were benefiting from the G.I. Bill. As these benefits declined, the amount spent by the college for this purpose

[48] Taken in abbreviated form from a report on the scholarship and student aid program at Amherst by Dean C. Scott Porter.

has appreciably increased so that in 1952-1953 it came to $146,940 as compared to about one-half that amount in 1930-1931.

However, disbursements for scholarships have not kept pace with other significant items. Thus, comparing 1930-1931 with 1952-1953, we find that:

Average scholarships per student increased	31 per cent
Endowment per student increased	45 per cent
Tuition per student increased	50 per cent

In 1930-1931, when the tuition per student was $400, the disbursement on scholarships would have provided full tuition for 189 students or 28 per cent of the whole student body. In 1952-1953, when tuition was $600, scholarship disbursement would have paid full tuition for 250 students or 24 per cent of the student body.

We had hoped to carry our financial analysis considerably farther. We believe it would be helpful to compare the trend of scholarship aid per student with other costs per student such as those for instruction (i.e., in the narrow sense of teachers' salaries), administration, buildings and grounds, etc. We had also hoped to be able to study the impact of the new curriculum upon the college finances. Such an analysis was not possible on the basis of information available from the Treasurer's office. So we merely present the financial data we were given. It appears in Appendix II.[49]

With these facts in mind we can now recur to the recommendations by the Long Range Policy Committee. The first of these falls into two parts: (1) the establishment of a minimum academic requirement of 75 per cent for sophomores, and (2) that, *so far as possible*, no scholarships be made available to juniors and seniors who are not candidates for the degree with distinction. The minimum requirement for a scholarship in all the upper classes is now 75 per

[49] The financial reports made available by Amherst College are probably not less intelligible than those of most privately endowed colleges. However, we are convinced that both the alumni and the faculty of this college, and of other colleges as well, are entitled to more meaningful financial reporting than is now the case. Some day the privately endowed colleges may, we hope, adopt a uniform accounting and reporting procedure which will (1) give an intelligible and reasonably detailed breakdown of general accounting items; (2) make possible reliable comparisons over a period of time for a given institution; (3) facilitate comparisons among institutions.

cent.[50] But at the time this recommendation was made the college average was under 76 per cent while today it is over 81 per cent. Thus the difference between the minimum requirements (72 per cent for sophomores, 74 for juniors, and 76 for seniors) during the prewar years and the college average was less at that time than it is now. To this should be added the fact that the percentage of scholarships awarded to students in the three upper classes whose averages are below the present college average is now considerably greater than it was during the prewar years.

The members of this committee agree with the majority of the Long Range Policy Committee that the minimum requirement for holders of scholarships was too low at the time the report was written. Therefore, we regard the present situation as worse than it was at that time. The present minimum is now at least six points below the college average. We believe that the minimum requirement should be brought into line with the college average. The required minimum for sophomores should now be 80 per cent.

The second part of the recommendation, that, *so far as possible*, no scholarships be made available to juniors and seniors who are not candidates for the degree with distinction, was never adopted. The normal minimum average required to be eligible for honors is 80 per cent. If, then, the minimum requirement for a scholarship were raised to 80 per cent, the scholarship group would *ipso facto* be restricted to those who are eligible for honors.

The Long Range Policy Committee asserted that the greatest single need of the college was a larger endowment for scholarships. An endowment for scholarships was the memorial to alumni who perished in World War I. The committee believed that such an endowment would again be the most fitting kind of war memorial. However, for World War II, it was decided to build a monument and an intramural playing field to be called Memorial Field.

The committee's recommendation, that a system of competitive

[50] The official statement reads: "The awards are competitive and are seldom made to students who barely meet the minimum requirements of a seventy-five average. Generally, a student who is seeking scholarship aid should strive for an average of eighty or better." At Wesleyan in 1950-1951 the minimum academic average required of *all* students to retain a scholarship was 83.3 per cent, and the college average was 80.47 per cent. *Facts About Admission to Wesleyan in 1951-1952*, p. 6.

regional scholarships be established, was adopted and tried on a small scale. These scholarships, announced in February, 1945, were intended solely for high school graduates in rural areas. They amounted to $400 each. Recipients were to have them for so long as they maintained a satisfactory scholastic average. This plan was given up after a few years, however, because of an almost total lack of response. The Lord Jeffery Amherst Scholarships, eight regional scholarships formerly offered, were not resumed after the war.

Experience with regional scholarships at Amherst—and, we believe, elsewhere as well—has led to the conclusion that a more flexible system is to be preferred. Restrictions on the basis of area sometimes prevented giving the larger scholarships to applicants who were better qualified but from another part of the country. As a substitute, the college is offering at the present time a number of special grants, called the Alumni Scholarships, with stipends up to $1500.

Although Amherst has, at present, $1,500,000 in endowment funds reserved exclusively for scholarship grants, we believe that a much larger sum is needed. Additional amounts for scholarships come from contributions of alumni and friends of the college and from general funds. The decrease in the relative amount disbursed for scholarships during the postwar years presumably represents a diversion of expenditures from general funds to other purposes. This has been possible because, for the restricted clientele from which Amherst draws her students, college education has become a bargain commodity. We noted earlier that the "invisible scholarship" given to a student who pays all fees has risen from $360 in 1940-1941 to over $1400 in 1953-1954. It has been estimated that since 1941 the average family income has gone up about 150 per cent whereas the cost of attending Amherst has advanced (as of 1954-1955) only 58 per cent since 1941. (The average cost of all college fees throughout the country has risen during this period about 75 per cent.)[51]

This diminishing need for assistance through scholarships is not, in our opinion, an argument for following the policy we *have* followed, of decreasing the relative amount spent for that purpose. On the contrary, it *is* an argument that we are in a good position at the present time to increase scholarship expenditures for the purpose the

[51] J. Edward Saunders, "Are Scholarships Improving Education?" *The College Board Review*, May, 1953, p. 363.

Long Range Policy Committee advocated, to widen the social basis of our student body.[52] It should be possible to offer more large scholarships, which could be used as a means of obtaining a greater number of students, including Negro students, from the lower income groups—students to whom otherwise it would be quite unthinkable that they could attend this college.

The next major recommendation of the Committee on Long Range Policy was the appointment of an assistant officer of admissions. What the committee had in view was that this person should devote his time to the recruiting of students from a carefully selected list of high schools in the smaller cities and larger towns. When this recommendation was made there was one full-time dean and one full-time assistant dean who was the director of admissions. In 1946-1947 a full-time assistant dean who would also be assistant director of admissions was appointed primarily for this purpose. Yet the hopes of the committee were frustrated. The number of applications for admission from returning G.I. students and from secondary schools rose sharply, as was the case everywhere, with the result that much more time was required merely to deal with those applications the office had on its hands. In addition, the new Dean was given responsibility for enforcement of the regulations governing class attendance, for a good deal of the veterans' counseling, and for supervising student employment. These and other preoccupations left him with little time for visiting schools. Since the college annually sends representatives to from eighty to a hundred schools, most of his share of these visits was perforce to institutions from which we are already receiving students. In 1953-1954 still a fourth full-time man has been appointed to the dean's office as an assistant dean and assistant director of admissions.

We agree with the committee and with our present director of admissions that, while the effort to tap new sources brings slow returns, it is worth making. Though 92 per cent of all secondary school students are enrolled in public high schools, 6 or 7 per cent in private denominational schools, and only 2 per cent or less in private non-denominational schools, approximately half our students are admitted

[52] It is also in our opinion a strong argument for increasing tuition to the point where it will cover at least the same relative part of the costs of a student's education that it did in 1941.

from private schools. In an elaborate study of the question of who should go to college, made for the Commission on Financing Higher Education, it is estimated that on a conservative basis there were in the year 1951 at least 68,000 high school graduates of high ability who wanted to go on to college but were unable to do so for financial reasons.[53] To this should be added, of course, the much larger group of equal ability whose choice of a college is restricted by financial considerations. For example, we have in the town of Amherst a state university which at the present time has an enrollment of about 4000 students and which, it is anticipated, may well reach an enrollment of 10,000 by 1960. This immense growth is due to a demand for increased educational facilities by the citizens of the state. A large proportion of these students come from high schools which rarely, if ever, send a student to Amherst College. It seems obvious enough that there are great untapped resources for students of high ability. Cannot the means be found for attracting some of them? Certainly, the real hope of obtaining a student body more representative of the population as a whole and of raising still higher the level of ability among our students is through an intensive effort to recruit applicants from public high schools which do not ordinarily send anyone to places like Amherst. We hope, since the strength of the dean's office has now been doubled, that this effort will be made.

As adjuncts to the recommendation that the college appoint an assistant admissions officer to work in the high school field, the Long Range Policy Committee made two further suggestions: (1) that the cooperation of the alumni be enlisted and (2) that a serious effort be made to obtain more good Negro students.

The first of these suggestions was adopted. There are now some thirty-five alumni scattered throughout the country who assist in the recruiting of students. The results are mixed. Some are excellent at interesting good students in Amherst; others do little but follow up requests for information. The chief difficulty with this kind of assistance, as was to be anticipated, is that many alumni have a stereotyped notion of what the college wants—or should want. Some of them tend to look for what has been categorized as "nice boys," and to overlook, or even discourage, youths with good minds who do not fit their idea of personal qualifications. It seems likely, however,

[53] Byron S. Hollinshead, *Who Should Go to College?* (New York, 1952), pp. 79-82.

that an increasingly useful group of alumni to assist with admissions can be developed.

A real effort has been made to get Negro students, but this for several reasons is difficult to achieve. The number of Negro boys who are adequately prepared for a college like Amherst is limited. Today many more first-rate colleges are offering generous scholarships to Negro boys of high ability. Many Negro institutions have so greatly improved that there is less inducement for Negroes to go to a college where there will be only a few members of their own race. During the year 1953-1954 there were eight Negroes in Amherst. For the class of 1957, which contains two Negroes, there were about eighteen applicants, most of them qualified. The problem is largely one of scholarship funds. If more large scholarship grants could be made, it would be possible to have more Negro students.

The fourth way in which the committee thought the total number of applications from good students might be increased was the adoption of more flexible admission requirements. The detailed proposal made by the committee was adopted, with some minor changes, by the faculty in 1946. In view of the character of the required courses during the first two years, the reduction of the formal requirements to a minimum may seem a Pickwickian gesture. In fact, it is not feasible to admit students who have not had at least two and a half years of mathematics. But there are occasions when an applicant with irregular schooling or a deficiency in foreign languages is yet a good prospect for admission. It is a distinct advantage not to be hampered by formal requirements in selecting the best students from all those who apply.[54]

As a coda to their consideration of the problem of increasing the number of well-qualified applicants from high schools the committee considered the objection "that while the present geographical and social distribution leaves something to be desired the present quality of our student body is about as high as we can obtain." To answer this objection the committee examined the relative achievement of preparatory and high school students. What they found was that preparatory school students as a group were inferior in achievement

[54] Since 1947 the Director of Admissions has sent to a large number of secondary schools a statement in which he gives statistics on applications vs. admissions and explains the criteria used for admission. That there is a good deal of preselection is evidenced by the increasing proportion of applicants who are qualified.

during their college course and that it was the preparatory school students admitted from the third and fourth quarters of their classes who pulled down the averages of that group.[55] The committee concluded that

> . . . if we could increase our applications, particularly from high school students, to the point where the great majority of these third and fourth quarter preparatory school students could be replaced by students from the upper half of their school, public or private, the intellectual life of the college would be greatly improved.

What, then, is the situation now? The average college board scores for the two groups are presented in the following table:

AVERAGE COLLEGE BOARD APTITUDE SCORES
(V—Verbal Aptitude M—Mathematical Aptitude)

Class	Public Schools	Public and Private	Private Schools
1951	566 V—583 M	542 V—564 M	569 V—587 M
1952	589 V—591 M	562 V—596 M	582 V—619 M
1953	567 V—580 M	569 V—591 M	583 V—586 M

The next table compares the achievement of three classes during their freshman year in college:

SUMMARY OF DATA FROM THE DEAN'S REPORT ON FRESHMAN CLASSES ENTERING AMHERST IN 1948-51-52

	Number		College Grade	
Standing in Preparatory School	Private Schools	Public Schools	Private Schools	Public Schools
1st quarter	233	316	80.60	79.82
2nd quarter	125	53	75.38	75.41
3rd quarter	48	14	73.17	75.79
4th quarter	8	3	73.79	73.33
	Total 414	Total 386	Average 77.78	Average 78.84
	Total Number 800		General Average 78.29	

[55] See p. 110.

Finally, we give (1) the awards of the degree with distinction and (2) elections to Phi Beta Kappa for the years 1949, 1951, 1952, and 1953:

DEGREE WITH HONORS

Class	Total	Public Schools		Private Schools		Public and Private	
1949	65	38	58.5%	14	21.5%	13	20.0%
1951	81	36	44.4%	29	35.8%	16	19.8%
1952	105	53	50.5%	33	31.4%	19	18.1%
1953	94	53	56.4%	31	33.0%	10	10.6%

PHI BETA KAPPA

Class	Total	Public Schools		Private Schools		Public and Private	
1949	28	16	57.1%	7	25.0%	5	17.9%
1951	37	17	45.9%	16	43.2%	4	10.8%
1952	36	15	41.7%	16	44.4%	5	13.9%
1953	37	30	81.1%	5	13.5%	2	5.4%

A comparison of these tables with those given in the Long Range Policy Report indicates that the inferiority in academic aptitude and achievement of students entering from private schools which the committee's data revealed no longer exists. Undoubtedly, this is due to the large relative decrease in the number of students admitted from private schools who were in the third or fourth quarter of their class.

The final recommendation in this section of the report is that a Committee on Admissions and Scholarship Policy which would include faculty representation be established. A committee of this sort consisting of the President, the Deans, and a member of the faculty has been created. It has been active in respect to admissions, not merely dealing with questions of policy but participating in the choice of applicants as well. It had not, up to 1954, participated in the awards of scholarships. Recently, the administration of scholarships, of loans, and of student employment has been concentrated in the hands of a single person. It is to be anticipated that the committee will now function also in that field.

It is our opinion that, on the whole, there has been a distinct improvement in the administration of admissions and of scholarships. We hope that means will be found to progressively increase the number of well-qualified students entering from high schools until the proportion of these students is a decisive majority of, say, at least 65 or 70 per cent. And we believe that the amount of money expended for scholarships can be and should be greatly increased, not merely to improve the quality of our student body but with the specific object of broadening so far as possible its social basis.

ORIENTATION AND GUIDANCE

In this field more than the Committee on Long Range Policy had expected has been done.

The recommendation of the program of orientation for freshmen described in the report (pp. 116-117) was adopted. During the years it has been in effect various plans lasting from periods of four to seven days have been tried out. Freshmen and sophomores, as well as members of the administration and faculty, have been asked to criticize these variants.

At present the freshmen arrive five days before the beginning of classes. They have all received, as prospective students, an attractively printed and illustrated pamphlet entitled *This Is Amherst*. The five days give ample time in which to realize the objectives stated in the report and also afford opportunity to give the class their physical examinations, reading-speed tests, and language tests. In addition, freshmen receive during the first semester instruction in the use of the library, and the Freshman Dean meets several times with the entire class to discuss some of the problems of adaptation to a college environment.

The report discusses in some detail the problem of academic guidance. The committee emphasized the need for a freshman-sophomore dean who would be in charge of the counseling of the lowerclassmen and for the establishment of a small group of capable advisers really interested in their assignment who would "work as a corps under the close supervision of the Dean to carry the students through the first two years." Things have worked out a bit differently from this. Instead of a full-time freshman-sophomore dean we have, at present, a Director of Admissions and Dean of Freshmen who performs this function for the first-year class while the Dean of the College undertakes the academic guidance of the three upper classes. There are also an Associate Dean and an Assistant Dean who assist both in various ways. Altogether, the four deans manage to give a considerable amount of academic guidance.

The two upper classes, since they naturally depend for the greater part of their advice upon members of the faculty in the fields of their majors, are adequately served. The Freshman Dean makes up a "predicted average," on the basis of his records, for each freshman. In this way he is able to locate the students who may be "underachievers" and does what he can to deal with each individual case. But the suggestions of the committee that a picked corps of advisers be established and that in "the second term, during the period preceding consultation with advisers and elections for the sophomore year, there should be a series of talks on courses and departments, roughly divided into three groups, natural sciences, social studies, and humanities, all dealing specifically with the requirements, type of work involved, typical programs, and as clearly as possible outlining the purposes of a major or major with honors in that particular field" (p. 117) were not put into effect. Apparently it was supposed that since the students would be getting acquainted with a large number of faculty members in their small seminar or laboratory sections adequate guidance of this sort would spontaneously occur.

It is now belatedly realized that the freshmen and sophomores do not receive adequate advice on the use of their limited electives. The result is that a good many juniors make a shift in the field of their majors. Most of these mistakes, costly to the individual who makes them, could be prevented. A proposal similar to the suggestions made by the committee providing for a corps of advisers and a series of meetings prior to registration is now before the faculty. We hope that it, or something like it, will be adopted.

On the subject of personal counseling and psychiatric aid the report said: "There is a need for some sort of psychiatric aid in dealing with certain individuals in every college but we have no clear idea what a college in Amherst's situation should do about it" (p. 114).

Here is where developments went beyond the committee's expectations.

In 1951-1952 Amherst, with the aid of an anonymous gift from a foundation, entered for a five-year period upon an experiment hitherto untried in a small college: to include a student counselor on the faculty, a clinical psychologist with special experience in vocational and student counseling and equipped to deal with the many sorts of personal difficulties encountered by undergraduates. The Student Counselor is also a regular member of the Department of Psychology who gives a part of his time to teaching. About 10 per cent of the student body consult him annually. In three cases out of four, on the average, their problems are of a relatively simple kind which can be dealt with effectively in a few interviews. Two-thirds of the students come to the Counselor of their own accord, without being advised to do so by a teacher or a dean—in contrast to a large institution like the University of Michigan where only about 13 per cent of the cases are "self-referrals." The experiment, now in its third year, has proved successful—so much so that it is no longer regarded as an "experiment" but as a permanent addition to our educational resources. It has provided, we believe, one good answer, at least, to the question left unanswered by the Long Range Policy Committee.

In concluding this section, one recent development should be mentioned. A Committee on Guidance and Counseling has been established. It brings together all the persons principally concerned with academic and occupational guidance and with religious, personal, and psychiatric counseling. The activities of this committee should result in improved communication and cooperation between those working in this diversified field—and, hence, a more effective program.

SOCIAL LIFE AND ACTIVITIES

This section of the Long Range Policy Report posed the basic question of the role of social life and activities as follows: "Do the activities serve and express the native 'resistance' of a boy to education, do they help him to prolong his adolescence and defer the arduous business of growing up; or are they a means of enabling him to reach social and intellectual maturity?" We shall first sketch briefly postwar developments in the three fields discussed by the report—student government, the fraternities, and physical education and athletics; then we shall state our opinions on the degree to which the hopes of the Long Range Policy Committee have been fulfilled. It will be most convenient for our purposes to reverse the order in which these topics were treated in the report.

The recommendations of the Long Range Policy Committee for physical education and athletics were based upon the premise "If competitive sports are really good, there should be competitive sports for all." This presumption was corroborated in the program worked out independently by a majority of the members of the Department of Physical Education and submitted to the committee. The committee therefore endorsed their proposal because it "really merges physical education, intramural athletics and outside competitions into one over-all program." (See above p. 146).

The essential gains made under the present program have been stated by Professor A. W. Marsh in a memorandum to this present committee as follows:

The Department of Physical Education prepared, and received faculty approval for, a group of requirements for graduation from the department and hence, the college. These are:

a. Standards of fitness
b. Standards for swimming ability
c. Participation in at least one competitive team sport
d. Participation in at least one recreational sport

These requirements assured an all-round training for all men.

The Department recommended, and the Administration appointed, a Director of Freshman Physical Education and Athletics. This assured the freshmen of more careful attention and care in regard to the requirements, particularly fitness.

Greater participation in intercollegiate athletics was stimulated by the addition of informal sports to the upper class program, and several sports were added to the freshman program. Of the present (normal) senior class (1951) 65 per cent have been on either freshman or varsity intercollegiate sports teams playing through the entire season.

The Department of Physical Education and the Department of Intercollegiate Athletics have been merged into a single Department of Physical Education and Athletics. This assures the integration of the program and the possible realization of many of the objectives of a well rounded program.

In addition, the program of intramural sports has continued to flourish. Typical figures for participation in all sports are these for 1952-1953:[56]

INTRAMURAL AND INTERCOLLEGIATE PARTICIPATION,
COLLEGE YEAR 1952-53

Seniors—Total: 222 men
154 participated in intramural athletics, or 69%
50 participated in intercollegiate athletics, or 22½%
Juniors—Total: 249 men
189 participated in intramural athletics, or 75%
73 participated in intercollegiate athletics, or 29%
Sophomores—Total: 290 men
219 participated in intramural athletics, or 75%
130 participated in intercollegiate athletics, or 45%
Freshmen—Total: 262 men
105 participated in intramural athletics, or 40%
165 participated in intercollegiate athletics, or 63%

What eventuated then, though undoubtedly an improvement over what we had, is *not* the full program suggested by the department and recommended by the committee. The existing program deviates in three essential respects from the recommendations made in the report: Physical education is required for only two years instead of four; intercollegiate competition for freshmen (on freshman teams) has been continued; and the Long Range Policy Committee's recommendation that an opportunity should be given all students who are physically fit and wish to do so to participate in intercollegiate sports was not adopted.[57]

[56] It may be of interest to compare the amount of participation in nonathletic activities:

CLASS OF 1951—TOTAL 257 STUDENTS

	Number	Per Cent
Freshman year	92	36
Sophomore year	118	46
Junior year	149	58
Senior year	141	54

[57] When asked about what proportion of the upperclassmen really could make some team if they wished to do so, it was estimated by a member of the department that perhaps an additional 10 per cent of the students could qualify. However, increasing the size of squads as they are now constituted would decrease each individual's opportunity to participate in the games.

Professor Marsh has listed the factors causing these modifications as follows:

The general post-war retreat from emphasis on fitness for war following demobilization (i.e., obstacle courses, service swimming courses, etc.) and the peacetime preparation for civilian life through general sports participation.

The return of many veterans and the greatly increased enrollment, particularly in the freshman class, which made the five hour program for freshmen practically impossible.

The decision of the Faculty Committee on Athletics to encourage freshman intercollegiate sports which in large measure supplanted the junior varsity sports for upperclassmen. This decision was largely influenced by the belief that freshman intercollegiate sports offered an incentive to freshmen hoping to enter Amherst as other colleges were planning to carry on the freshman sports.

We recognize, as did the Long Range Policy Committee, that to require physical education throughout the college course and also to devise a program of intercollegiate athletics which allows every undergraduate who wishes it an opportunity to participate in them is expensive and would encounter many practical difficulties. However, upperclassmen have many competing interests. Those especially who are engaged in honors work and preprofessional preparation or who are taking the R.O.T.C. course in addition to their regular work might in many cases prefer the alternative of continuing their physical education in the upper two years by electing to engage in the individual sports rather than the more arduous and time-consuming intercollegiate competitions. The rapid decline in the percentage of upperclassmen participating in intercollegiate athletics, even of the sophomores (who are required to take physical education), may be an indication that this supposition is correct. And if it is correct, that would make the problem easier of solution.

We believe that the Committee on Educational Policy advanced sound reasons for their basic contentions: that physical education is just as important as intellectual education and therefore should be required of all students throughout their four years; and that intercollegiate athletics are too important (as a part of physical education) to allow the opportunity for engaging in them to be restricted to a minority, the physically elect.

The fathers of liberal education, the Greeks, considered it obvious, says the report, that music and gymnastics are equally important for education. If they were right in believing that these are the two complemental aspects of the curriculum, and we believe that they were right, why should not the college follow their example?

We have noted that the question whether the fraternities should be reinstated or abolished was one needing an early settlement. The Long Range Policy Committee (Professor Brown dissenting) had recommended their abolition. The faculty supported this recommendation. The vote was 47 for abolition, 26 for retention of the fraternities. (Absent members of the faculty were polled by mail.) As a supplement to this action twenty-five members of the faculty sent a letter to the trustees in which they made concrete proposals for the institution of a house plan similar to one suggested in the majority report of the alumni subcommittee on activities.

Meanwhile, this subcommittee on student activities, under the chairmanship of Mr. Ordway Tead, had, on the basis of arguments similar to those in the faculty report, voted four to one (Mr. R. H. Gregory dissenting) in favor of their abolition. On the subcommittee report the General Committee, consisting of the four subcommittee chairmen and the over-all chairman, Charles W. Cole, made this comment:

> Three members (Downey, Greene, Tead) endorse the majority report on this issue. Two members (Bixler, Cole) endorse the minority report with this reservation: that five years after the fraternities are reinstated the matter should be studied again by the trustees, the administration, the faculty, the alumni, and the students; if at that time it cannot be shown that the fraternities are making a positive and wholesome contribution to the intellectual, moral and social objectives of the College, then the recommendations of the majority report should be put into effect.[58]

Meanwhile, another group of alumni, a Committee on Post War Fraternities, appointed by the members of the Fraternity Business Management, issued a third report recommending that, with certain reforms, the fraternities be reestablished. This report appeared in February, 1945. Finally, the Alumni Council had sent out with the report "Amherst Tomorrow" a questionnaire on this and other

[58] "Amherst Tomorrow," *Alumni Council News*, 18 (1945), 126.

topics. The votes on the questions dealing with fraternities were as follows:

	Alumni Vote		Executive Committee Vote	
Do you believe that the Amherst fraternities should be abolished at once?	Yes	195	Yes	0
	No	666	No	7
If retained, do you believe that				
(a) Pledging should be postponed until the opening of the sophomore	Yes	303	Yes	0
year?	No	299	No	7
(b) Stricter supervision should be	Yes	443	Yes	5
maintained by the faculty?	No	159	No	2

With all of this before them, the trustees considered the question and concluded that the fraternities should be retained. At their meeting on June 2, 1945, the trustees adopted a statement in which they reached the following conclusions:

1. That the fraternities have failed markedly in recent years to make a positive contribution to college life.
2. That the interests of the College can best be served at this time by a program of radical reform rather than by one of abolition, with its inevitable untried substitutes.[59]

Final action by the board was taken the following December when they unanimously adopted a resolution providing:

I. In reopening the fraternities, the College shall make available such additional facilities as may be needed to provide living quarters and appointments for social life equal to those now available at fraternity houses, to the end that each member of the three upper classes who wishes to join a social organization may have the opportunity of doing so.

II. No freshman shall be permitted to be pledged by, or join any fraternity. No rushing shall be permitted until after the final examination at the end of the freshman year.

III. Fraternities shall not be permitted to operate dining rooms, and members of the upper three classes shall not be permitted to eat in fraternity groups.

IV. The Student Council shall be reorganized so as to exclude fraternity and house representation.

V. It shall be a condition of the reopening of each fraternity that it

[59] *Amherst College Bulletin*, 35, no. 1 (1945), 9.

formally recognize that the College Administration has the same control over the maintenance and operation of fraternity buildings and social life in the fraternity as it has with respect to the dormitories.

VI. National dues and all other national costs to the undergraduates at Amherst shall be drastically reduced.

VII. The present Fraternity Business Management Committee shall be continued.

VIII. There shall be established as promptly as possible a committee to consist at the outset of one alumni representative from each fraternity or house and, as soon as feasible, an undergraduate from each fraternity or house, and to include the Fraternity Business Manager as Secretary. This Committee shall be known as the House Management Committee, and shall elect its own chairman and a working executive committee, and adopt such other rules of organization as it may desire.

This committee shall

a. Formulate and implement a program for reestablishing rushing, bidding, and the initiation of fraternity members, both until normal conditions are established and thereafter—including regulations for the size of fraternities and delegations.
b. Prepare a code of conduct for the members of fraternities.
c. Establish, in cooperation with the faculty, a system of faculty advisers for each fraternity.
d. Take such steps as may be found necessary to effect a drastic reduction of National charges now made by each fraternity, exclusive of cost of the pin.

IX. Fraternities shall be permitted to reopen in the fall of 1946, or as soon thereafter as is feasible in the opinion of the House Management Committee and the College Administration.

X. A standing committee of the Board of Trustees on Fraternities shall be established, with the understanding that this Committee shall present annually to the Board a written report on the fraternity situation at Amherst College with recommendations of such further action as may appear to be necessary.[60]

In respect to most of these reforms there was little or no controversy. The only provision in respect to which there appeared to be a serious division of opinion at the time was that which provided for delayed rushing.[61]

[60] *Amherst College Bulletin,* 36, no. 2 (1946), 19-21.

[61] In January, 1948, the rushing period was moved to spring vacation of freshman year. There is general dissatisfaction among students and faculty alike at the way rushing interferes with academic work. The proper time at which to have it remains an unsolved problem.

On April 20, 1946, the board supplemented these regulations by voting: "That on or before October 1, 1948, each chapter of a fraternity at Amherst College shall formally advise the Board of Trustees of Amherst College that there is no prohibition or restriction by reason of race, color, or creed affecting the selection of the members of such chapter." The date was subsequently set forward to February 1, 1949, and again to February 1, 1951, at the request of several fraternities. This stipulation has also been a subject of controversy.

In accordance with Section I of these provisions the college acquired a house which was remodeled to provide suitable housing and social facilities for the members of the nonfraternity organization, the Lord Jeffery Amherst Club.

Of the two basic charges against the fraternities, that they were anti-democratic and anti-intellectual, it is plain from the character of their reforms that the first weighed most heavily with the trustees. Presumably they hoped that the newly instituted House Management Committee might with the aid of the faculty advisers do something toward stimulating the fraternities to "make a positive contribution to college life." In any event, it is in reducing discrimination that real progress has been made.

At the time of their resolution of April, 1946, five Amherst fraternities had discriminatory clauses in their charters or bylaws. The national organization of one of these fraternities, Delta Tau Delta, refused to permit the local chapter to reopen because of its dissatisfaction with the way in which fraternities were being treated at Amherst. This group became a local fraternity under the name Kappa Theta.

Clearly, the requirement that these clauses be deleted was as much as the trustees could do toward effecting an abolition of discriminatory practices. That this formal action was insufficient for the purpose was dramatically illustrated when in April, 1948, Phi Kappa Psi pledged Thomas Gibbs, a Negro student. Though this fraternity was one of those which had no discriminatory clauses in its constitution and bylaws, strong objections were made by some other chapters with the result that the Amherst chapter was directed by the national organization not to initiate Thomas Gibbs. The undergraduate members of the chapter had taken it for granted that their charter gave them freedom of choice. They did not anticipate trouble and they had "bid" Thomas Gibbs simply because they wanted him as a person to be a member of their group. Faced with this choice, the members of the chapter voted unanimously to keep their word. The national organization suspended the chapter and later revoked its charter. Phi Kappa Psi also became a local fraternity under the name Phi Alpha Psi.[62]

Perhaps the best comment on this episode is an editorial entitled "Victory at Amherst" in the *New York Times:*

> The Amherst College football team beat Williams on Saturday by a score of 13 to 7, but it may be that another sort of victory, won on the Amherst campus on Friday, will be longer remembered. Until Friday, Amherst had a chapter of the national Phi Kappa Psi fraternity. On Friday that chapter was suspended by the national executive committee for "unfraternal conduct." This conduct consisted in a decision to go ahead with the initiation of a respected and popular student who happened to be a Negro. The Amherst chapter chose to defy this dictate of intolerance. In taking this position it was in line with the declared policy of the Amherst College trustees, adopted two years ago, and, we hope and believe, with student opinion on the Amherst campus.
>
> The general public can have no concern with college fraternities, but it is rightly concerned with the prevalence of the democratic spirit in institutions which receive tax exemptions and other forms of public support. In this episode we see the real meaning of a liberal education. An Amherst degree has always been respected. It will be more respected now.[63]

[62] A graphic account of the affair is given in Alfred S. Romer, "The Color Line in Fraternities," *Atlantic Monthly*, June, 1949. Since then a number of similar incidents have occurred at other eastern colleges.

[63] By way of contrast, consider this statement made by David A. Embury, chairman of the National Inter-Fraternity Conference, in a speech at the thirty-ninth annual convention as reported in the *New York Times*, November 29, 1947:

"Mr. Embury charged that subversive elements on the nation's campuses were mostly responsible for the widespread protest movement against restricted fraternities and sororities. . . .

"Saying that people should 'stop shivering at the word "discrimination,"' Mr. Embury asserted that he 'would sing the praises of the term.'

"'I love the discriminating tongue, the discriminating eye, and the discriminating ear, and, above all, the discriminating mind and soul,' he said. 'The person for whom I can find no love and no respect is the indiscriminate person. To be indiscriminate is to be common, to be vulgar.'"

Of the four chapters which had discriminatory clauses to get rid of, only one, Phi Delta Theta, found its difficulties interminable. The system of checks and balances in the constitution of the national organization made it extremely difficult for the local chapter to get the clause rescinded. Extensions of time were granted the chapter by the trustees. Meanwhile, the undergraduates disregarded the clause when considering persons for membership. An open challenge to the national organization by the Williams chapter forced the national organization to take a definite stand on the issue, and as a result the Williams and Amherst chapters were suspended in May, 1953, for violating the discriminatory clause of the constitution. Phi Delta Theta at Amherst became a local fraternity, Phi Delta Sigma.

It is evident that Amherst has made substantial progress toward the elimination of discriminatory practices in pledging. Perhaps, though, other fraternities have been intimidated by the expulsion of chapters here and at Williams, Wesleyan, and Bowdoin, rather than encouraged by their example. An editorial in the *Amherst Student* for October 18, 1951, raises the question: "How many other fraternities are there on campus who have no clause of discrimination in their charter but who would have difficulty if they 'stepped out of line'? How many houses have gentleman's agreements with their national organizations? How many houses would not even consider doing something 'unfraternal' for fear of trouble, though no agreement exists? How many houses hesitate?" And the writer of this editorial goes on to say, "There are houses on campus which have been able to remove their discriminatory clauses only by instituting strong tacit agreements in their place."[64]

Even more important than this direct attempt by the trustees and by the undergraduate members of the fraternities to abolish discrimination is the grass-roots movement for "total rushing." Since the war rushing has been operated through a complicated system of preferential card bidding combined with quotas for each house. Under this system only a proportion, though a large one, of those students who wished to join a fraternity could be pledged. Those left out had the choice of remaining independent or becoming members of the Lord Jeff Club, which accepts all students who apply. However, in 1950-1951, in part no doubt because of apprehensions about the draft,

[64] So far as we are aware, these charges were never substantiated.

so many freshmen were pledged during the original rushing period that the students requested a further period for supplementary over-the-quota rushing. The result was that all but two men of that freshman class joined a fraternity or the Lord Jeff Club. Then, some time before the rushing period in 1952, three undergraduates, Peter Schrag, David Gyger, and John Herzog, devised and proposed an ingenious plan for over-the-quota rushing whereby it would be at least possible for all freshmen who wished to do so to join a fraternity. The scheme caught on and was adopted, with some modifications, for that year, with the result that in 1951-1952 total rushing was achieved. Of the 286 freshmen who indicated their interest in joining a social organization fourteen preferred to join the Lord Jeff Club, and the remaining 272 were all pledged by the thirteen fraternities. This, we believe, is the first instance in which total rushing has occurred at any fraternity college. Thus initiated, total rushing has held on. The following year all but one man were pledged. Since he had refused an opportunity to join a fraternity because it was not the one he wanted, total rushing was in effect achieved. And again in 1953-1954 all the students who expressed the wish to join a fraternity were bid.

How did this come about? The most important factor, we believe, was the continual discussion on the campus of the moral issues involved, generated by the trustees' requirement that restrictive clauses be removed. A whole series of events—the expulsion of Phi Kappa Psi from the national organization, similar incidents in sister colleges, the trials of Phi Delta Theta in trying to get its clause removed, the constant agitation by an aggressive and influential element in the Lord Jeff Club—kept this issue before the minds of the undergraduates and cumulatively built up a climate of opinion favorable to the proposal for total rushing when it appeared. It looks now as though that ineluctable entity, a "tradition," is being established.

However, the very success of voluntary total rushing creates a difficulty which may endanger its continuation. *Voluntary* total rushing depends upon the existence of the Lord Jeff Club. Not only does the club serve as a safety valve by preventing the fraternities from feeling that they are expected to take everyone, it also is there *for* the student who does not wish to join a fraternity and who does want to belong to the type of social organization which the club represents. As a group, the members of the club favor total rushing. But total rushing has had the result that very small numbers of students are now joining the club. If the success of the principle for which the club stands were to extinguish it, a difficult situation would be created. It is quite possible that under those circumstances the fraternities would be forced to choose between reverting to their former practices and *compulsory* total rushing; and, in the event they did adopt the latter, the students who do not wish to join a fraternity would have no place to go.

Since the fraternities were reestablished there has, then, been a substantial reduction of their former exclusiveness. But it is not at all evident that they have been less inimical to the intellectual life of the college. The charge made by the Long Range Policy Committee was:

> The fraternities represent an entrenchment of the world without inside the college community. They are the center of a kind of social education that reinforces the conventional values of our society in an environment where those values are being analyzed. Hence, there is a real and natural antagonism, which anyone at all acquainted with them will recognize, between the fraternities and the college.

Opinions on this subject are difficult to verify, but we have no reason to believe that, as yet, the fraternities have changed. We have carried forward the tables presented by the Long Range Policy Committee on the annual awards of the Treadway Trophy for interfraternity scholarship, for degrees *summa cum laude* or *magna cum laude*, and for elections to Phi Beta Kappa.[65] The results are shown in the accompanying tables.

AWARDS OF THE TREADWAY TROPHY, 1943-44 TO 1952-53

Academic Year	Fraternity or Group
1946-47	Lord Jeffery Amherst Club
1947-48	Lord Jeffery Amherst Club
1948-49	Phi Gamma Delta
1949-50	Phi Alpha Psi
1950-51	Lord Jeffery Amherst Club
1951-52	Lord Jeffery Amherst Club
1952-53	Lord Jeffery Amherst Club

(No awards were made in 1943-44, 1944-45, and 1945-46)

[65] See above pp. 132-133.

Degrees Summa Cum Laude or Magna Cum Laude Conferred at Commencements from 1943-44 to 1952-53 Inclusive Analyzed by Fraternity Membership

Group	Summas	Magnas	Total	Percentage
Highest fraternity	3	18	21	10.0
Second highest fraternity	1	16	17	8.2
Third highest fraternity	1	15	16	7.8
Nonfraternity	12	48	60	29.0
	—	—	—	—
	17	97	114	55.0
These four groups	17	97	114	55
Ten other fraternities	12	81	93	45
	—	—	—	—
	29	178	207	100

Elections to Phi Beta Kappa from 1943-44 to 1952-53 Inclusive

Group	Elections		Percentage
Highest fraternity	29		
Second highest fraternity	27		
Third highest fraternity	23	Three fraternities	29
Nonfraternity	70	Nonfraternity	26
	—		—
	149		55
These four groups	149		55
Ten other fraternities	121		45
	—		—
Totals	270		100

Note: The three highest fraternities in the second table are the same ones as in the last. Two of these three highest fraternities are the same as the two highest listed in the Long Range Policy Report. Two fraternities were singled out in the Long Range Policy Report as being consistently the lowest in attaining honors and elections to Phi Beta Kappa. These two fraternities are still consistently and markedly lower than any others.

The Long Range Policy Committee concluded "that there has not been maintained a healthy and reasonable balance, in the matter of high scholarship, among the different social groups of which the college is composed." This apparently is still true.

Yet there now are circumstances which should help to produce some improvement in this situation. First, the great increase in the number of applicants for admission has enabled the college to raise its standards far above those of the prewar level. The present student body is presumably more intelligent—as judged by the criteria for admission—and it is unquestionably more industrious. To the degree that intelligence and industry combined are correlated with intellectual interests (and to some degree this must surely be the case), the fraternities presumably are less anti-intellectual than they were. Certainly, the playboy is less in evidence.

To this it should be added that an indirect effect of total rushing is to reduce selectivity among the houses, making each more nearly representative of the student body as a whole. During the years prior to total rushing the membership of the Lord Jeff Club was large. Undoubtedly, it contained an undue proportion of those students who were markedly individualistic and of those (frequently the same persons) who would be classed as "intellectuals." Some of the students were in the club by choice, others were there because the fraternities had passed them over. In fact, the club drained off a good deal of the leaven in the lump. It helped the fraternities as a group to preserve their social and intellectual mediocrity. Total rushing will lead to a dilution of this "typing." As each fraternity becomes more representative of the student body as a whole, it will be a better agent for the social education of its members, and its will to resist the educational aims of the college will diminish.

But these statements should not be taken to mean that all is now well and getting even better. During recent years the President has repeatedly been forced to criticize the fraternities for their failure to develop "a mode of social life consonant with the aims and purposes of the whole college." "The trouble with the social life of the students," he has said, "is that there is too much of it." The social life of the campus as focused in the fraternities has "come to be over-developed, over-emphasized and confused." With this opinion we agree, and we intend to make our own comments on the general attitude of the student body toward their social responsibilities at the end of this section.

The Long Range Policy Committee had urged: "It is of the greatest importance that when the college returns to normalcy every effort be made to institute and maintain a proper form of real student government, one organized on a basis similar to the one destroyed in 1938" (p. 124). This formal restitution the trustees effected by directing that "The Student Council shall be reorganized so as to exclude fraternity and house representation." But the restitution was with one vital difference: the trustees also provided at the same time for a House Management Committee to be composed of one alumni and one undergraduate representative from each fraternity or house. To the House Management Committee was assigned jurisdiction over the rushing rules, a mandate to establish a system of faculty advisers for the fraternities, and the duty to prepare a code of conduct for the members of fraternities and houses. Though it was not expressly stated, the House Management Committee would presumably have the power to enforce its rulings.

While it was remembered that conflicts among the fraternities had led to the overthrow of a similar type of student government in 1938, no one seemed to have looked far into the consequences of dividing the functions of student government between two entirely independent bodies, the Student Council and the House Management Committee. Though the constitution of the student government naïvely states that the first purpose of the organization shall be "To provide a controlling and directing force for every phase of undergraduate activity" (Art. II, sec. 1), it has no jurisdiction over the most important phases of student activity. Its actual business is to deal with *relatively* peripheral matters, chiefly the supervision of extracurricular activities.[66] The real core of student government is what it always was, regulation of the social groups into which the student body is divided. It is no surprise, therefore, to find it said in a survey of the college made by the student paper:

[66] It should not be presumed, however, that these functions are unimportant, or that the officers administering them lack prestige. The presidency of the Student Council is the most highly prized position on campus. The Council has the responsibility of appropriating more than $20,000 for undergraduate activities; it has a good deal of real authority in the regulation of sports; its president is a member of the Committee on Intercollegiate Athletics; a representative of the Council sits on the Chapel Committee; the Council appoints the members of an undergraduate Curriculum Committee which consults with the faculty Committee on Educational Policy and the faculty Lecture Committee; it is, of course, the representative of the student body in dealing with the administration; and it is consulted by the administration on all important disciplinary problems.

Actually of course student government at Amherst insofar as most students come into contact with it is centered around the social organizations. It is the fraternity goat which is Amherst's expression of the *vox populi*. Few Amherst men, the poll shows, even know what the council does because they have little or no direct contact with it. And of course class organization is recognized as outmoded and replaced by the social organization. The House Management Committee, in fact, is more a subject of campus knowledge and interest than the Student Council, because the student has contact with the former through reports in goat by the HMC representative.[67]

Gone are the days when the capture of offices was the objective of "combines" and the occasion of bitter internecine strife, when student government resembled the turbulent politics of ancient Greek city-states. While there is an occasional flare-up over some matter of general interest to the undergraduates in which the Student Council is involved, student government is now generally equable because it is innocuous.[68]

Evidence that student government is peripheral to the basic interests of the undergraduates is afforded by their reaction to the question whether the honor system should be reestablished. This question was used in the spring of 1954 as one of the topics in the required course, Problems of American Civilization. Because the sophomores spent two weeks in the study of this problem, it became a subject of discussion by all undergraduates. The results, judged by the papers submitted and the opinions expressed in seminar meetings, are interesting. Approximately one out of three of the sophomores was in favor of an honor system, though most of these opposed any plan which involved reporting another student. Few even of the students

[67] *Amherst Student*, May 14, 1951.

[68] If the present segregation of powers was made in the interests of efficiency, we doubt whether even that object has been attained. The alumni members of the House Management Committee are helpful in the formulation and administration of rushing rules; here their opinions are respected and their judgment is influential. But in respect to the vital matter of a social code, the alumni group cannot be very effective. The alumni group has no intimate contact with the student body. Consequently, in this area they have no prestige. The students feel, quite naturally, that the alumni group has an insufficient acquaintance with their problems to really understand them, and suspect that any policy they may advocate is inspired by the administration. In exercising this function the House Management Committee is generally regarded as the agent of a disguised paternalism.

in favor of an honor system felt any strong sense of group responsibility; rather they favored an honor system because they did not like being watched during examinations or vaguely apprehended that, somehow, to be for it was getting over on the side of the angels.

The opposition was based chiefly upon an unwillingness to take responsibility. A typical attitude was this: The teacher makes out the exams, let him proctor them. I don't cheat (unless it is justifiable, as when a course is not well given or the exam is unreasonable) and I don't see why I should have any responsibility for others. The Amherst attitude is to "stay loose." (This was a favorite phrase.) We are individuals and we want our freedom. We resent the prep school rules restricting women and liquor in fraternity houses and requiring class attendance. If we had an honor system, it would take a lot of time and trouble to run it and it would undoubtedly be a failure as students would cheat more even than they do now and decent Amherst students would certainly not report on each other.

The apparent success of the honor system at such places as Princeton and the University of Virginia was attributed to the existence of a tradition which did not exist at Amherst. The notion that such a tradition might be developed here appealed to few. Most of the students seemed to feel it was not worth the effort and was probably impossible anyway. And the attitude of upperclassmen, at least as reflected by the Student Council, was even less favorable to the assumption of responsibility than that of the sophomores. The question having been brought before the Council, that body voted "by an overwhelming majority to table indefinitely any further investigation of the possibility of instituting an honor system on the campus." Their reason was that a great majority of the students did not want it, and, as one Council member explained, "We feel that you cannot legislate an attitude."[69]

What a preponderant group of the students want, then, is freedom without responsibility. The prevalent attitude is expressed by the injunction "Stay loose."[70] In consequence, the faculty and administration are forced to take the initiative in formulating rules governing

[69] *Amherst Student*, May 21, 1954.

[70] We doubt that this attitude is at all peculiar to Amherst. It appears to be widely prevalent in this postwar generation. One interesting discussion of some possible causes is David Riesman's *The Lonely Crowd: A Study of the Changing American Character* (New Haven, 1950).

the behavior of the undergraduates. Whenever these rules become too constrictive of their precious freedom, the students cry out against paternalism.

President Cole has commented on this attitude in a chapel address entitled "Paternalism and Responsibility." He summarizes his point as follows:

What I have been trying to say is that what looks like existence or extension of paternalism in a college where all those in authority believe strongly and deeply in self-government always has another aspect. Turn the coin of paternalism over and look at the other side: it is always the failure of undergraduates to assume or to fulfill responsibilities. Such failure leaves a vacuum and those responsible for the future of the college, and for its present, must fill the vacuum. They do it hesitantly and reluctantly, but fill it they must.

And he concludes that

Paternalism in a college like this arises only when it is called into being by a lack of maturity among the students. If they do not act like mature and responsible men, then they must be governed as if they were not mature. . . . It is not too much to say that it is a matter of world importance whether, in colleges like Amherst today, young Americans are learning that they must be steadily responsible, not only for themselves and their own development, but also for those with whom they are associated and the institutions to which they belong. If such men do not learn that for their freedom they must ever pay in responsibilities eagerly assumed and gladly fulfilled, if such men in such surroundings do not learn this lesson and learn it well—then the lights of freedom may burn low and flicker out in this nation and in all lands.[71]

The more thoughtful undergraduates recognize the inconsistency in this prevalent attitude. But they also realize that it is not wholly the fault of the students themselves. One undergraduate has stated the point in this way:

It cannot be denied that the student body has had a notable lack of success in achieving solutions to its common problems; nor has it exerted itself to do so in any unified fashion. As a case in point, fraternities at Amherst are not cohesive, purposive units, and they have largely abdicated from any responsibility for the social behavior of their members.

[71] *Amherst Alumni News*, 6, no. 2 (1953), 2-3.

To the extent that the undergraduates have not learned how to participate in such group and community efforts, they have not been educated. To the extent that the College has not pointed the way for the undergraduates to solve their own problems, it has failed in its educational task of preparing them to accept their social responsibilities.[72]

We agree with this judgment. President Cole's address is an eloquent statement of the clear and present danger in demanding freedom without accepting responsibility, but it gives no constructive answer to the charge: "To the extent that the College has not pointed the way for the undergraduates to solve their own problems, it has failed in its educational task of preparing them to accept their social responsibilities." The question, then, is how the administration and faculty of the college can fill this "moral vacuum." To say that paternalism arises when it is called into being by lack of maturity emphasizes only the negative possibility. The effect of this kind of "paternalism" is to maintain the state of immaturity. To exercise it is a confession of failure. But there is another kind of paternalism, of the parent who recognizes that maturity is gradually acquired, and that to foster growth in the ability to accept responsibility is the parent's duty. Every person confronted with the demand that he accept a new responsibility finds in himself an ambivalent attitude—he fears and resents it and at the same time he finds it a challenge. The more immature a person is, the more he needs the authority of a parent, not to accept the responsibility for him if it is truly *his* responsibility, but to give him the support he needs in order to meet that challenge and accept the responsibility for himself. This is the way in which individuals can become free, and this is a sound working definition of "education for democracy." For democracy may best be defined as the maximum diffusion of responsibility, the maximum, of course, that is reasonably possible—the principle being that every individual should be given as much responsibility as, for his given abilities and stage of maturity, he can reasonably bear.

This is why the Long Range Policy Committee did not compose a report dealing merely with the curriculum. The committee recognized that any such report would be a travesty of their mandate to reconsider the *educational* policy of the college. The educative effect,

[72] C. M. Grimstad, *Amherst Student,* June 12, 1954.

for better or worse, is the impact upon the individual of the total environment in which he spends his four college years. Accordingly, the committee was concerned with "the quality and character of the life of the institution as a whole."

What the committee hoped was that a real integration of "college life" and the "curriculum" might be achieved. "If," they said, "the college can make itself a democratic intellectual community, profoundly interested in the welfare of the society of which it is a part, its future will do honor to its past."

So far as the college community is not democratic it has also failed to become intellectual. Evidence for this is given by the students themselves. According to the survey of the state of the college made by the staff of the *Amherst Student*, the undergraduate "lives on two levels." Studies, they say, seem to be

> . . . something which you work at for an average of 15 to 20 hours a week outside the classroom (as shown in the poll) and then forget about in social problems and extra curricular life. . . . It can certainly be said that at Amherst very few students apply the same kind of analysis—and then act upon it—in their social life as they do in their courses. All of the preceding merely emphasizes the fact that for the Amherst man studying has its place and the first commandment about studying, as about everything else, is "Stay loose!"[73]

And this conclusion is corroborated by the student commentator we have previously cited. There is, he thinks, an "element of sterility" in the education our students receive because "the ability of the Amherst student to pass judgment on academic matters does not seem to be effectively applied to the formulation of standards for social action."

The basic aim of the Long Range Policy Committee was to show how Amherst College might help to produce men elected, in Jefferson's words, "for genius and virtue" to serve our democracy. We do not believe that this is a utopian hope. But that aim will not be fulfilled until a great deal more that *can* be done *has* been done to foster among our students the freedom which comes from self-reliance. If we expect them to become mature, then we must *require* them to accept all the responsibility for their own conduct that they can

[73] *Amherst Student*, May 7, 1951.

possibly bear. They should become working partners in the administration of the college. At this crucial point the "new program" has not been put into effect. Until it is, the administration and faculty of this college cannot truly say *with* the committee "that it is the purpose of the college to give young men of superior endowment the knowledge and training that they need to make them leaders in a democratic community."

THE RELIGIOUS LIFE OF THE COLLEGE

We have noted the action on the recommendations of the Long Range Policy Committee that attendance at church services be made voluntary and that college chapel be continued. In October, 1945, the faculty approved the committee's recommendations on church and in April they voted that chapel should be resumed the following academic year. These actions were ratified by the Board of Trustees. Since it was recognized by everyone that a "voluntary" service would not be practicable and that all of the town churches would welcome those students who chose to attend them, college church services were discontinued.[74]

The argument of the Long Range Policy Committee was based upon this presumption:

> Under these [early] conditions it would have been pointless, in fact impossible, to distinguish between religion in Amherst College and the Christianity of Amherst College. Today it is equally impossible fruitfully to discuss the question without making that distinction. For now, only one teaching member of our faculty, the professor of religion, is a clergyman, and church and chapel are no longer the powerful institutions they once were.

That was not, however, the tone of this section of the alumni committee's report. All but one of the members of the sub-committee on religion were graduates of theological seminaries. Their discussion, if we understand it rightly, does *not* proceed from a distinction between religion in Amherst College and Christianity in Amherst College.

[74] A questionnaire sent out by the Alumni Council with the report of the Alumni Committee on Postwar Amherst gave the following results:

Do you favor compulsory church? Yes, 392; no, 390.

Do you favor compulsory chapel? Yes, 593; no, 195.

The members of the Council themselves voted unanimously against compulsory church and in favor of compulsory chapel.

Perhaps this difference in tone can best be indicated by quoting their opinion on the question whether church attendance should be voluntary:

Although a large proportion of alumni opinion favors compulsory church, there is also a minority group which states that "religion and compulsion are incompatible." To this group we may say that it is true that religion cannot be forced upon anyone, for response to it must come from within. However, this response cannot be expected of the religiously illiterate person. Therefore, it might well be considered an obligation of the College to see that students are acquainted with the basic characteristics of religion—and thus receive an experience comparable to rudimentary training in other disciplines—as part of the well-rounded educational process. Thus, in their maturity men will have some knowledge and experience upon which their capacity to respond to religion may be based.[75]

The alumni committee assumed that juniors and seniors were sufficiently mature to know their own wills in this matter and accordingly recommended that the attendance of only the two lower classes at the College Church (or at a town church) should be required.

The same difference between the two reports comes out in their treatment of chapel. The view of the faculty committee was:

Chapel and church were both originally religious services. Chapel was the continuation in college of family prayers. It should not now, however, be considered a service of worship. The two questions of church and chapel are, in our opinion, different ones and therefore should be treated separately.

The alumni committee did *not* regard the two questions of church and chapel as "different ones" which "should be treated separately." Their position was:

If the religious ideas taught by the College are to become effective in the lives of students, some way must be found of providing experiences by which classroom instruction is translated into decision and action. Chapel and Church are here of the first importance. . . .

The objections by students, faculty, and alumni to the prewar "chapel" services held during the week have centered in their lack of direction and purpose as religious exercises. These objections are probably legitimate,

[75] "Amherst Tomorrow," *Alumni Council News*, 18 (1945), 108.

since under the name of "chapel" differing types of exercises have been conducted, ranging from religious services to talks on vocations.[76]

To answer these objections they recommended that the four meetings a week be divided: two times a week "a student meeting," preferably to be known as an "assembly" and not as "chapel," "should be held"; the other two times should be given to a "voluntary chapel service" which would "always be religious in nature."

Beyond the retention of compulsory chapel, neither committee's recommendations were followed in practice until about two years ago. What has been called "an ambiguous mixture" has been the rule.[77] The ambiguity is nicely expressed in the official pamphlet, *This Is Amherst*:

Services are held in Johnson Chapel on week-day mornings, as they have been for more than a century. There are four such services a week, and attendance at at least two of them is required of all undergraduates. Each service consists of an appropriate religious framework (doxology, prayer, hymn, benediction) and a short talk on either religious or secular matters. The latter are concerned with topics of current interest at the College, or subjects drawn from the history of the College and the town, or from the theater of national and world events.

Those who agree with the alumni committee object to having a doxology, prayer, hymn, and benediction when the "short talk" is on "secular matters"; those who believe with the faculty committee that chapel should not be compulsory if it is "a service of worship" object to those services in which the "short talk" is on "religious matters." It is unlikely that the alumni committee's way out, two required "assemblies" and two voluntary "chapels" a week will be adopted. One difficulty is the fact that Johnson Chapel can accommodate only about half of the present student body. Moreover, the experiment was tried for a short while of having some purely secular assemblies. It was the opinion of the Chapel Committee that these were distinctly unsuccessful—the traditional framework seems to be needed—and so the "assemblies" were discontinued. What we have then is what we had—long before the committees made their reports: required chapels

[76] *Ibid.*, p. 107.

[77] By John B. Coburn, formerly chaplain of the college, and James A. Martin, professor of religion, in a joint memorandum to the present committee.

some of which are "religious" and some of which are "secular," both with the traditional framework.

As everyone knows, an intermittent agitation against required chapel by the undergraduates is endemic on those campuses where it still exists. On chapel there is always an open season. The assaults come in waves which relapse and, after a while, rise again. The most recent attack by the students found its rationale in this ambiguous mixture. The result of student agitation was that two secular and two religious chapels a week were *scheduled*. This was not novel; the novelty consisted in giving advance notice of the days on which each type of service would be held.

Obviously, a minor modification is not to the point. The point is that those who are responsible for religious activities on the campus believe that chapel *should* be a religious service in their sense of the term; they are not willing to allow *all* chapel services to become convocations—religious only in the sense that they express the corporate unity of the college.

There may be no way out of this impasse. We have one suggestion to make, however, which *could* be put into partial effect even though the usual number of chapels which are services of worship is maintained. What the faculty committee said in 1945 is true now: "If Chapel is to survive, every effort must be made to make it interesting." Though it might linger on for quite a while as an otiose custom, the real question is: How *can* it be made interesting? And the only answer is: By recovering its *former* importance. When chapel was the continuation in college of family prayers, it was also the *peculiar* responsibility of the President. In conducting chapel he stood in the relation to his students of *paterfamilias*. Thomas Le Duc, describing Amherst during the administration of President Seelye (1876-1890), says:

> The focus of the official college life was still the chapel. Here the students gathered with their teachers for morning prayers and a brief word from the president. Few of Seelye's notes for these talks on homely subjects have survived, but one reputable alumnus speaks of them as "full of moral elevation and practical wisdom."[78]

[78] *Piety and Intellect at Amherst College* (New York, 1946), p. 57.

It is easy to be nostalgic about the good old days, especially if they are so old you were not then alive, yet there can be no doubt that the president of a small college was and still is in a position to exert a unique and invaluable influence upon the student body—and that it is in the conduct of chapel that this influence can be most effective.

Certainly our attitude should *not* be: "Chapel is a revered institution and we must try to keep it going with a minimum of discontent." By taking that attitude a great opportunity will be missed. Ideally, chapel would "go" of itself because it had a maximum of consent. It is the engineering of this consent which is the locus of the problem. Now it suffers from the distemper of heterogeneity, a mélange of seven-minute speeches assigned by a Chapel Committee to various members of the faculty and administration. Yet chapel *should* perform an integrating function throughout the students' undergraduate course. We have tried at Amherst to construct a plan of study which will enable our students to acquire a more coherent understanding of the bewildering world in which they must live. The curriculum has, we believe, a considerable degree of intellectual integration. What we lack is a form of personal integration. Chapel should be made the focus of this personal integration—as it was in President Seelye's time. We believe that, so far as possible, chapel should be what it was in Seelye's time—the President's course, *his* four-year course required of all students. In giving his course the President is not relying merely upon himself. No classroom teacher does so. The teacher represents his subject. And the President speaks as one who is also invested with the dignity of his office and who represents to his auditors the traditions of the college.

This is where a President can make one of his most significant contributions to the intellectual and moral life of the college. We realize that nowadays college presidents have many more duties and distractions and that the assumption of this additional responsibility would be a heavy burden. In fact, it would be under existing conditions a burden so heavy that its full assumption is impracticable. When the chapels were primarily religious meetings, the President could be expected to take charge of them often. All he ordinarily had to do was read a passage from the Scriptures and make that the basis of some edifying comments. But for the President to conduct secular chapels often would put him in the position of the daily columnist—and that is certainly a full-time job. Furthermore, to introduce any real continuity for the student auditors into the chapel meetings is made extremely difficult if not impossible because the room holds only something more than a half of the present student body.

All we are entitled to ask for, then, is an improvement of existing practices. In the last few years the quality of the chapel services has been bettered, chiefly by more careful planning of assignments to the speakers. The students are decently attentive, and most of them would probably say—after their graduation—that, on the whole, chapel was worthwhile. But we do believe further improvement is possible; there ought to be a closer approximation to the ideal we have stated, that chapel should be the President's course. For it is only in terms of *this* ideal that we can defend our affirmative answer to the question: Why should attendance at chapel be *required?*

SOME PROBLEMS OF ORGANIZATION AND GOVERNMENT

In this final section of their report, the Committee on Educational Policy discussed the following topics: "divisional organization of the faculty; tenure, appointments and promotions; acceleration of the college course; the size of the college; and the corporate life of the college." We shall comment briefly upon each of these in turn.

The committee's recommendation that general courses and group majors be given departmental status was, as we have noticed, put into effect, and their warning against any further strengthening of the divisional organization of the college was heeded.

On tenure, appointments, and promotions the procedure recommended by the committee was adopted by the administration. At a meeting of the Committee of Six, the executive committee of the faculty, on December 16, 1946, the President considered with them the question of tenure. The minutes of the Committee of Six summarize the results of this meeting as follows:

> After an extended discussion, the consensus of opinion was that, while a formal statement of tenure approved by the Trustees would be desirable, it would be better at the present time to have an informal understanding that the cases of all instructors and assistant professors should be reviewed during their fourth year at Amherst, and a definite decision should

be made concerning their continuation in Amherst by the end of either their fifth or sixth year.

There still is no provision respecting tenure in the Statutes of Amherst College beyond the vague statement of Chapter II, section 3:

All officers of instruction shall serve either at the pleasure of the Trustees or for limited terms. In the latter case their connection with the College shall automatically cease at the end of the term specified, unless they are reappointed. Administrative officers shall serve at the pleasure of the Trustees.

There have been no breaches of academic freedom at Amherst, nor is it likely—considering the temper of our faculty and students together with the loyalty of the trustees, administration, and alumni to the ideals of liberal education—that any action subversive of academic freedom will occur, in the foreseeable future, from within the corporate life of the college. Today the greatest threat to academic freedom comes from without. An institution as respected and powerful as Harvard has been attacked by these subversive groups. Under the circumstances, well-defined standards for eligibility to tenure on the faculty can be a bulwark of defense, even for the trustees themselves. In recognition of this fact, the board has, we understand, taken the question of formulating these standards under consideration.

The committee was opposed to acceleration of the college course, with one exception already noted—the recommendation that some unusually mature and well-prepared students who have completed the equivalent of only three years of secondary school might be admitted to the college. This provision was voted by the faculty and under it an occasional student has been accepted. In those cases where a student is able to satisfy any of our requirements for the first two years he is, naturally, excused from taking them. But with the exception of the language requirement, which a small proportion of our students satisfy in advance, this form of acceleration is even rarer.

In our experience acceleration is so unusual that it is unimportant. The chief argument for it is that there is a considerable degree of overlap between the last two years of secondary school and the first two years of college. This appears to be true of many colleges. Hence, the report of a committee composed of members of the faculties of Andover, Exeter, Lawrenceville, Harvard, Princeton, and Yale, entitled *General Education in School and College*, advocates "*the adoption of a coordinated seven-year program for qualified students* as an alternative to the usual four years of secondary school and four years of college leading to a B.A. degree."[79] And, as everyone interested in the problem is aware, the Ford Foundation is at the present time conducting an extensive experimental study to determine the feasibility of accelerating the student's progress through secondary school and college.[80] We await with interest the final conclusions to be drawn from the results of this large-scale project. What we expect will come from it is an enhanced realization that the students in many colleges are not in fact making what the Long Range Policy Report characterized as "an adult departure" in their freshman year. Certainly it is our experience under the new program that we have virtually no students who cannot profit and profit well from the full four years of their education here. And this applies even more emphatically to our honors students than it does to the *rite* group.

In their discussion of the size of the college, the members of the Long Range Policy Committee were motivated by an anxiety lest pressures for expansion jeopardize the educational values of the program they had formulated.[81] Accordingly, the committee recommended:

> . . . that the size of the entering class be limited to not more than 250 students and that the size of the junior and senior classes be regulated by the elimination of the most unsatisfactory students, at least by the

[79] *General Education in School and College* (Cambridge, 1952), p. 112. This study was subsidized by the Ford Foundation.

[80] For a summary of the results to date, see *Bridging the Gap Between School and College—A Progress Report on Four Related Projects Supported by the Fund for the Advancement of Education*, published by the Ford Foundation in June, 1953.

[81] The committee noted the tendency of large institutions to absorb an ever larger proportion of the total student body. This trend has been intensified since the war. In 1951 there were thirty-two institutions of higher education with an enrollment of over 10,000 students, and half of the entire enrollment was in 116 of the 1854 institutions in the United States. Moreover, the pressure of population is increasing. It has been estimated that by 1970 the number of young people of college age will be about 70 per cent greater than it was in 1953.

end of the sophomore year, in such a way that the total size of the college will be not more than 800 students.

The alumni committee concurred in the recommendation that Amherst remain small, though they did not venture to suggest a definite size for the college.[82] It is fortunate that everyone concerned recognizes the unique contribution which should be made by institutions of Amherst's sort and is prepared to resist these pressures.

At the close of the college year in June, 1946, the enrollment was 464. The next fall Amherst opened with 1154 students. For the successive years 1947 to 1953, enrollments were 1163, 1201, 1192, 1051, 1077, and 1063. These persistently higher enrollments made it look as though Amherst would be definitely committed to some figure well above a thousand students. Several years ago the President decided that it was necessary to formulate a policy concerning the future size of the college. He sent a memorandum to those involved in administration asking what they considered an ideal size of the college in terms of our physical facilities. The answers were almost all in the range of 900 to 1000 and the median was about 960. Shortly thereafter, he sent a questionnaire to each faculty member asking what he considered the ideal size of the college from an educational point of view, irrespective of physical plant or financial considerations. The variation here was extremely wide (115-3000), but the median was 965. Since that time, it has been assumed that the objective is to get the college to about 965 in size. We have not yet done so because of a series of miscalculations based on the supposition of a larger attrition rate (military and otherwise) than actually occurred. The college should be under 1000 after the graduation of the class of 1955. It is planned to admit, for the long run, about 250 students a year, with the possibility of adding a few transfers.

The difference between the number of 800 suggested by the Long Range Policy Committee and the number now proposed is mainly due to the great improvement in the average of ability among our students. As a consequence the college average has risen from around 75 per cent to over 80 per cent, and there has been a sharp decrease in the attrition rate. In his annual report for 1951-1952, President Cole pointed out that since 1947 no class has graduated less than 85 per

[82] "Amherst Tomorrow," *Alumni Council News*, 18 (1945), 63-64.

cent of those entering, and for the five classes of 1947-1951 the average has been just under 88 per cent. Under present circumstances, then, limiting the entering classes to 250 students would result in a college of about 875 to 900 students. Presumably the size of entering classes and the number of transfers will be determined from year to year in order to approximate the present goal, a college of 950 to 975 students. While this figure is a good deal higher than the one suggested by the committee, it is, we hope, low enough to insure preservation of the values of a small college.

The final topic dealt with in the report is the corporate life of the college. With the views expressed by the committee concerning the respective duties and responsibilities of the trustees, the administration, the faculty, the students, and the alumni as agents within the corporate life of Amherst we are in complete agreement. We should like to add only one further suggestion, which is in the nature of a codicil to their remarks about the respective spheres of the trustees and the faculty. In the over-all government of the college, the primary responsibility for educational policy rests with the faculty while financial policy lies in the hands of the Board of Trustees. In matters of detail this becomes a meaningful and useful division of labor. In matters of policy, however, it is a time-honored myth, for in actual fact educational and financial or budget policy are two sides of the same coin and cannot possibly be separated. Major questions of educational policy inevitably have an import for the budget, and few important financial decisions can be made which are not reflected in educational policy.

This being the case, we are impressed with the importance of a close working relationship between the Board of Trustees and the faculty of the college. Their coordination is, of course, a primary function of the President, one which, in our opinion, is performed by the present administration with exceptional skill and sincerity. Nevertheless, we believe the problems of educational policy are so dependent upon the over-all decisions of the Board of Trustees that we should strive for an increased coordination in policy determinations. Two years ago, Professor Willard L. Thorp, then a trustee, was appointed to the faculty and retained his position as a trustee. We welcome this development and believe that the Board of Trustees should give consideration to instituting a system by which one or two members of the faculty would serve regularly as members of the board.

This concludes our review in detail of Amherst's new program. In the final section we shall comment on it in more general terms.

ON "EVALUATION"[83]

Boswell once said to Dr. Johnson that: ". . . he would suffer vexation if he were in Parliament and saw things going wrong. 'That is cant, sir,' said Johnson. 'Clear your mind of cant. You may talk as other people do: you may say to a man, 'Sir, I am your most humble servant.' You are *not* his most humble servant. You may say, 'These are bad times; it is a melancholy thing to be reserved to such times.' You don't mind the times. You tell a man, 'I am sorry you had such bad weather the last day of your journey, and were so much wet.' You don't care sixpence whether he is wet or dry. You may *talk* in this manner; it is a mode of talking in society: but don't *think* foolishly."

Now the curse of educational discussions is *cant*. We all know that the usual commencement address is in Boswell's mode of speaking; and the discourses of the professional writers on the subject are infested with such words. Indeed, a special canting dialect has been invented for this subject. The late Dr. Wallace Butterick of the General Education Board named it "Pedigese." Three of the key terms in this strange language are "objectives," "evaluation," and "integration." The first two of these, "objectives" and "evaluation," are of course correlative. What I should like to do is examine briefly the questions: What residuum of good sense, if any, can be found in these words? and, more briefly still, What sense of this kind is there, if any, in Amherst's curriculum?

Professional "educationalists" want, of course, to be "objective" and "scientific." They make a great to-do with these magic words "objectives" and "evaluation." In simple cases this *does* make sense: If, for example, one wishes to evaluate two methods of typewriting, the "hunt and pick" versus the touch system, the objectives, speed and accuracy, are simple and the way of testing, trial runs of each method, is obvious. But how does one test a whole liberal arts program? What are the measurements which show the superiority of one pattern of liberal

[83] This section was originally published as an article by Gail Kennedy entitled "Is There a Way out of Educational Confusion?" in the *Amherst Alumni News* for March, 1953. While it is an expression of the author's personal opinions, the other members of this committee are in general agreement with his position.

education over another? For it should be noted that the process of evaluation is circular. Thus, in the typing instance, the objectives (speed and accuracy) are set in advance and the tests test the degree of achievement of these predetermined objectives. To take a second illustration, what do intelligence tests test? If, for example, one problem in the Simon-Binet tests is to repeat numbers backward, then what is tested is the ability to repeat numbers backward. Accordingly, you must conclude that intelligence tests test what intelligence tests *do* test. Again, in the field of ethics, we find Aristotle saying that only the good man can judge what is truly good. But who is to judge who *is* a good man? The answer has to be, of course, only a man who is *good* can be the judge of who *is* a good man. Equally, it follows that only the well-educated man is competent to judge what constitutes a good education. Is the setting up of objectives and the evaluating of them in this case parallel to that of deciding between two alternative methods of typewriting? I consider that a rhetorical question.

Let me illustrate by reference to the planning of the new curriculum by the Faculty Committee on Long Range Policy. Just what were the objectives the Long Range Policy Committee set up in formulating the new program? Now it can be told: there was no real discussion of objectives in the committee. Shortly after getting organized the committee did send a five-page mimeographed flyer out to the faculty—as a trial balloon. This proved to be, in essentials, a summary of the report so far as the freshman-sophomore program is concerned. But there was very little discussion of the "principles" involved in this outline of a program for the first two years. In fact, there were hardly any real discussions of the basic questions of educational theory or policy throughout the deliberations of the committee. That part of the proceedings in which they considered courses was all most practical and matter of fact—devoted chiefly to what came to be called "curricular arithmetic." The real problem was to find ways of implementing the program, such things as squeezing into the student's working day enough of each of the things they wanted him to do. It was *means* the committee was concerned with; *ends* hardly preoccupied them at all.

True, the first part of the report of the committee is entitled "Objectives of the Liberal College in a Changing Society" and is a discussion, hopefully, of the general principles which underlie the specific recommendations made in Part II of the report, but that introductory section was written by the chairman after Part II had been completed and approved by the members of the committee. Similarly, there was virtually no discussion of educational principles or of general objectives in the faculty meetings at which the recommendations made in the report were considered. All the motions discussed and voted on were motions dealing with ways and means.

By way of contrast, I know of a not dissimilar institution which some time later set up a similar committee. This committee began by discussing "objectives." It promptly split into a conservative wing and a progressive one. The more these two factions attempted to adjudicate their differences the deeper became the rift, and the more tenacious each side was in holding to its convictions. Their intellectual integrity was now involved. As a result two rival reports were submitted to the faculty. The faculty in turn, with these reports before it, broke into not two but several opposed groups. Both reports, after a good deal of futile debate, were rejected and nothing at all was done.

The moral is that in fact policies are not formed by abstract analysis and discussion. Policies grow out of specific decisions and commitments. This is true, is it not, of the development of a foreign policy—say, American foreign policy during the period between the two world wars? And any other example of the development of an actual policy under complex circumstances will serve as well. In fact, the abstract approach to questions of policy is quite literally doctrinaire; and if the conditions are complex, that approach produces division rather than agreement.

Evaluation of the new program is a most subtle and elusive thing. I cannot imagine a simple and objective way of doing it. Actually the "evaluation" would have to be a continuing process of analysis and amendment in terms of the interaction between students and teachers. Education is a process. Evaluating it is a little like evaluating a marriage. The real test, then, of our new program, in my opinion, is this: Is there a growing consensus among the teachers? Is enthusiasm and morale among them sustained? Do they feel a real satisfaction in their day-to-day job, or is there an increasing sense that things are not going well and that there is need for a change? Similarly, do the students feel that they are gaining in that intangible quality, intellectual maturity, that they are growing up intellectually? Can they, when juniors and seniors, perceive a real and valuable difference between what they were as freshmen or sophomores and what they are now?

Members of the faculty, looking back over these six years, should ask: What should be changed? What hasn't worked to my satisfaction and why? Each student should ask: If I had it to do over, how might I have better invested my energy and my time? Which were the mistakes in this for me? Such a continuing process of criticism means that the program will not petrify into a static set of conventions about what every young man should know, but will be altered for the better with growing experience. This is the only kind of evaluation that counts.

Now, I wish similarly to consider that other magic word, "integration," again with some reference to Amherst's educational program.

The opposite of integration is certainly confusion, and all the pundits and publicists agree in referring to our times as an age of confusion. As far back, at least, as Matthew Arnold, this is the common refrain. In one of his poems he expresses it as

> . . . this strange disease of modern life
> With its sick hurry, its divided aims,
> Its heads o'ertaxed, its palsied hearts.

This confusion is reflected in our educational system. The cause, I should think, is obvious. It is a result of the constantly increasing division of labor. The multiplication of specialties leads to a dispersion like that at the Tower of Babel. Every fission of subject matters into new courses compounds the confusion until one begins to lose all hope of an effective way of dealing with the problem. Pseudo solutions are easy to arrive at: spending four years with the great books at St. John's College is, I believe, one of them; and its polar opposite, a tailor-made curriculum for each individual student, as at Sarah Lawrence, on the basis of that student's supposed "needs" or "interests," is, I believe, another.

Surely, no one who tries to think seriously about the matter can fail to come squarely up against this problem. Whitehead, in his book, *The Aims of Education*, has expressed it this way:

> The fading of ideals is sad evidence of the defeat of human endeavour. In the schools of antiquity, philosophers aspired to impart wisdom, in

modern colleges our humbler aim is to teach subjects. The drop from the divine wisdom, which was the goal of the ancients, to text-book knowledge of subjects, which is achieved by the moderns, marks an educational failure, sustained through the ages.

If integration is to occur at all, then, it must occur in the student's mind. No mere juggling of courses and scrambling of course contents will achieve it. Such a procedure will give us just another kind of encyclopedic knowledge about something of everything and an actual acquaintance with little or nothing. "The secret of the mediocrity of the learned world," says Whitehead, "is its second-handedness." Do you not notice that people who read widely and voluminously have, often, dull and unperceptive minds? Erudition, no matter what kind of can you put it in, is a denatured food. Once more, I must quote Whitehead: "Knowledge," he says, "keeps no better than fish."

How, then, can we achieve the sort of integration that bespeaks strength of mind? Is there any way out of intellectual confusion? Clearly, not dear old Matthew Arnold's recipe, an acquaintance with the best that has been thought and said. No wonder, having tried that remedy himself, he became infected with

> . . . this strange disease of modern life
> With its sick hurry, its divided aims,
> Its heads o'ertaxed, its palsied hearts.

At the risk of seeming like another Jack Horner, I think there *is* a way out and that it is adumbrated faintly, at least, in the Amherst curriculum. I refer particularly to the course in American Studies, the part of this new program with which I am best acquainted and which, in my opinion, exemplifies the *kind* of reorganization of our educational procedures that is necessary if we are going to have any chance at all of stemming the tide of disintegration in the modern world.

The present curriculum is, I think, good—as a lusty infant's first step. Yet it covers very little of the distance that we are going to have to traverse in order to bring our collegiate institutions into line with the existing world. The colleges are perhaps the worst sufferers from cultural lag. Even many churches seem progressive beside them. They become only too easily citadels of what Santayana called the "genteel tradition," the home of lost causes and impossible hopes. As a consequence, they lose all sense of real direction. The pervading atmosphere within a college is one of chronic restlessness and dissatisfaction —for, after all, what does the conventional program consist of? One takes a course in mathematics—from which nothing follows, a course in literature—from which nothing follows, a course in history—that leads to nothing, etc. And then some people wonder why it is so much easier to teach football.

The source of our intellectual confusion, then, is this kind of aimlessness. Football is easy to teach not because it is an easier subject (I am sure there are some courses at least that could be called "guts" by comparison) but because it has an obvious and immediate relevance to the life that the students are leading in college. Football is genuinely a part of "college life." In what sense, though, can it be said that the conventional subject-matter courses are parts of college life? They are the truly extracurricular activities.

If this is so, why is it so? To answer that question one must, I think, consider what education has always been in societies simpler than ours. There it was essentially a matter of growing up within the context of the daily activities of that society and gradually acquiring by coming to participate in more and more of its business a working knowledge of what to do and how to do it. The young gained most of their education by participating in the activities of the group. Under such conditions one acquired his whole education in the same way that in any society, our own included, one learns to speak his native language. Discord intrudes upon this idyllic situation only when the growing division of labor compels the segregation of a part, at least, of the educational process in the formal institutions we call schools. Here is the beginning of aimlessness and with it of confusion. It is only in schools that you are taught such things as mathematics that leads to nothing, and history from which nothing follows.

Now Whitehead has said that while knowledge is not wisdom, wisdom *is* the way in which knowledge is held. What that means can be easily illustrated. The story is told of the great scientist Clerk-Maxwell that, when he asked the questions which any intelligent child is constantly asking his elders, he would refuse to be put off with the kind of vague, general answer usually given by ignorant and impatient adults and insist, "But I want to know the particular go of it." Anyone who is a parent will realize what a dangerous boy Clerk-Maxwell must have been.

The infant Clerk-Maxwell had placed himself instinctively on the path to wisdom. He realized that mere *knowledge about* things is of no use unless one has real *acquaintance with* them. It is mere knowledge about that produces what Whitehead calls "inert ideas," and it is inert ideas which cause mental dry rot. The only possible way, therefore, of obtaining an education is through active participation in some type of project. It is this participation which brings us into real contact with things and makes us genuinely acquainted with them. And it is for this reason that Whitehead defines education as "the acquisition of the art of the utilization of knowledge." For, by what other means can one acquire any art except by practice?

This is the part of Amherst's "new" curriculum which, wherever you find it in the new curriculum, is, for a college course, really new. I mean that when one attempts to teach the art of utilizing knowledge, one deliberately gives up the attempt to teach subjects and instead more modestly tries to initiate the student into the kind of work that is done by the professors of those subjects. An illustration of this is to be found in the sophomore course in American Civilization. When a group of us had about finished outlining the list of problems we were going to use in the first year of that course, someone suddenly came to and in genuine surprise exclaimed: "Why, we haven't included the Civil War. What kind of course is that?" The answer is that we do include the Civil War; we include it about every third year on the average, but if we do include the Civil War, we are pretty sure to omit the Revolution. That is how the American Civilization course deals with the problem of integration. For the truth of the matter is that one cannot integrate by using the encyclopedic approach. Such omnibus survey courses must progressively include less and less about more and more. How can they be anything but repositories for all the best certified inert ideas? Their sole utility, so far as I know, is to prepare one for competing in the Information Please type of radio programs. And the only alternative to them is the way of participation. Apprenticeship was the original form of education and it still remains the unique mode of education. For general ideas can become meaningful only in so far as one sees into their concrete consequences.

What, then, should we do? We should, I believe, follow the example of the law schools and medical schools. To me it seems beyond doubt that the kind of education one receives in the best of these law and medical schools is incomparably superior to that offered by the conventional liberal arts college. In those places law and medicine are as well taught as football is taught at the college level. Yet at one time this was not the case. Those institutions also confined themselves to teaching out of the book. What gave them their present vitality was the development of the clinical methods of teaching in the medical school and of the case method in the law school.

Recall here Kant's dictum that "concepts without percepts are empty while percepts without concepts are blind." What liberal education needs is a much stronger infusion of perceptual content. If only we can learn how to develop throughout the whole of the student's four years here, and in every course, the mode of approach which treats the student as an apprentice, which attempts to give him some training in the *kind of work* which is done by those who are proficient in that subject, and not to hand him the ready-made products of someone else's work, as though that could mean anything to him, we shall have followed through to the end something which has been barely begun in what we call the "new" curriculum. In such a college any student fit to attend it could never be tempted to classify his academic work as the extracurricular activities. To graduate from such a college and to go into any business or profession would not constitute the break, the "commencement" as we ironically call it, that it does now. Such a type of schooling would quite break down the distinction between liberal and vocational education. In so doing it would be graduating students with the kind of genuine culture which prepares them for the liberal exercise of their vocations.

APPENDIXES TO PART III

I. SPECIMEN ASSIGNMENTS, ETC., FROM SOME COURSES IN THE NEW CURRICULUM

A. *Science 1-2* Experiment No. 4

CENTRIPETAL FORCE

In this experiment you will make measurements which are directly concerned with the concepts of angular velocity, centripetal acceleration, centripetal force, etc., as developed in class and lecture. Come to the laboratory prepared to define these quantities and derive the relations among them.

Start your notebook write-up thus: Suppose you take a mass at the end of a string and whirl it around in a circle, the circle lying in a horizontal plane. Make a list of the quantities which you must measure in order to *compute* the centripetal force acting on the mass. Describe very briefly in terms of actual operations how each quantity *might* be measured.

Now examine the equipment which is available to you. Note that it simply creates the situation described above and incorporates means for measuring the quantities you have already listed. Play with the apparatus until you understand exactly what is involved and *how each measurement is to be made*. Consult an instructor about anything regarding which you are uncertain, but do so only after having honestly tried to answer the questions yourself. Note that the results of your examination of the equipment automatically become your notebook description of the apparatus and of how the experiment is to be performed, so keep writing while conducting the examination.

Next proceed to make the measurements described and compute the centripetal force acting on the mass.

Now let us approach the same problem from a slightly different point of view: The centripetal force you have just computed was supplied by the spring to which the mass was attached, the magnitude of the force being determined by the extension of the spring. Since you now know how far the mass was from the axis of rotation while it was being whirled, it is possible to devise a very simple method for measuring *directly* the force which must have been acting. The method referred to *does not involve whirling the mass again*. Decide how to make this measurement, describe your procedure, carry it out, and compare the result with the previous computation.

Discuss any resulting discrepancy *convincingly* in terms of possible sources of error and the possible *magnitudes* of such errors. A haphazard list of every speculation which enters your head is of no value per se. A guess as to a source of error is acceptable *only* if you can say something about the actual *amount* of error you can ascribe to it.

B. *Science 23-24: Evolution of the Earth and Man*

LABORATORY EXERCISE 17

Dental Formulae for Representative Mammals
The Kinds of Primates: skeletal differences (Biology Lab.)

References: Sedgwick, *Textbook of Zoology*, Vol. 2
Parker and Haswell, *Textbook of Zoology*, Vol. 2
Hooton, *Up from the Ape* and *Man's Poor Relations*
Howells, *Mankind So Far*

I. Purpose: This exercise is designed to show you:
   a. the characteristic tooth differentiation found among the different orders of mammals, and
   b. the important skeletal differences found between the different groups of *one* of the orders of mammals, namely, the *Primates*.

II. *Dental Formulae*

The teeth of most mammals, unlike other vertebrates, are differentiated into incisors, canines, premolars, and molars. Learn to recognize them and their uses. Each order shows a certain characteristic differentiation of the groups of teeth which matches the feeding habits of the animals. Often different genera show a characteristic number of teeth of each kind. Living mammals and especially fossil skeletons can often be identified by the teeth alone.

1. Skulls of the following mammals are placed on the table:

a. cat, dog, or bear	d. deer	g. opossum
b. pig	e. beaver	
c. horse	f. man	

The teeth of each species are described in the dental formula as follows:

$$\frac{\text{Number of teeth in one side of upper jaw}}{\text{Number of teeth in one side of lower jaw}} \text{ as follows } \frac{\text{i c p m}}{\text{i c p m}}$$

List the skulls; record the dental formula for each. Refer to textbooks, especially Sedgwick, Vol. 2, and Parker and Haswell, Vol. 2.

III. *The Kinds of Primates*

Order Primates

Suborder	*Tupaioidea*—Tree shrews
Suborder	*Lemuroidea*—Lemurs
Suborder	*Tarsioidea*—Tarsius
Suborder	*Anthropoidea*
Infraorder	*Platyrrhini*
Family	*Hapalidae*—Marmosets
Family	*Cebidae*—Capuchin and howler monkeys
Infraorder	*Catarrhini*
Family	*Cercopithecidae*—Proboscis monkeys, guenons, macaques (1), baboons, mandrills
Family	*Hylobatidae*—Gibbon (2), siamang
Family	*Simiidae*—Orang-utan (3), chimpanzee (4), gorilla (5)
Family	*Hominidae*—Man (6)

IV. a. *Skeletal Differences Between Primates*

Bodily proportions of anthropoids and man.

Work in pairs and handle all skeletons with extreme care.

1. Secure a yardstick and tabulate the measurements indicated for each of the following (1), (2), (3), (4), (5), (6).
   a) Total height, ankle joint to top of head
   b) Top of head to shoulder level on spine
   c) Top of head to hip joint
   d) Breadth of shoulders, outside of humerus
   e) Length of arms, shoulder to fingertips
   f) Breadth of pelvis, outside of femur
   g) Length of legs, hip joint to ankle joint
   h) Foot length
2. From these measurements construct a row of proportion figures on the same base line running the long axis of the page to the scale of one inch to one foot. Follow the diagram on the blackboard.

3. State the principal differences in bodily proportions between apes and man shown in 2.

b. *The Vertebral Column and Appendages of Primates*

The skeleton of all vertebrates is divided into the axial skeleton, including the skull and the vertebral column, and the appendicular skeleton including the girdles and limb bones.

1. *Axial skeleton.* In addition to the skull, the vertebral column consists of vertebrae articulating with each other and supporting the head and ribs. Each includes a *body* or *centrum,* and an arch covering the spinal cord, the *neural arch.*

   There are five groups of vertebrae:

   a) *cervical* or neck vertebrae with a short bifid spine
   b) *thoracic* vertebrae which bear ribs
   c) *lumbar* vertebrae of the mid-body with large centra
   d) *sacral* vertebrae, fused together into one bone, the sacrum
   e) *coccygeal* vertebrae, tail or tail vestiges

   In certain forms, there is an S-shaped curve of the backbone in the lumbar region (in a side or lateral view), known as the lumbar curve.

2. *Appendicular skeleton.* The girdles are the bones by which the trunk is supported by the limbs.

   a) The pectoral girdle consists of the scapula and the clavicle. Identify in each skeleton. Identify also in the arm: humerus, radius, ulna, carpals, metacarpals, phalanges.
   b) The pelvic girdle. The pelvic bone on each side is formed of three elements: the dorsal wide ilium, and the ventral pubis and ischium. These bones are fused in the adult in one bone, the pelvis, but all three can be seen in the young chimpanzee or human baby skeletons.
   c) Identify also in the leg: femur, tibia, and fibula, tarsals, metatarsals, phalanges.

   Learn the bones of the pectoral and pelvic girdles and limbs. *You will be given an oral quiz on them before leaving the laboratory.*

C. List of Problems Used in *American Studies 21-22*: *Problems in American Civilization*

Altogether, forty different problems were used during the first five years of the course. Those which have been published are:

Puritanism in Early America
The Causes of the American Revolution
The Declaration of Independence and the Constitution
Hamilton and the National Debt
The Turner Thesis concerning the Role of the Frontier in American History
Jackson Versus Biddle—The Struggle over the Second Bank of the United States
The Transcendentalist Revolt Against Materialism
Slavery as Cause of the Civil War
Reconstruction in the South
Democracy and the Gospel of Wealth
John D. Rockefeller—Robber Baron or Industrial Statesman?
Roosevelt, Wilson, and the Trusts
Pragmatism and American Culture
The New Deal—Revolution or Evolution?
Franklin D. Roosevelt and the Supreme Court
Industry-wide Collective Bargaining—Promise or Menace?
Education for Democracy—The Debate over the Report of the President's Commission on Higher Education
Loyalty in a Democratic State
Immigration: An American Dilemma
Pearl Harbor: Roosevelt and the Coming of the War
The Great Tariff Debate, 1820-1830
William Jennings Bryan and the Campaign of 1896

Some of the other problems which have been used are:

Economic Planning
The United Nations and World Security
International Control of Atomic Energy
National Health Insurance

D. *Humanities 1-2* Reading List 1952-1953

First semester:

Homer, *Odyssey*, trans. E. V. Rieu, Penguin Books.
Selections from the Old Testament, in *The Bible: Selections from the Old and New Testaments*, ed. A. G. Chester, Rinehart Editions.
Aeschylus, *Prometheus Bound*, trans. Edith Hamilton.
Sophocles, *King Oedipus*, trans. W. B. Yeats.
A third play chosen by the section instructor. (These in *Greek Plays in Modern Translation*, ed. Dudley Fitts, Dryden Press.)
Plato, *Euthyphro* and *Apology*, trans. F. J. Church, rev. ed. R. D. Cumming, Liberal Arts Press.
Plato, *Phaedo* (cut), trans. F. J. Church, ed. F. H. Anderson, Liberal Arts Press.

Thucydides, *History of the Peloponnesian War*, trans. R. Crawley, rev.-ed. Sir R. Livingstone, Oxford University Press (World's Classics).

Second semester:

Selections from the New Testament (text as above).
Lucretius, *The Nature of the Universe*, trans. R. E. Latham, Penguin Books. (Portions only.)
Dante, *The Divine Comedy, I. Hell*, trans. Dorothy L. Sayers, Penguin Books. (Slightly cut.)
Chaucer, selections from *The Canterbury Tales*, in *The Portable Chaucer*, trans. Theodore Morrison, Viking Press.
Shakespeare, *Othello*, ed. Mark Eccles, Crofts Classics.
Montaigne, *Selections from the Essays*, trans.-ed. D. M. Frame, Crofts Classics.
Swift, *Gulliver's Travels*, Rinehart Editions. (Portions only.)
Conrad, *Lord Jim*, Modern Library.
Malraux, *Man's Fate*, trans. H. M. Chevalier, Modern Library.

E. Questionnaire Given in *Humanities* 1-2 (1948-1949) and the Replies

Please answer the questions below by inserting the *number* as shown in the list.

(1) Homer: *Odyssey*
(2) *Bible*—selections
(3) Aeschylus: *Prometheus Bound*
(4) Sophocles: *Antigone*
(5) Euripides: *Alcestis*
(6) Thucydides: *Peloponnesian War*
(7) Plato—selections
(8) Lucretius: *On the Nature of Things*
(9) Dante: *Divine Comedy*
(10) Shakespeare: *King Lear*
(11) Montaigne—selections
(12) Lyric poems
(13) Goethe: *Faust* I
(14) Forster: *A Passage to India*

Questions:

1. Which assignments did you find most enjoyable?
First choice:______
Second choice:______
2. What assignment did you find least enjoyable? ______
3. Which assignments did you find most profitable?
First choice:______
Second choice:______
4. Which assignment did you find least profitable? ______
5. Which of the readings had you already read, complete or extensively?
Numbers:______________________________

Humanities 1-2: Questionnaire results, June, 1949

1. Most enjoyable, 1st choice:

70 *Faust*
41 Odyssey
35 *A Passage to India*
34 *King Lear*
13 *Antigone*; Lucretius; lyrics
7 Montaigne
6 Thucydides; Dante
4 *Prometheus Bound*; *Alcestis*; Plato

Most enjoyable, 2nd choice:

60 *Faust*
43 *A Passage to India*
40 *King Lear*
36 Odyssey
20 *Antigone*
12 *Alcestis*
9 Dante
8 *Prometheus Bound*; Lucretius; Montaigne
7 Lyrics
6 Thucydides; Plato
3 Bible

3. Most profitable, 1st choice:

53 Montaigne
50 Plato
44 Lucretius
42 *A Passage to India*
18 Dante
12 Bible
11 *King Lear*; *Faust*
5 Odyssey; Thucydides
1 *Prometheus Bound*; *Antigone*; *Alcestis*; lyrics

Most profitable, 2nd choice:

43 Plato
39 Lucretius
35 *A Passage to India*
26 Dante; Montaigne
21 Thucydides
17 *Faust*
14 Bible
12 *King Lear*
5 *Antigone*
4 *Prometheus Bound*; *Alcestis*
3 Odyssey; lyrics

2. Least enjoyable:

64 Montaigne
58 Dante
31 Lucretius
30 Thucydides
25 Bible
20 Plato
12 Lyrics
7 *Prometheus Bound*; *A Passage to India*
2 *King Lear*
1 Odyssey

4. Least profitable:

68 Lyrics
39 Thucydides
27 Montaigne
24 Dante
16 Bible
15 Odyssey
12 Lucretius
8 *King Lear*
7 *Prometheus Bound*; Plato
6 *Alcestis*
4 *Faust*

5. Previously read:

128	*Odyssey*	15	*Alcestis*
108	Bible	13	Montaigne
69	*King Lear*	12	Dante
54	Lyrics	11	*A Passage to India*
26	*Antigone*	10	Thucydides
22	Plato	9	*Faust*
16	*Prometheus Bound*	3	Lucretius

(In 8 sections, 36 students said they had read nothing on the list. Answers to this question were not reported from one section.)

F. *Humanities 21-22: An Introduction to Fine Arts, Music and Drama*—typical material studied

DRAMA

Anonymous:	*Abraham and Isaac; Everyman, Quem Queritis; Second Shepherd's Play*
Aeschylus:	*Agamemnon, The Furies, The Libation Bearers*
Anderson:	*Winterset*
Chekhov:	*The Sea Gull*
Dryden:	*All for Love*
Hellman:	*The Little Foxes*
Ibsen:	*A Doll's House; Ghosts; Peer Gynt*
Marlowe:	*Doctor Faustus*
Miller:	*Death of a Salesman*
Rostand:	*Cyrano de Bergerac*
Shakespeare:	*Antony and Cleopatra*
Sophocles:	*Electra; Oedipus the King*
Wilde:	*The Importance of Being Earnest*

MUSIC

Anonymous: Entre copin et bourgois (13c); Mira lege (11c); Veni Sancte Spiritus (10c)

Bach: Ich ruf' zu Dir; Invention in F; Little G Minor Fugue; Second Orchestral Suite; Toccata and Fugue in D Minor

Beethoven: Symphony No. 3; mov. 2 of Symphony No. 7

Brahms: Academic Festival Overture

Chopin: Prelude No. 20 in C Minor

Handel: Hallelujah Chorus from *The Messiah;* mov. 4 of Concerto Grosso, Op. 6, No. 3

Haydn: Quartet in G Minor (Op. 74, No. 3); mov. 2 of Symphony No. 97; Piano Sonata No. 37 in D
Honegger: March from *Le Roi David*
Mozart: "Dalla sua pace" from *Don Giovanni;* Overture to *The Marriage of Figaro*
Palestrina: Sanctus and Benedictus from *Missa Papae Marcelli*
Raimbault: Kalenda maya (12c)
Stravinsky: Soldier's Violin, Waltz and Ragtime from *Histoire du Soldat*
Wagner: Act I of *Die Walküre*

Fine Arts

First semester: Examples of art representing all media, from a variety of periods and most geographical areas. Selection is made in every case on the basis of excellence as a demonstration piece, but other criteria include: the importance of the object, its potential as representing more than one point, and its usefulness in both semesters.

Second semester: the study focuses on a few major monuments.
Parthenon—architecture, sculpture
Temple of Zeus at Olympia—architecture, sculpture
Hagia Sophia at Istanbul—architecture, mosaics
Cathedral, Pisa—architecture
Cathedral, Chartres—architecture, stained glass
St. Peter's and the Vatican—architecture, sculpture, painting
Versailles—architecture, painting
French and American Romantic painting of the nineteenth century
Rodin, the man and his works
Frank Lloyd Wright

G. *English 21-22* *Othello* Exercise

I. Object

Your object in this exercise is to discover and evaluate an element of pervasive design in *Othello.*

II. Preparation

1. Read and interpret the speech of Othello at II, i, 181:

It gives me wonder great as my content,
To see you here before me. O my soul's joy!
If after every tempest come such calms,
May the winds blow till they have waken'd death!
And let the labouring bark climb hills of seas

Olympus-high, and duck again as low
As hell's from heaven! If it were now to die,
'Twere now to be most happy; for I fear
My soul hath her content so absolute
That not another comfort like to this
Succeeds in unknown fate.

a. What mood of Othello at this moment do these lines express? Analyze the uses of language by which this mood is projected.

b. Notice especially the words

If it were now to die,
'Twere now to be most happy . . .

What meaning do they have for Othello? What different meaning do they have for a spectator who is aware of the sequel? How would you characterize the emotional response which accompanies this perception?

2. Now read and interpret the speech of Othello at V, ii, 1-22:

It is the cause, it is the cause, my soul.
Let me not name it to you, you chaste stars!
It is the cause. Yet I'll not shed her blood,
Nor scar that whiter skin of hers than snow,
And smooth as monumental alabaster.
Yet she must die, else she'll betray more men.
Put out the light, and then put out the light.
If I quench thee, thou flaming minister,
I can again thy former light restore,
Should I repent me; but once put out thy light,
Thou cunning'st pattern of excelling nature,
I know not where is that Promethean heat
That can thy light relume. When I have pluck'd the rose,
I cannot give it vital growth again;
It needs must wither. I'll smell it on the tree.
(He kisses her.)
O balmy breath, that dost almost persuade
Justice to break her sword! One more, one more!
Be thus when thou art dead, and I will kill thee,
And love thee after. One more, and this the last!
So sweet was ne'er so fatal. I must weep,
But they are cruel tears. This sorrow's heavenly;
It strikes where it doth love. She wakes.

a. What mood of Othello's at this moment do these lines express? By what uses of language is this mood projected?

b. Consider especially the words

So sweet was ne'er so fatal.

By these words Othello expresses an evaluation of the situation. How does the spectator's evaluation differ from his? What sort of emotional response accompanies the perception of this difference? (Is there a sense in which these words could be the spectator's verdict too?)

3. How are these two passages alike? Find and analyze at least one other passage of the play which resembles them.

4. You have now noticed at least three moments of the play in which the spectator's evaluation differs from Othello's. How, because of these differences, *must* a reader view Othello?

III. Writing

Incorporate your findings in a readable essay of not more than three pages.

(This exercise was prepared by Professor John A. Moore.)

H. The Degree with Honors: Theses Submitted by Students in the Class of 1954

American Studies

(The Department of American Studies requires two theses of its honors candidates)

Albert, Burton, "The Regulator Movement in North Carolina, 1765-1771" and "Passion, Propaganda and Prejudice: A Group Study of the Scottsboro Case"

Allen, Harry S., "The Quaker Merchants of Colonial Philadelphia: A Case Study of the Rise and Fall of an Elite Group" and "The Tidelands Oil Issue"

Clapp, Roger H., "James Madison, Father of the Constitution. His Early Political Philosophy" and "Prelude to the Four A's: The Development of Advertising Agency Associations in U.S. 1865-1917"

Goldberg, David R., "The Clipper Ship Elite" and "The Unionization of Teachers"

Gove, Gilbert E., "Conflict of Elites: The Faction and the Moderates in Massachusetts, 1670-1695" and "Group Interest and the St. Lawrence Seaway"

Hunziker, Robert M., "A Study of the Elite of the Silk Industry in

Paterson, New Jersey, 1860-1900" and "The Repeal of the 18th Amendment"

Mahar, Anthony S., "An Analysis of the opposition to Horace Mann's Educational Reforms, 1837-1845" and "Hyphenated American Groups and the Treaty of Versailles"

Mitchell, Matthew P., "The Leaders of the Know-Nothing Party: An Approach to a Problem in Historical Causation" and "Richard Wright and Ralph Ellison: A Study in Recent Negro Fiction"

Price, Meridith, "The Struggle for Leadership in the South following the Civil War: Thomas Nelson Page and Walter Hines Page" and "An Examination of Group Action: Segregation in Washington, D.C."

Rutter, Marshall A., "Jeffersonian Republicanism in Connecticut 1793-1818: A Study of Its Leadership and Urban Character" and "A Voice Beyond the Veil: The Life and Thought of W. E. B. Dubois."

Biology

Benneyan, Robert N., "The Effect of X-radiation on Genetic Crossing-over in *Drosophila melanogaster* as Modified by Infrared Pre-treatment"

Black, Craig C., "A New Species of Mesogaulus in the Miocene of Wyoming with Notes on Variation of Cheek Tooth Pattern due to Wear"

Brown, Kenneth A., "A Comparison of the Myology of *Dasyprocta columbiana* with that of Other Members of the Genus"

Bryant, Frederick C., Jr., "Birds of Amherst"

Carter, Joseph H., Jr., "A Study of the Effects of Stimulatory Substances on the Growth of *Drosophila* Raised Under Aseptic Conditions"

Cattell, Hereward S., "The Effects of Ultraviolet Radiation on Reversion in *Salmonella* 549-59-19"

Fisher, William H., Jr., "The Effects of Skin Removal and Traumatization in Limbs of Late *Rana clamitans* Tadpoles"

Freeman, John M., "The Use of Chelation Techniques in Studies of the Inorganic Requirements of *Tetrahymena pyriformis* Strain W"

Gotoff, Samuel P., "The Effect of X-radiation at Low Dosages on the Rate of Egg Lethality of *Drosophila melanogaster*"

Hilgartner, C. Andrew, "On the Causes of Dominant Lethality"

Ickler, John L., "A Preliminary Study of Nucleic Acid Starvation in *Drosophila melanogaster*"

Kaplan, Richard N., "The Effect of Low Dosage Gamma Radiation upon the Frequency of Sex-Linked Recessive Lethals in *Drosophila melanogaster*"

Lessell, Simmons, "Fossil Geomyoid Rodents from Muddy Gap, Wyoming"

Lindberg, Donald A. B., "The Effect of Xenoplastic Adrenal and Other Transplants upon Regeneration of Limbs in Hypophysectomized Newts"

McIntosh, Duncan A., "A Study of the Processes of Post-amputational Healing in the Limbs of Young Rats Under Various Experimental Conditions"

Pellman, Carl M., "The Effect of Hypertonic Salt Solutions upon Regeneration in Hypophysectomized and Normal *Triturus viridescens*"

Schapiro, Robert H., "Studies on the Succinoxidase System in *Tetrahymena pyrformis*, Strain W"

Smith, Charles M., "Significance of Delayed Reverse Mutations in *Salmonella typhimurium* Induced by Ultraviolet Radiation"

Spiegelman, Irwin M., "In Vitro Studies on the Effects of Irradiations on the Mitochondria. The Effect of Ultraviolet Radiation on the Cytochrome Oxidase"

Tulgan, Henry, "A Study of the Chromosomal Aberrations Induced in Two Lines of Irradiated *Drosophila melanogaster*"

Turner, Raymond W., "The Metabolism of *Glaucoma scintillans* Regarding Source of Organic Carbon"

Wilcox, William W., "The Delayed Appearance of Mutations in *Salmonella typhimurium*"

Chemistry

Baumann, Jacob B., "Some Attempted Syntheses of Pyridyl Isocyanates and Isothiocyanates"

Fendrick, Gerald M., "Studies in the Chemistry of 'Meldrum's Acid' (2,2-Dimethyl-1, 3-dioxane-4,6-dione)"

Gebauer, A. George, "Measurement and Interpretation of the Faradaic Admittance on a Dropping Mercury Electrode"

Hanselman, Raymond B., "Preliminary Investigation into the Size, Shape, and Molecular Weight of Desoxyribonucleic Acid Prepared According to the Methods of Simmons"

Kambour, Roger P., "Analytical Applications of the Pseudo-Capacitance and Polarization Resistance at the Dropping Mercury Electrode"

Oxman, Leon M., "A Comparative Study of Various Methods for the Isolation of Desoxyribonucleic Acid from Calf Thymus"

Rassweiler, John H., "An Attempt at Synthesis of Ethyl 4-(x-Pyridyl)-acetoacetate"

Soffer, Richard L., "Studies of *Syn-anti* Isomerism in the Phenylhydrazone Series by Infrared Techniques"

Economics

Daugherty, James C., "The Taft-Hartley Injunction"

Edelstein, Haskell, "The New England Woolen and Worsted Textile Industry"

Fieleke, Norman S., "The Motel Industry: An Economic Analysis"

Galef, Andrew G., "Lloyd's of London"

Jones, David O., "The Factor of Competition in the Air Industry"

Leviston, William B., Jr., "Depletion of the New England Fishing Industry"

Nixon, James A., "The Economics of Innovation—A Case Study of the Automobile Industry"

Oresman, Stephen B., "Lewis Mumford and the Economics of City Planning"

Pagter, Ralph G., "Depletion Allowances and the Oil Industry"

Purdy, John E., Jr., "Longshoring on the New York Waterfront"

Rosenthal, Jon K., "The Relationship Between the Internal and External Equilibrium of the Swedish Economy"

Weil, Frederic E., "The Classical Long-Playing Record Industry"

Werner, B. Kay, "A Study of Workmen's Compensation Insurance"

Whitney, William E., Jr., "The British Cotton Textile Industry and the Decline of British Cotton Textile Reports"

Wilbor, Guy W., "Problems of Military Aircraft Production"

Willemson, Richard M., "A Study of Investment of Insurance Company and College Endowment"

Williams, John A., "Federal Estate Taxation, Federal Gift Taxation, and Life Insurance"

English

Armstrong, John H., "*Tristram Shandy*, by Laurence Sterne: The Motley Novel of a Gentleman-Jester"

Blackburn, Thomas H., "Truth and Imagination—A Study of the Poetry of William Butler Yeats"

Corson, Edward W., Jr., "Beyond Life and Death—An analysis of the Merits and the Limitations of Ironic Structuring in the Poetry of E. E. Cummings"

Lundeen, David F., "The Critics, The Poetry and Robert Frost"

Millis, Walter, III, "Translating Fortune—A Study of Some Early Works by Ernest Hemingway"

Silbaugh, Hugh R., Jr., "Lord Byron and the Indestructible Hero—A Study of the Narrative Poetry of George Gordon, Lord Byron"

Spofford, Edward W., "An Analysis of the Movement of Dialogue in *Julius Caesar* by Shakespeare and *Death of a Salesman* by Arthur Miller"

Storms, Clifford B., "The Tribute of the Current to the Source—A Critical Study of the Poetry of Robert Frost"

Taft, William W., "The Experience of Satire—A Reading of Jonathan Swift"

Tayler, Edward W., "The Garden of the Mind—A Study of Some of Andrew Marvell's Poems"

Whitmore, Stephen C., "Faulkner: Style and a Definition of Nature"

Fine Arts

Childs, Maurice F., Jr., "A Proposed Amherst Alumni House"

Miller, J. Arthur, "A Regional School for Amherst"

Geology

Bassett, William A., "Experimental Study of Uranium Precipitation in Various Environments"

Linehan, David C., "Lithium"

Patten, J. Michael, "Experimental Study of the Acquisition and Precipitation of Uranium from Sulphate Solutions"

Schreiber, Hans W., "Migration of Uranium and Radioactivity"

German

Townsend, Vincent F., "Gottfried Keller: A Study of Idealism and Realism in His Work"

History

Barnes, James J., "The Novel and the Historian: A Study of Four Novels of Victorian England"

Deutsch, Irwin F., "The Innkeeper of Europe: An Inquiry into the Ideas of Voltaire"

Elden, John A., "The Clash Between the United States and Japan from 1918-1932"

Gamble, Richard R., "The Responsibility for the Jameson Raid"

Grimstad, Charles M., "The Impact of the French Revolution on the Domestic Policy of William Pitt, 1791-1795"

Hodgen, Robert T., "Archbishop Cranmer and the Rise of Protestantism in England"

Jenkins, Thomas S., "Some Aspects of the Interaction of Economic Factors and Government Policy in the Development of Economic Institutions in Spain from 1492 to the Death of Philip II"

Jordan, Richard D., "The Comparison of the Ambassadorships of Sir Nevile Henderson and André François-Poncet, the British and French Representatives to Berlin in the Years Prior to World War II"

Lacey, E. Bradford, "The Second Afghan War, 1878-1880"

Pastore, Richard S., "Nuremburg: Milestone in International Justice with Respect to War"

Pfund, Peter H., "The Political Education of Thomas Mann"

Rohde, Harry G., "Cesare Borgia and the Problem of the Unification of Italy"

Warner, Edwin G., II, "Thomas Cromwell: Burgess and Protestant Reformer"

Mathematics

Barnaby, Charles H., "Surfaces of Center"

Gould, Roderick, "Surface Transformations"

Longsworth, Maurice A., Jr., "Geodesic Curves, Geodesic Curvature, Geodesic Torsion and Related Topics"

Perez, Giovi, "The Moving Trihedron"

Redner, Keith H., Jr., "Lines of Curvature"

Sherwood, Peter F., "Minimal Surfaces: Their Origin and Properties"

Winter, Donald F., "A Dissertation on the Concept of Total Curvature"

Physics

Dean, Lee W., III, "The Hall Effect in Cuprous Oxide, and the Construction of a Magnetic Field Strength Meter Using the Principle of the Hall Effect"

Norman, Hilary M., "Construction of a Cryostat for Research Between 1 and 4 Degrees Absolute, and the Measurement of the Specific Heat of Tin in This Range"

Political Science

Culver, Fred A., "A Study of Majority Suppression in the Union of South Africa: Fear, Frustration, and Apartheid"

Dubin, Seth H., "Some Connotations of Treason"

Ewing, John T., "Transitional Government in Communist China"

Griffin, Burt W., "Foreign Policy: Democracy's Dilemma—A Study of the Domestic Politics of Marshall Plan Legislation"

Kirsch, David A., "The Histradut: A Critical Examination of the World's Strangest Trade Union"

Little, Thomas M., "The Road to Security: American Military Organization in the Twentieth Century"

Seham, Martin C., "Organized Bigotry and Its Effect on Public Policy"
Sherman, John C., "British and American Relations with China"
Vander Clute, Norman R., "Corporation Government in the Middle Eastern and Venezuelan Oil Communities"
Werner, Frederic P., "A Federal History of the Self-Incrimination Clause Regarding the Problem It Presents Today as a Bulwark of Liberty and a Shelter for Criminals and Subversives"

Psychology

Bauer, William A., "The Relative Difficulty of Concepts Involving Color, Number, and Form"
Hornberger, Robert H., "The Effects of Anxiety on Learning Under Conditions of Experimentally Induced Failure"
Underwood, David G., "An Investigation of Group-Influenced Judgments as Related to Selected Personality Factors"
Walter, Eugene J., "An Investigation of the Influence of Novelty as a Factor in Gaining and Holding Attention in Magazine Advertising"

II. DATA ON POSTWAR COSTS OF OPERATION OF THE COLLEGE, SCHOLARSHIP FUNDS, ETC.

The table which follows supplements that given in the appendix to the original report of the Faculty Committee on Long Range Policy. These data are submitted as prepared by the Comptroller of the college. In arriving at the figures presented here the Comptroller has, where possible, adjusted prior years' figures to present conditions rather than eliminating items from present years' figures to make them comparable with earlier figures. Comparison of these data with those provided in the Appendix of the earlier report should be made with the foregoing statement in mind and with the qualifications noted in the statement accompanying the table in that report.

Graphical representation of these data has not been attempted as in the earlier report. We have come to the conclusion that unless the data available are much more detailed such analysis is not enlightening. Thus the item "Instruction" includes not only teachers' salaries but also outlays for research, intercollegiate athletics, departmental expenses, etc.

STATISTICAL SUMMARY

	1930-31	1940-41	1946-47	1952-53
Endowment	9,131,219	12,162,610	13,383,666	20,123,572
Per student	13,588	14,275	11,597	19,695
Plant investment	3,441,517	5,296,665	6,346,034	7,180,029
Per student	5,121	6,217	5,499	7,026
Number of students	672	852	1,154	1,022
Expenses				
Instruction (including Research)	403,901	533,482	745,449	1,075,484
Per student	601	626	645	1,053
*Relative change per student	100	104	107	175
Library	38,085	53,065	74,055	87,704
Per student	57	62	64	86
Relative change per student	100	109	112	151
Administration	94,873	103,817	171,941	252,482
Per student	141	122	149	247
Relative change per student	100	87	106	175
Buildings and grounds, etc.	149,038	184,770	241,232	372,451
Per student	222	217	209	364
Relative change per student	100	98	94	164
Scholarships and student aid	75,695	89,916	40,478	149,940
Per student	113	106	35	147
Relative change per student	100	94	31	131
Auxiliary enterprises	7,713	54,797	585,789	708,900
All other expenses	23,210	24,561	19,977	35,949
Total expense	792,515	1,044,408	1,878,921	2,682,910
Total excluding auxiliary enterprises	784,802	989,611	1,293,132	1,974,010
Per student	1,168	1,160	1,120	1,930
Relative change per student	100	99	96	165

* = Ratio to 1930-31

Set in Linotype Electra
Format by Edwin H. Kaplin
Manufactured by The Haddon Craftsmen, Inc.
Published by HARPER & BROTHERS, *New York*